SUPPLEMENTARY MANUAL

FOR TEACHING

ENVIRONMENTAL LAW and POLICY: NATURE, LAW, and SOCIETY

AS A FIRST LAW COURSE

Zygmunt J.B. Plater
Robert H. Abrams
William Goldfarb

West Publishing Company
1992

Special thanks to a cohort of hardworking associates at Boston College Law School for help in preparing this manual:

- Researchers and general factota: Steve Bunyak, J.D. '94, Patrick Ratkowski, J.D. '94

- Law student teachers who offered this course in the Boston College political science department, as part of a law-teaching seminar practicum, in the course of which they prepared extensive syllabus drafts and exam materials:

  Nancy Adams, '92; Bert Cooper, '92; Dan Cronin, '92; Elise Feldman, '92; Dan Goerke, '92; Jeff Henricks, '93; Craig Kelley, '93; Patricia Lapid, '93; Andrew Lee, '93; Lucy Manning, '92; Deborah Morazzi, '93; Sean Murphy, '92; Aniello Siniscalchi, '93; Nancy Snyder, '93; Aaron Toffler, '92; Kevin Viola, '93

- Wordprocessing:

  Fran Piscatelli, Kathleen King, Brenda Pepe, Susan Noonan, Mary Curran

And to colleagues who have offered the course in graduate and undergraduate programs, or as a first-year law school legal process course, for their advice and shared experiences with the book and its predecessor materials:

- Professors Harry Bader at the University of Alaska; Orlando Delogu at Bowdoin, Jeff Haynes at University of Michigan-Flint, Leighton Leighty at Michigan State, Armin Rosencranz at Berkeley, and Michael Wolf at the University of Richmond.

August, 1992

ISBN 0-314-01382-2

Note: Part of this and the main teacher's manual for ENVIRONMENTAL LAW AND POLICY: NATURE, LAW, AND SOCIETY are designed to be photocopied by teachers as handouts for student use in the course (particularly the materials in Part Three of each manual).

1st Reprint—1992

Table of Contents

There is hardly a political question in the United States which does not sooner or later turn into a judicial one.

Alexis de Tocqueville
Democracy in America, 1848

PART ONE: DESIGNING THE COURSE

A. How to Use This Manual

B. On Teaching Nature, Law, and Society as a First Law Course

C. Designing the Course: Approach, assignments, term paper, exams, etc.

IA. How to Use This Manual

This manual is designed to be used as a supplement to the main manual for the coursebook ("A Teachers Manual to Accompany Environmental Law and Policy: Nature Law and Society," published June 1992, with green cover). The main manual was designed for use in teaching upper-class elective law school courses. This supplementary manual is designed to facilitate teaching environmental law outside the elective law school curriculum — as a legal process course in the first year of law school and in graduate and undergraduate non-law school programs.

Although primarily offered in law school courses for second and third-year students, the coursebook (which we often refer to as "NLS") and its predecessor materials have been used successfully in more than a dozen courses offered outside that elective law school curriculum. NLS has been used in several law schools as a vehicle for an introductory first-year course in legal process, and in other schools as a graduate or undergraduate course in the political science department, environmental and natural resource studies, business and management programs, and the like. When taught as a first law course, adjustments have to be made in page assignments (basic readings constitute about 500 of the book's 1000+ pages) and teaching approach. The book's design, however — building step by step from common law foundations of liability and remedies to sophisticated public law regulatory schemes, with consideration of constitutional and other over-arching theories like the public trust doctrine — has made it accessible to students who have never previously studied law, in a way that most environmental law textbooks are not. Its organization — based on legal process rather than discreet physical science categories like air, water, solid waste, toxics, etc. — guides students into consideration of the law as a body of techniques and principles, rather than just an accumulation of environmental regulation and policy.

This manual is structured very much like the main teachers manual. The major function of this Part One is to facilitate the designing of the course syllabus; the main function of Part Two is to provide ideas and direction step-by-step for classes throughout the course; and Part Three provides background information and useful handouts to accompany the course. Because this manual is conceived of as a supplementary guide, we recommend that teachers, in preparing each class, read it along with appropriate sections in the main teachers manual.

One of the first tasks for the teacher in this setting is to define exactly what s/he wants to accomplish in the course. As noted below, most teachers and students in the first-level offering of this course are not primarily interested in it as a substantive environmental policy-science-and-economics course. That agenda is available and better covered in other areas of the curriculum. Rather the point of the course seems to be to teach the structure and process by which our legal system responds to the challenges of environmentalism, with details of the various approaches and techniques which have been brought to bear in that process. Although the course offers a wealth of fascinating perspectives on environmental science, policy, economics, and ethics, its organizing focus is as a course in the legal system and principles of modern environmental law.

Most of the charts, exercises, and comments in the main teachers manual will be directly useful in offering the course as a first law course. Nevertheless, teaching this course outside the elective law school curriculum is a sufficiently different context that some of the suggestions in this manual will override those made in the main manual. Later in this Part One, for instance, in section C, "Designing the Course," we recommend substantially shorter assignments and often emphasize different readings First-time students of law need far more focus on the fundamentals of the legal system, so we are more assertive in proposing what readings to assign and not to assign in this format. In our Part Two recommendations for class preparation, especially in the beginning weeks of the course, we choose to emphasize the teaching of legal system fundamentals, with major consequent changes in allocations of time from the main manual. In Part Three, many of the handouts are designed for basic overview and introduction to the court system, the design of a cause of action for launching a court case, the progress of a case step-by-step through the litigation process, the justices of the Supreme Court, etc. Part Three also includes the federal constitution, readings and citations on how to study for a law course, and updated material for several recent cases and the 1992 Rio Conference. You should review the collection to see what interests you for handouts and for your own class preparation.

You should spend some significant time reviewing and second guessing our syllabus proposals in Part One (C), shaping them to your own ideas and the amount of time you have available through the duration of the course. Recognize that class progress, especially at first, will be fairly slow since most students are novices in confronting the structure and character of the legal system. The character of your institutional offering and your student enrollment will play a major role in defining your approach to the course.

If you are teaching the course in the first-year curriculum of a law school, it is likely that the legal process aspects of the course (introducing, broadening, and deepening technical understanding of the various components and tendencies of the legal system and its jurisprudence) will provide the dominant focus. Law students, even those who are personally interested in environmental law, will typically have to be reassured that this course is being used as a vehicle to give them some basic legal fundamentals that they need to become legal professionals. (This manual is written as if all students are total beginners in legal studies. Where the course is being offered in the *second* semester of a first-year law school curriculum, further adjustments will be useful in accommodating the students' prior law course exposure.)

If you are teaching the course in a program outside the law school curriculum, defining your approach will be more relative. In some offerings, for instance, environmental studies and natural resources students will predominate; in those classes the particular features of environmental law doctrine may be more consistently the focus of student and departmental interest. In other settings — where, for instance, pre-law students predominate — the legal process dynamics of the material may appear especially relevant to your students. In either event the material of this course is likely to insinuate a double focus. And ultimately, of course, you will and should teach the kind of course that interests you.

Some further practical notes:

- The first printing of the coursebook regrettably contained a number of typographical errors and slips, many of which were corrected in the August 1992 second printing. You may wish to get a corrected second-printing version of the book for your teaching copy by contacting West Publishing Company's Jon Olson (who has consistently provided gracious and valuable support during the coursebook's publication) at 612-687-7629.

- Also available from West Publishing if useful to your course preparation:
  - A loose-leaf 3-ring binder version of the coursebook which may help organize notes and text.
  - We are preparing occasional updates in the form of edited late-breaking cases, materials, and questions to be available as update supplements to the teachers manuals prior to the beginning of the school year.
  - Some of the charts for teaching legal fundamentals had to be reduced and page-split for inclusion in this manual (e.g. Charts A and C). If you would like legal-sized copies of these charts for improved clarity of reproduction, Jon Olson has master copies.

IB. On Teaching NLS and Environmental Law as a First Law Course

Many students know the legal system only through shows like LA Law, Hill Street Blues, Night Court, and movies like To Kill A Mockingbird. Most have a recollection of eighth-grade civics, but no realistic sense of how legislatures, agencies, courts, corporations, and citizens interact.

In this setting, most students (even those who think they know the legal system) are likely to have only scattered disjointed knowledge of the legal system as a whole. Even first-year law students who take this course in their second semester have only glimpses of what law is.

Environmental law is both fascinating in its own details and can also provide a remarkable array of different approaches — statutory, agency regulatory, common law, ADR, etc. — by which the law can be directed toward accomplishing society's goals. Environmental law also is remarkably complete in its cumulation of legal issues — different theories of fault and responsibility, legal and equitable remedies, procedural requirements and burdens of proof, degrees and postures of judicial and administrative discretion and deference, and an overview of the historical development and evolution of legal principles, the technical details of the litigation process and legislation, the intersection of politics and law in courts, legislatures, and government, and so on.

The challenge, of course, is to teach a coherent course in spite of the extraordinary variety of different themes, materials, and distractions that environmental law produces. Our answer to this is that it is consistently fun to teach environmental law as a first course in law. In part it is because most students have a deep or awakenable interest in the subject matter of environmentalism, and most are pleased to have one discrete subject matter carrying them through the entire legal system. Tying together all the diverse elements of law, and revealing age-old mysteries of this secret profession, usually prove to be both exciting and engrossing to students. We have been consistently surprised by how much energy students pour into the course. They often welcome extra exercises, such as mock trials or writing briefs. It is exciting to hear them ask about judicial politics, to see them figure out how to read a case or statute, and to help them second-guess legal controversies they have heard about in their own lives.

For this reason, as noted in Part One above, the fundamental theme that runs through the course whenever we or others of our colleagues have offered it is its theme of step-by-step illumination and exploration of the nooks and crannies of the legal system. Learning technical procedures and terms seems to be a turn-on even for students whose particular interest in natural resource and environmental studies substantive material brought them to the course in the first place. What this course provides is a technical understanding of how issues of social policy and economic analysis can be made *functional*. Law is something with which people *do* things. It offers an understanding of a system for going beyond the academic cloister in which many of them have spent so many years of their lives. On the other hand environmental law has many wonderful elements in and of itself. The environmental movement has led to important new discussions about public values and public policies. These discussions have changed the workings of our legal system, producing imaginative use of old doctrine and creating effective types of new doctrine.

Thus in prior offerings of NLS as a first law course, there has always been that double approach — teaching *law*, and teaching *environmental* law. So long as the readings are kept within bounds, class discussions can develop both these themes concurrently throughout the semester.

We have found that it is worthwhile to presume no knowledge on the part of any of our students, and to build up the entire course from scratch. In this course setting, even the brightest students seem to welcome a step-by-step building process beginning from the most basic foundation.

Professor Goldfarb has found it useful to trace a common theme — the concept of balancing tests — through the entire course. His students have appreciated having a consistent frame of reference for all of this new and disparate material. What follows is a short discussion of how to weave such a theme into the course.

> Except for the welcome but rare "win-win" situation, all public policy decisions create winners and losers. Public policy formulation and implementation involve comparing the benefits and costs of a proposed policy in order to reach an optimum solution. With regard to environmental policy, sometimes private economic loss (e.g. compliance cost) is balanced against public environmental gain. Conversely, as in the *Boomer* case, private environmental loss may be balanced against public economic gain. In other cases, the risks raised by a proposed policy (e.g. encouragement of biotechnology) are weighed against the economic and social benefits that might be realized if the proposal be implemented. Benefit-cost analysis, defined in the most general sense (see Chapter 2), pervades environmental policy. For example, what are the benefits and costs of replacing salting of roads with another deicing method?
>
> The legal system serves both to make and carry out public policy. Doctrines developed through the case-by-case evolution of the common law may be legislatively codified (see Chapter 6). These statutes, which are then subject to administrative and judicial interpretation, become a primary mode of policy implementation. The balancing of benefits and costs is thus an important element of environmental law. Various manifestations of the balancing test in environmental law differ with regard to terminology used, factors to be balanced, weights accorded to each side of the balance (translating into different burdens of proof), and modes of accounting for scientific uncertainties. In some cases (e.g., "economic isolationism" in dormant commerce clause analysis — see Chapter 10) a balancing test is explicitly foregone in favor of a categorical rule of testing legality of particular conduct. But it is important to recognize that a categorical rule is one way of balancing private loss against public gain in a situation that lawmakers perceive as extreme.
>
> It is a useful teaching tool to trace the balancing concept through this coursebook. Analyze it as it appears in 1) common law causes of action like private and public nuisance, 2) remedies such as punitive damages and injunctions, 3) categorical rules of liability such as joint and several, strict, and retroactive liability under CERCLA, 4) criminal law doctrines of knowledge and intent, 5) the public trust doctrine, 6) "takings," 7) concepts of judicial review of administrative action, and 8) statutory tests such as NEPA's "systematic balancing," the definition of "critical habitat" under the Endangered Species Act, public resource management tests such as multiple and dominant use, "unreasonable risk" under FIFRA and ToSCA, standard-setting methodologies such as the harm-based and technology-based approaches, RCRA's "land-ban," etc.
>
> The balancing test concept can serve as a consistent frame of reference through which students can cope with this new, disparate, and frequently confusing material.

As to actual teaching style, we have found that students are often galvanized — especially outside law schools — by the law class mode of teaching. Pure lecturing misses this opportunity. The course has typically been offered as at least a modified lecture, with semi-socratic questioning, dialogue, role-playing, classroom argumentation between plaintiffs and defendants, spin-offs on current events, and so on. Students outside law schools typically are extremely pleased not to be stuck in the old lecture recitation model of course work.

We have noted that — whether because of the nature of environmentalism or the particular setting of the course — the relationship between students and teachers in most offerings of this course has often tended to be somewhat more informal/collegial than in other courses. Students often feel encouraged to analyze and wrangle over issues about which they have strong personal feelings, "conservative" as well as "liberal." The teacher-as-authoritarian does not necessarily fit this model of inquiry and discourse well.

The following excerpts from a short article by Bill Goldfarb, writing on his experience teaching NLS and environmental law outside the law school curriculum, may be helpful to you in defining the goals and process of the course:

GOLDFARB, LAW COURSES FOR NON-LAW STUDENTS
(adapted from Fall 1991 PLANC POINTS,
the publication of the Pre-Law Advisors National Council)

William Goldfarb, J.D., Ph.D.
Professor of Environmental Law
Cook College, Rutgers, The State University of New Jersey

It has been twenty years since my first stint as a Pre-Law Advisor, and, concurrently, since I first began to teach Environmental Law to non-law undergraduate and graduate students as a full-time faculty member. There is some controversy among law school faculty and pre-law advisors about whether pre-law students should take courses in law. I'm an unabashed advocate of the "do it" school, and in this article I'll explain my reasoning.

In 1970, after five years as a practicing attorney and a return to graduate school in order to obtain a doctorate in English and Comparative Literature, I was teaching Humanities in a college of engineering when the first "Earth Day" stimulated another change in my career plans. On that epochal day, I decided to become an environmental lawyer, and to teach my subject to non-law university students. The following fall I introduced what has become the longest-running undergraduate Environmental Law course in the United States.

I could go on about the advantages of a law course to those students who, as non-law professionals, will frequently be working with the law and lawyers. In fact, two-thirds of my Environmental Law students are undergraduate and graduate students-mostly in the sciences and engineering-who aspire to careers in Environmental Management. Over the years, many graduates have told me how important a law course had been in preparing them to understand legal problems, legal concepts, legal language and lawyers.

But let's talk about pre-law students. Many of them, for better or worse reason, are drawn to law courses, and some academics are concerned that taking law courses will narrow or dilute an undergraduate's education. I would argue, on the contrary that a few wisely-chosen undergraduate law courses can only enhance the undergraduate's educational experience.

Our American system of legal education is not the only possible system. In England, for example, law students "read" (major in) law as undergraduates, and then qualify as barristers or solicitors by passing examinations and serving periods of apprenticeship. Without commenting on the relative merits of the American and British systems of legal education, it's clear that most students who enter American law schools have had no background in law whatsoever. Some of them may have taken undergraduate courses in the politics or sociology of law, or else courses in law taught by political scientists or sociologists, but they've generally not taken a law course taught by a lawyer.

Now, as pre-law advisors, we know that college graduates go on to law school for all sorts of reasons: for example, some to please their parents, some because they've become enamored of "L.A. Law;" some because they've heard that lawyers make loads of money and hold positions of power; and some because they believe that law is the best way to change the world. Some of these students belong in law school and some don't, depending on their aptitudes, their enjoyment (or lack thereof) of legal studies, their dedication, their work habits, their temperaments, etc.. But the point is that those students who don't belong in law school won't find that out until it's too late-until they've invested so much time, energy , and money in their legal educations that they can't abandon them and do what they should have done in the first place. The first year in law school is a matter of survival, a rite of passage. Law students really don't begin to evaluate their career goals until their second year, and then they've invested so much that they might as well finish up.

For the ordinary American college senior, going to law school is a blind leap in the dark. This situation is unfair not only to the student, but also to the law schools that will be asked to educate students who find out too late that they'd rather not be lawyers, and to those other undergraduates, better suited to legal education, who might be competing for places in law school first-year classes.

My undergraduate Environmental Law course is taught like a law school course. I use law school coursebooks, concentrate on close readings of cases, statues, and regulations, and emphasize legal reasoning and the structure of the American legal system. The major differences between my course and a law school course are that my course moves at a considerably slower pace; there is no required legal research or writing; less use is made of the so-called "Socratic Method;" and more attention is paid to the policy aspects of the subject. Nevertheless, when a student completes my course , she/he knows what the law is and does, and what legal studies entail.

Time and time again, I've had students come up to me at the conclusion of the course and say something like, "Professor Goldfarb, thanks for an enjoyable course. I was pre-law before this course, but I now realize that I'm not proficient enough at working with this material and I don't enjoy studying it enough to make it my career. So thanks, I've learned a lot, but I think I'll do graduate work in ecology (or business, or psychology, etc.)." At this point, I feel terrific. I've corrected a misguided career choice and saved the student a good deal of wasted time, aggravation, and money.

But undergraduate law courses work the opposite way too. Just as many students who, before taking my course, were majors in Environmental Science, Economic, Business, etc., decide to become lawyers after completing (and doing well in, and greatly enjoying) the course. These are students who would not be pre-law had it not been for their exposure to legal studies at a time when they were still in a position to make an informed career choice.

So, undergraduate law courses (of course, taught by lawyers) are beneficial for pre-laws who shouldn't be, and for non-pre-laws who should be.

What about undergraduate law courses for pre-laws who are headed in the right directions?

First, we need to dispel some myths. Undergraduate law courses don't give a student an advantage in the law school admissions process. Rightly or wrongly, law school admissions officers are not impressed by these courses. Undergraduate law courses, by themselves, don't hurt an applicant's chances, but they don't help them either. Moreover, experience with legal studies in college doesn't give an entering law student an appreciable advantage over her/his classmates. One's first year in law school is a unique experience — a trial by fire for which no prior experience can prepare one.

Nevertheless, pre-laws should take at least one undergraduate course in law. First, a positive experience in such a course can confirm an undergraduate's choice of careers — no small matter in these times of vocational uncertainty. An outstanding performance in a law course might even help a student to convince his/her parents to contribute to his/her legal education. Second, attaining a high grade in the course will probably enable a student to procure a strong law school recommendation from the instructor, who may have achieved contacts and credibility with law school admissions officials. I'm convinced that my personal assurance that one of my students would excel in law school has, on more than one occasion, made the difference between acceptance and rejection. Third, I've often been told by former students that my course has, by educating them in legal reasoning, prepared them for the LSATs in a way that no "cram course" ever could. And finally, an undergraduate law course can familiarize a student with the relationships between law and public policy, a nexus that is not generally emphasized in law schools.... Taking a "non-professional" law course permits the student to perceive the law in a broad social context....

Ic. Designing The Course

As noted above, the nature of your students, your own aspirations for the course, and the objectives of your institution in offering NLS, all enter into the process of designing the course you will offer and your approach to the materials. Your approach will differ depending on whether, for example, you have 20 or 120 students enrolled in the course, whether you are an adjunct faculty member with a demanding full-time job elsewhere or a full-time faculty member teaching this and other graduate courses — a large Environmental Law class and two other medium-sized classes. As a general rule, the more students and less time that you have, the more you will have to rely on the "examination - weekly quiz" mode of grading. Guiding and grading papers takes a great deal of time. In a smaller group or graduate seminar setting, you can do more with papers, role-playing, mock trials, debates, etc.

Our caveat to you at this point is that, whatever approach you choose, by the end of the semester you will undoubtedly wish you had much more time. Constraining the volume of material covered and the degree of detail in dispensable areas of coverage will be an important part of designing a successful approach to the course.

In the main manual we discuss the term paper and exam requirements of the course. In this non-law school elective setting, in an area so new to the students, it is especially important that they get some kind of feedback during the course of the semester. For this reason NLS courses have often had short written exercises — a legal memo, a mini-brief re-arguing a case in the text, or a short mid-term exam — in addition to the major graded course assignments which are typically due at the end of the term.

LEGAL RESEARCH TERM PAPERS

As to a term-paper, in Part Three of this manual we set out several models that have been followed successfully at different schools in past offerings. A five-page term paper is a sufficient challenge; it need not be longer to be of great value. We have consistently found, however, that it is best to require that the term paper be a *legal* project, not an analysis of environmental policy or factual issues. Most such legal term papers require some law library research (whether closed-horizon or wide-open research). Indeed, the challenge of working with legal materials seems to be what most students seek from the exercise. Be sure to coordinate beforehand with law librarians, especially reference librarians, to prepare for the arrival of novice legal researchers, but the endeavor is one we recommend.

In some instances, classes have been assigned the same or a choice of one of three issues — e.g., whether strict liability applies in a particular toxic setting, the applicability of primary jurisdiction, the availability of coming-to-the-nuisance defenses, etc., where each student must write from the position of plaintiff or defendant in a different jurisdiction. At other times students are given a range of possible legal topics or advised in their own selection of a legal topic. In addition to such a term paper assignment, or in substitution thereof, some course offerings have had students brief and present an appellate argument in a moot court setting, and in at least one case present the complete trial of a pollution tort. The bottom line is that students in this course do not have to be shielded from some hands-on work with legal materials; quite to the contrary, they seem to thrive upon such assignments in this new field.

When you assign the research paper we suggest you choose between the approaches set out in the draft Research Paper Prospectus in Part Three of this manual, labelled Formats 1, 2, and 3. There are further points to be noted: Besides warning the law library staff that this assignment is coming, and having them assist in making plans, you should also decide whether students will be allowed to use WESTLAW and LEXIS; the learning exercise is more useful if confined to hardcopy reporters and digests, with the possible addition of state codes annotated. You also could decide to make the Format 1 assignment a "closed horizon" exercise, where all cases that may be used are pulled and put on reserve for ready access by all; this approach may be necessary if there is no law library available, but misses the actual library exploration that most students enjoy and value.

EXAMINATIONS

Examinations are always the worst part of teaching a course. Some past examination questions are set out in the main teachers manual. In Part Three of this manual there is a further selection of midterm and final exam multiple choice and essay questions that have been used in offerings of the course to first-time law students. Midterm exams can be useful to students and teachers alike, although they divert student energies and are a burden to grade. The unfortunate fact, however, is that environmental law seems to require at least a final examination. If course credit is based solely on one or two writing assignments, students tend to delve deeply into the narrow area involved in those exercises, but not to force themselves to integrate the entirety of the course. Exams force everyone to "pull it all together," and allow the teacher to assess which portions of coverage need to be reworked for subsequent offerings.

DESIGNING THE SYLLABUS

In terms of designing the course itself throughout a semester (or two semesters if you are so lucky) as noted in the main manual, the critical question is the amount of time available. A typical offering will be fourteen or fifteen weeks, with three or four class hours a week. (We would not advocate teaching the course at less than three credit hours.) Professor Goldfarb has the luxury of teaching the course in more than seventy hours of actual classroom time over two semesters. Most people will be more likely to teach in the range of 35-40 class hours for the entire course.

In designing the course, you should look briefly at the course-design material provided in the main manual, pages 9-36. In this manual, however, we are slightly more prescriptive.

What follows here in this section, pages 12-20, is a draft syllabus with options for designing a first law course. (Final draft versions of this syllabus and others are printed at pages 72-84 herein.)

The bold portions of the running page blocks in this draft compilation are basic core assignments, totaling approximately 535 pages out of the coursebook's total 1039 pages.

The page blocks set out in smaller regular font type are our suggestions for potential add-on readings, totaling another 95 pages.

Separate free-standing optional classes also appear in the draft syllabus, totaling another 195 pages.

These possibilities, of course, are not dispositive. Some useful material has undoubtedly been left out of our proposed drafts. To assist you in further efforts in designing your own syllabus, in Part Three we provide a comprehensive raw syllabus worksheet, setting out a running page block inventory of all the materials in the book; if you so choose, you can thereby make your own selections on a clean slate.

The draft syllabus is designed more or less in one class-hour blocks. If your course is offered in two 1 1/2-hour sessions per week, it will require appropriate adjustments. Similarly, on many of these assignments you will be strongly tempted to extend class coverage for another hour. For that reason, extra time has been built into the proposed syllabus to be used through the sequence of assignments as necessary (i.e. this syllabus includes only 27 stipulated assignments, with 9 add-ons. A fourteen week course, meeting three times a week, equals a total of forty-two class meetings.

[As to materials you choose not to assign, it is always worth skimming them to consider whether to bring them into class discussions as professorial asides, and background.]

A DRAFT FORMAT SYLLABUS FOR NATURE, LAW, AND SOCIETY AS A FIRST LAW COURSE,

With optional add-on assignments

[SEE ALSO PROPOSED FINAL VERSION IN PART III.]

bold, larger type = suggested basic assignment pages
plain text = possible add-on or skim assignment pages

Class hour	Page assignment	Coverage	Chapter	(Notes to teachers)
1.	**xxiii-xxxvii** **1-4** 4-6, 6-7, 7-10 11-15	**INTRODUCTION** **THE BREADTH & SCOPE OF ENVIRONMENTAL PROBLEMS** Ecology — Rachel Carson, Aldo Leopold, What on Earth Are We Doing? Ethics — Leopold, and text	1	
	15-17, **17-27**	**The highway salting problem** **Environmental analysis & legal strategies**		
*	OPTIONAL CLASS [33-91]	A class hour may be added here on economics, risk, and corporate cost externalization: Select from pages 33-91 (using worksheet, Part III herein): Hardin, Kepone case, *Wilsonville*, Sandman, Huber, *Reserve Mining, Corrosion-Proof Fittings* (in main Teachers Manual page 279), and text. [See handout charts in main Teacher's Manual at 277-278.]	2	(If you skip this so that class can go right into the *Boomer* case, this material can be integrated into following assignments.)
2.	**33-40,**	**MORE ENVIRONMENTAL ANALYSIS — the tragedy of the commons — Hardin**	2	
	102-112, HANDOUTS: **legal process charts A, B**	**Traditional common law theories** **The *Boomer* case, to be read initially for facts and for analyzing the development of a law case**	3	(Handout charts are in Part III of this manual. You may also wish to hand out the Glossary from Part III of this manual.)

3.	**Re-read 102-112, 112-116** **HANDOUTS: legal process charts C, D**	***BOOMER*** **A prima facie tort case: private nuisance, intentional**	3	
4.	**117-121**	**DEFENSES IN ENVIRONMENTAL TORT SUITS**	3	
5.	**121-130,**	**A COMPENDIUM OF TORT CAUSES-OF-ACTION: Public nuisance —** ***Schenectady Chemicals, Spur Industries***	3	(Handout Spur map missing from p. 129 in first printing, from main TM at 289-290.)
	131-142	Trespass, negligence, strict liability cases		
6.	**148-159,** 159-163, **163-170**	**REMEDIES: civil damages available** Long-distance indirect economic damages — *Pruitt*: Kepone and Chesapeake Bay **Natural resources damages**	3	
7.	**142-148,**	**EQUITY AND INJUNCTIONS**	3	*Wilsonville*, 66-78, can be added here as a restoration injunction case.

8.	171-176,	NEW LESSONS FROM TOXIC TORTS Multiple parties, litigatability, class actions	4	(See *Biechele* class action notice (in Part III) as possible handout.)
	176-180, 196-198, comments 5 and 6, [epidemiological proof of causation]	Joint and several liability — *Velsicol*		
	199-210	**A toxic tort case: logistics, theory, proof — *W.R. Grace,* the Woburn, Mass. chemicals case**		
9.	**224-232**	**ENVIRONMENTAL REMEDIES FROM OTHER FIELDS OF LAW:**	5	
	and/or	**corporate law—*Pacific Lumber;***		
	232-237	**Property & contract law — strip-mining cases**		
10.	**241-244,**	**FROM COMMON LAW TO PUBLIC LAW**	6	(The indented pages can be assigned here or with the chapter 21-22 assignment. Accommodate this assignment to your chapter 21-22 assignment.)
	42-49,	**The *Kepone* case — Goldfarb**	2	
	244-258,	**Statutes and *Kepone***		
	260-266,	**Statutory liability — Rich**	6	
	[266-279, 285-287 here or with Chaps. 21-22]	Parties liable under CERCLA and RCRA — *NEPACCO* *Wade II*		
	287-292,	Joint and several liability — *Monsanto*		
	skim 301-313	**The effect of environmental statutes on common law — *Silkwood***		
11.	**322-327,**	**THE 1899 REFUSE ACT, ENVIRONMENTAL CRIMINAL LAW REDISCOVERED**	7	
	327-330,	***Film Recovery***		
	330-335,	**Criminal prosecution**		
	335-336,	Fifth amendment and the corporation		
	336-343	**Difficulties in proving collective activity crimes — *Kepone* — Goldfarb**		

Class	Pages	Topic	Chapter	Notes
12.	365-376,	**THE PUBLIC TRUST AS QUASI-CONSTITUTIONAL ENVIRONMENTAL RIGHTS — Sax**	8	(You may wish to do a mini-lecture on constitutional claims of environmental rights, 357-364.)
	376-381,	**Applying the modern public trust doctrine — *Paepke***		
	394-405	**How far does the public trust go? — *Florissant***		
13.	381-393,	**PUBLIC TRUST CONTINUED —*Mono Lake***	8	(*Mono Lake* can be switched with *Florissant*.)
	405-412,	**Public trust and private property rights — Sax**		
	414-420	***National Gettysburg Tower***		
14.	425-429,	**PROPERTY RIGHTS AND ENVIRONMENTAL LAW — EMINENT DOMAIN**	9	
	429-435,	**Challenging an eminent domain condemnation — Poletown**		
	436-442	**Inverse condemnation —*Thornburg***		
15.	442-448,	**PROPERTY RIGHTS CONTINUED — regulatory takings and the case of wetlands**	9	
	449-452,	***Johnson***		
	452-453,	***Sibson***		
	453-457,	**Assorted tests — *Pennsylvania Coal***		
	457-464	**Residuum test**		
16.	465-472,	**NO REMAINING ECONOMIC USE?**	9	(Add *Lucas* excerpt from Part III.)
	Handout: *Lucas*			
	472-473,	Takings remedies		
	473,	Amortization and offsets		
	474,	Exactions and *Nollan*		
	474-475	Due process and innocent landowners		

*	OPTIONAL CLASS	**FEDERAL-STATE ENVIRONMENTAL ISSUES:**	10	
	476-482,	**preemption under the supremacy clause**		
	504-508,	Basics of dormant commerce clause adjudication — Philadelphia v. N.J.		
	512-520	**Balancing burdens — *Procter & Gamble***		
*	OPTIONAL CLASS	**SPARE DAY: review, catch-up**		
17.	**544-561**	**ENVIRONMENTAL ADMINISTRATIVE LAW — *Overton Park*** **Administrative law in a nutshell**	11	(Note here, or later, the taxonomy of statutes pages 535-536)
18.	**561-570,**	**THE CITIZEN'S ROLE IN ADMINISTRATIVE LAW —*Scenic Hudson* and citizen standing**	11	
	574-580, **Handout: Lujan v. Defenders**	**Standing — Lujan v. NWF [BLM public lands]; Lujan v. Defenders of Wildlife [international endangered species]**		(Add new *Lujan* material from Part III herein as handout. Note further areas of deference — on procedure and on statutory interpretation.
	581-589	Attempts to expand agency procedures — *Vermont Yankee*		
19.	**596-603,**	**NEPA**	12	
	603-609,	**The Chicod Creek case, NRDC v. Grant**		
	609-624,	***Grant,* continued**		
	624-625,	***Grant* (1972)**		
	625-630	***Grant* (1973)**		

*	**630-636,**	**NEPA CONTINUED — Content of an EIS**	12	We recommend teaching *at least* one additional class on the NEPA material.
	637-644,	EIS process — *Kleppe* (Sierra Club)		
	644-649,	*Marsh*		
	649-655	*Robertson*		
20.	**656-659,**	**SUBSTANTIVE ROADBLOCKS: section 7 of the endangered species act of 1973, a stark prohibition statute**	13	(You may want to assign 659-665 as a skim assignment.)
	659-665,	***Hill,* The Tellico Dam/snail darter case**		
	674-684	**The spotted owl and logging our old-growth national forests**		
*	OPTIONAL CLASS **685-686,**	**PUBLIC RESOURCE MANAGEMENT STATUTES**	14	(Handout: checkerboard map from main Teacher's Manual, 304.)
	686-688,	**The public lands**		
	688-700, HANDOUT: MAP	**Multiple use mandate — Coggins**		
	707-716	Off-road vehicles		
21.	**717-719,**	**HISTORICAL DEVELOPMENT OF POLLUTION REGULATION**	15	
	719-723,	**Michigan's water pollution statute**		
	723-726,	**Utilex: water pollution case study**		
	726-731,	**Alternative approaches to standard setting**		
	731-737	**Modern permit processes**		

	Pages	Topic		Notes
*	OPTIONAL CLASS	**REGULATION OF MARKET ACCESS — Pesticides**	16	(Les v. Reilly handout is in Part III of this manual; *Corrosion-Proof Fittings* is in Part III of the main Teacher's Manual at page 279.)
	738-739,	Federal regulation of pesticides		
	739-741,	—Miller		
	Handouts: Les v. Reilly; skim *Corrosion-Proof Fittings*	**Les v. Reilly; skim *Corrosion-Proof Fittings***		
	747#8,	FIFRA licensing		
	748-750,	ToSCA — R. Druley		
*	OPTIONAL CLASS	**STARK STATUTORY POLLUTION STANDARDS — Auto emissions —**		
	760-764,	**Clean Air Act — Title II excerpts**	17	
	766-772	**Statutory overkill?**		
22.	**774-780,**	**THE CLEAN AIR ACT, ambient standards, the national commons and federalism; Harm as the threshold of regulation**	18	(Handout in class: chart from *Cleveland Electric* from Part III of main Teacher's Manual at 311.)
	780-783,	*Train*		
	783-787,	*Lead Industries*		
	787-790,	**Commentary and question on the Clean Air Act**		
	790-793,	The perplex of safety and risk assessment		
	800-811,	***Cleveland Electric***		
	Handout: Chart from *Cleveland Electric*			
23.	**825-831,**	**THE CLEAN WATER ACT AND TECHNOLOGY-BASED REGULATION**	19	(Handouts in main Teacher's Manual at 312 and 313.)
	831-835,	Conservation Foundation report		
	835-848,	***Rybachek***		
	Handouts: Chart and Average River problem,			
	856-859	CWA citizen suits		

*	**859-860,**	**ECONOMIC INCENTIVES AND ARTIFICIAL POLLUTION MARKET STATUTES**	20	
	860-863,	Ideal versus real — Latin		
	863-866,	Reforming environmental law — Ackerman		
	866-870,	Effluent taxes		
	870-876,	**Marketable permits — Hahn**		
	876-881	**EPA, Title IV acid deposition program**		
24.	**266-269,**	**TOXIC WASTE REGULATION — *NEPACCO*: a toxics case under RCRA and CERCLA**	6	
	926-928,	**Introduction to RCRA**	22	
	882-886,	**Introduction to CERCLA**	21	
	260-266,	**Statutory liability**	6	
	928-924,	More on RCRA	22	
	285-287,	Proof of causation — *Wade* II	6	
	287-292	Joint and several liability — *Monsanto*		
24.*	**Alternate 24.**	**TOXIC WASTE REGULATION —**	22	(Alternate assignment: If you gave fairly intensive coverage to liability in chapter 6.)
	928-940,	**tracking and controlling the life cycle of hazardous waste**		
	940-946,	**The "land ban" and the use of "hammers" to control agency action**		
	882-898	**'90 National Contingency Plan**	21	
25.	**911-923,**	**MORE ISSUES IN TOXICS REGULATION — EPA enforcement strategies — *Cannons Engineering***	21	(Assign 954-960 if not assigned in next class.)
	898-903,	**The costs of CERCLA — *Conservation Chemical***		
	903-908,	**Fairness — *Picillo***		
	924-925,	**EPA CERCLA §106 orders — Shifting to private cleanups**		
	954-960	**State hazardous waste facility siting statutes**	23	

*	OPTIONAL CLASS: 954-960, 960-967, 967-971, 972-975	**LAND USE IN ENVIRONMENTAL LAW** State hazardous waste facility siting statutes §404 wetlands regulation *Bersani* Regional planning — *Wambat* Subdivision regulations and zoning	23	
26.	**979-993,** 993-996	**ADR — ALTERNATIVE DISPUTE RESOLUTION** **A case study in EDR — Talbot** Negotiated rule making — Susskind	24	(See handout map of Hudson River in main Teacher's Manual at 316.)(Or do simulation? — available from Harvard Program on Negotiations at 617-495-1684.)
*	**Optional class: Main Teacher's Manual, 342-353**	**RACE, POVERTY, AND THE ENVIRONMENT**		TM 342-353.
27.	**997-999,** **999-1006,** **1013-1021,** **Handouts: Rio Earth Summit materials** 1021-1026, 1026-1027, 1027-1029, 1029-1030, 1030-1031, 1031-1033	**INTERNATIONAL ENVIRONMENTAL LAW** **The Sandoz spill — Schwabach** **Whaling — Birnie** Extraterritorial municipal law NGOs Intergenerational equity — Weiss "Soft Law" The North-South split One world/One tribe?	25	(Rio handouts in Part III.)

PART TWO: THE COURSE, Class-By-Class

This part of the syllabus provides structures and suggestions for teaching the class assignments noted in the draft syllabus set out in Part One above.

In the first weeks of the course we make special efforts to introduce students to the structure and characteristics of an environmental lawsuit. Legal mechanics are illustrated in a variety of charts and diagrams prepared as handouts, set out in Part Three of this manual, as referred to in the text below. The experience of past teachers of the course has been that although most of the mechanics of law are taught in the first weeks, they continue to be pulled into discussions throughout the course. For that reason, despite the fact that the readings tend to focus upon substantive matter in later weeks, teachers should be prepared to encounter legal process questions at every step of the way.

Class 1. Introduction to the Course

The first class hour is an opportunity to do a number of important things. Chicken-hearted teachers will use the first meeting only to explain the mechanics of the course — term papers, exams, the syllabus etc. — and then adjourn early, but we always try to cram more substance into the first class. It has been our experience that students come into their first environmental law class with anticipations of getting an idea of what this new kind of course will be, without much preconception of what to expect, and teachers do well to provide some glimpses of what is to come

So what can you do with the first class, noting that in many or most cases students will not have done any reading, even if reading was assigned? The class can nevertheless address the following four points:

• **The nature of an environmental analysis.** The highway salting example in the coursebook is a good teaching vehicle, even if students have not done the reading. Other options would be to choose a current environmental issue in the newspaper, a pollution tort case, or the like. In each case, however, the teacher should try to put on the blackboard some graphic representation of a controversy so that students from any background can relate to the problem, noting how the problem has been created by actor-decisionmakers who typically have been able to ignore the "externalized" "environmental" public costs of the action. It is important to remind students early on that most environmental problems derive from human actions that are made with a narrowed, insulated point of view that ignores or discounts environmental values and costs, and that environmental law is a way to change such behavior, retrospectively and prospectively, by "presenting the bill," or setting up legal procedures to force the market process to avoid or minimize those costs.

• **A flying survey of possible kinds of legal remedy** that might be applied to the problem at hand. In the case of highway salt, or in whatever other model controversy you choose, it should be possible to brainstorm a variety of different weapons that concerned citizens and officials might bring to bear upon the problem. You should remind the students that in our society the media and other extra-legal mechanisms are available, but that, in most cases at least, the potential for legal action is an important component of how issues are resolved. This flying survey should thus consider whether the private marketplace can handle the problem by itself, or why not; the availability of public law remedies, direct or indirect, through pollution statutes, regulations, and ordinances; the availability of common law theories, etc..... You can also foreshadow for the students the various kinds of technical issues that will be involved in these different areas. The course will discuss theories of liability, theories of defense, theories of remedy, the technical interplay between different branches of government, and the effect of constitutional principles upon the daily operation of such cases. The point is that students should walk out of the first class having a sense of the variety of legal topics that will be raised in the course, as they might apply to some real, comprehensible environmental controversy. Part of this exercise, too, especially for students outside law school, is to reassure them that they can cope with this somewhat mysterious and technical new field. It would be useful to state that all these legal inquiries are intended to make sense, building step by step along the way from a simple foundation, and that ultimately all the material in the course should be accessible to the entire class irrespective of their prior experience with the law, or lack thereof.

• **Your approach to the course, or theme.** This will have been illustrated by your presentation of the first two points.

A side note: Especially when you are teaching the book to first-year law students as part of a required introductory legal process course, it is useful to acknowledge at the outset the "bias" in much of environmental law (and in this coursebook, as discussed at page xxxv of the Introduction) in favor of environmental accountability and environmental plaintiffs. Legal process students must be reminded: that the subject matter is being used as a particularly apt vehicle for a comprehensive foundation course in the legal system, that environmental plaintiffs made environmental law so that their perspective must be understood in order to learn the field, and that all coursebooks have their biases but some hide them better than others. And even we are not consistently predictable in our positions on various issues in the book.

• **Course logistics.** Students of course want to know how they are going to be graded, and all the logistical details that lie between them and the ultimate grade. The course prospectus and syllabus (see drafts in Part Three herein) can provide them with most of this information. We typically try to cover these logistical points in the last five or ten minutes of the first class hour, so that they do not mushroom to take up the full session.

•***For the next class*** **:**

(a) (If teaching the following optional class on economics and risk at this point): Tell students to read the assigned materials for policy, rather than for legal process, noting the economic behavior of the relevant players and the difficult problems posed by risk and uncertainty when we don't know critical facts but downside dangers may be great.

(b) (If going straight to "Class 2" of this draft syllabus): Tell students, in preparing the assignment for class 2, to note briefly the various strategies for coping with pollution set out in Hardin's "tragedy of the commons" (a policy analysis refrain that leads into legal analysis), and then go to the *Boomer* case, approaching it as an exercise in learning how to read a legal appellate opinion; tell them to recreate in their minds the *factual story* of the environmental controversy. The legal mechanics of the actual *Boomer* case will be covered in depth in later sessions.

You may wish to give them in advance the Chapter 3 handouts (Charts A, B and possibly C from Part Three herein) which can be used to figure out how a lawsuit is put together and how it proceeds through the various steps of litigation and appeal. They are not supposed to understand the charts on their own, but may use them to prepare themselves for the legal process narrative that will begin in the next class.

---

* Optional Add-On Class (from chapter 2 materials on economics and risk)

[In many past offerings this Chapter 2 policy material has been postponed until later in the course. It has seemed wise to go straight to Chapter 3, so that students in their second day of the course can get right into the process of analyzing a legal case. Chapter 3's *Boomer* is the case that we highlight as the first case subjected to intensive legal process analysis (see "Class

2" following). The idea is that the material on economics, cost externalization and risk are much more concerned with substantive environmental policy than legal process, and students early in a first law course should have their focus directed to legal mechanics.

Nevertheless a number of people who have offered the course, including Professor Goldfarb, and others whose natural resources/environmental studies students are particularly interested in substantive environmental policy, typically work through the Chapter 2 materials at this point in the course sequence — Hardin's "tragedy of the commons" (which is also included in our draft "Class 2" below) is a wonderful paradigm to teach.

The *Kepone* case is a major case study which is brought into other chapter's discussions, and can be used to show how corporate decisionmaking typically attempts to internalize as much profit, and externalize as much cost, as possible.

The *Wilsonville* case is used by Professor Goldfarb as an intensive study of how a trial takes place, with discussion of expert witnesses, contending parties, politics, risk assessment, and the role of the judge. At this stage Prof. Goldfarb does not delve deeply into the legal theory of the tort cause of action, instead looking at the dramatics of the judicial forum and the policy questions that lie within the case.

The Sandman, Huber, and *Reserve Mining* materials are important in analyzing public reactions to environmental toxic cases, where politics reflect human reactions as much as statistical reality and scientific proof. (Note that *Corrosion-proof Fitting,* a case which can be substituted for *Reserve Mining* appears in the main teacher's manual at 279.)

If you follow the lead of the proposed draft syllabus and go straight into *Boomer* in class 2, much of the Chapter 2 material will naturally be brought into subsequent discussions. (See assignments for classes covering chapters 3, 6, 7, and 16.)

Class 2. Introduction to a Private Law Case — *Boomer* — Chapter 3

A good way to begin the second day of classes is to pick up again on some of the environmental/economic analysis of the first day's discussion. The Hardin "tragedy of the commons" material is classic, and may be familiar to several of your students. We use it to show how an unregulated market will tend to externalize costs and internalize the maximum amount of benefits from the decision, to the ultimate detriment of the whole.

The discussion then should be shifted into ways in which cost-externalizing onto the commons could be avoided:

- voluntary agreements, though they do not work reliably;

- privatizing the commons — as by putting a fence around each respective owners' share — is possible in the limited cow pasture setting, but obviously is not practical in a larger environmental setting (can you put a glass globe over the Atlantic Cement Company to force it to internalize its costs? could you require municipalities to locate their water intakes downstream of their sewerage discharges to force them to internalize their own water pollution?);

• if a statute can be passed prohibiting grazing beyond a certain number of cows, and can be administratively enforced, that provides an analogy to command and control pollution legislation, although it requires a careful specification of cow density/pollution in the first place, and administrative agents to monitor and enforce;

• there could also be an administrative lottery or other floating assignment of grazing credits;

• it is possible to have a combined market-regulatory system through the imposition of grazing/pollution taxes or fees, whereby every eligible person would have to pay the true cost to the public of the extra imposition of a cow unit upon the commons; such tax systems end up being extraordinarily complex and subject to political abuse, but are an important new approach in the U.S., chronicled in Chapter 20.

• (Most students will overlook this) another legal remedy for cow pasture overloading might be to file a lawsuit under some form of common law cause of action. You could ask the students whether a *Boomer* type lawsuit would seem appropriate; you might note for them that the *Boomer* precedent is not exactly on point because Hardin's commons is not private property, but there still might be a common law tort (public nuisance) that you will study subsequently that might provide the opportunity for legal remedies: damages and/or injunction.

Stepping back from this catalog, it becomes clear to students that unless there is an artificial, forceful imposition of externalized costs back to decisionmakers, the marketplace actors will be motivated to ignore them. You might say that much of the focus of environmental law is learning how to present the invoice for externalized costs to actors in the marketplace, so that more rational decisions ultimately will be made. Here, the "tragedy of the commons" example can be segued into the *Boomer* case, which provides an example of how one set of externalized costs is brought back into the corporate polluters' calculus by the legal system.

Rather than beginning with an environmental/economic analysis of *Boomer*, which can well be done later on in your *Boomer* class coverage, it may make sense to get right into the guts of *Boomer* as a legal case.

A good way to begin this is to replay *Boomer* as a recreation of what probably happened. The case began when Boomer and his neighbors became angry about the cement dust pollution. This narrative scenario is set out in part in the main teachers manual, pages 65-67. Boomer and his neighbors apparently presented a petition to the cement company (an appeal to the marketplace through non-legal means which was fruitless, but soon becomes immensely important in proving the "civil intent" of the company in its knowing continuation of harm to the plaintiffs). You might ask whether the Boomers and their neighbors could have gone elsewhere other than to court. Albany, the state capital, was only a few miles away from Coeymans, N.Y. where the case takes place, but obviously the state agency and local public authorities were not inclined to confront a major local employer (see NLS text 110-111). Note that if a state agency does decide to take on a case, it offers some real advantages: it has a large number of paid employees charged with investigation, laboratory testing, and enforcement, and theoretically can levy fines and administrative injunctions. Agencies, however, are often burdened by politics, inertia, or complex protracted procedures. The common law, moreover, offers damages to injured parties. So Boomer goes to court.

At some point here you will want to ask the students what it is they are reading when they read the *Boomer* case? Chart A (see Part III herein) is intended to show them the full course of a civil case at a glance. Note for them that the cases that are typically read in a law course are those written only at the end of the process, and include little or nothing of the actual trial. The process of reading a case thus is a process of imaginative re-creation on the part of the student, attempting to determine from a rather abstract appellate opinion what actually had gone on at trial in terms of relevant facts, the theory of the cause of action, and other issues including politics and atmospherics. (This is a good way to set up class 3, telling the students to reread *Boomer* for the next class session, noting what facts were pulled together to fit what cause of action (this is the meat of Chart C), creating a finding of liability in the trial court, which was upheld in the intermediate appellate court, awarding a permanent damage remedy instead of an injunction, and this was affirmed by N.Y.'s highest court, the Court of Appeals.)

Chart B sets out simplified schematic diagrams of the state and federal court systems. The court that wrote the *Boomer* opinion excerpted in the text would usually, of course, be called the state "Supreme Court." You, unfortunately, must tell students that states have different conventions and New York State's court names are very confusing — because the *trial court* in New York is called Supreme Court, while the highest appellate court in New York is the Court of Appeals. Thus at the end of the *Boomer* majority opinion, the case is remitted (remanded) to "Supreme Court, Albany County," which actually is a remand back down to the original trial court for assessment of damages. (In going through this in chart A or B, you might also want to take a moment to note that when plaintiffs file a case in state court they theoretically get a possibility for further appeal to the U.S. Supreme Court in the limited cases where a federal question is implicated. Further, you may wish to note at this point the plaintiff's opportunity to choose to proceed through the federal court system, on diversity grounds or otherwise.)

So Boomer chooses to go to a private attorney's office to seek a remedy and vindication. You might want to role-play this, as suggested above, putting a schematic diagram on the board as the pieces of information that Mr. Boomer would provide are contributed by students: location of the cement plant, location of the plaintiffs' houses, a smoke stack, vibrations, movement of cement dust from smoke stack to the plaintiffs' neighborhood (and beyond), the neighborhood petition, a chronology of these events to set up a coming-to-the-nuisance inquiry, an indication of prevailing wind direction, an opportunity to ask how difficult the proof of causation would be, an indication that cement dust actually goes far further than the plaintiffs' homes, inviting discussions of the degree to which this action fails to internalize substantial pollution costs, and the specifics (as far as we know them) about possible injuries to property and health.

To get into the legal process, you can ask students what Boomer wants. Does Mr. Boomer want to throw the corporate executives in jail? Clearly he'd be pleased to see them sent up the river, but his major interest is the remedy of getting paid for all of his economic losses, and the cessation of the noxious intrusions on his home and farm, including a remedy shutting down the plant if possible, but not criminal law sanctions. The attorney thus turns to private civil law, rather than statutory criminal or regulatory law.

You probably will not have time to get into the details of how the *Boomer* private nuisance cause of action was chosen and applied. That can be done in the next class, using Chart C. In this class you may merely decide to talk about the dynamics and logistics of how a case begins, noting that this case proceeds under the common law, and drawing policy observations about possible advantages of common law, corporate behavior, the diffusion of externalized costs in the cement dust case, the limits of law in achieving a full accurate accounting, and so on.

You may also want to highlight not only the chain of events that led up to the lawsuit, but also invite the students to imagine what evidence (testimony, exhibits, etc.) it will take for the Boomers to prove those facts in court.

If you have time, you may wish to start analyzing the formulation of the prima facie case in *Boomer*, using Chart C. (Discussion of the elements of a tort cause of action formula, using Chart C, is the focus of the next class.)

• ***For the next class:*** Tell students, in re-reading the *Boomer* case for the next class, to focus on the legal mechanics of how the attorney for Boomer built a "prima facie case," based on private intentional nuisance, and tell them to try to figure out Chart C.

Class 3. Building a Private Law Cause of Action — Private Nuisance — Chapter 3

This class is intended to pick up the many dangling threads left from the prior class introducing the *Boomer* case. This class focuses on the law of an intentional private nuisance cause of action. First you can ask the class to give as many particulars as they can figure out about the actual cause of action that Boomer's attorney chose to follow in the trial court, private nuisance as an intentional tort.

Chart C shows how an attorney can take a selection of facts from a controversy and apply them in a variety of possible causes of action so as to shape a prima facie case, leading to a finding of liability and some remedy for the client. Going through that Chart C spectrum checklist of possible causes of action, you can ask first whether the *Boomer* cause of action was a "constitutional" claim? If there were public power involved, it's at least possible that this could have been a constitutional "inverse condemnation" action. Federal statutory claims might also theoretically have been possible; under §304 of the Federal Clean Air Act, citizens have standing to file claims for enforcement of the federal statute, but of course that becomes immensely entangled in the complexities of regulatory proof, agency initiative, politics, etc. State statutes similarly might be the subject of a hypothetical lawsuit, especially as the state statutes are now part of the federal Clean Air Act's "State Implementation Plan" (SIP) program. Or local ordinances may be the basis of an action. But all of these public law remedies offer more difficulties than advantages, and do not produce compensatory damages for private plaintiffs. Turning to the common law, several causes of action are available, including private nuisance, public nuisance, trespass, personal injury negligence, and negligent nuisance, etc. — each requiring slightly different assemblages of the facts. At this point you should merely indicate to students the array of possibilities and have them identify private nuisance as the only cause of action that Boomer's attorney attempted. (It is important to note to them that a civil complaint can include as many causes of action as appear to be applicable, including pleading in the alternative; "piling-on" is illegal in football, but not in law.)

Private nuisance is a common law claim, deriving from the 13th century judicial formulas for granting redress in the kings' courts rather than a statutory cause of action. You may want to talk a bit about the common law and how it does not derive and usually is not found in modern statutory compilations, but yet is part of the inherited law which Anglo-American courts apply.

For your own use we have included a brief nutshell on old forms of tort action in Part Three of this manual.

Picking up on the discussion of how a cause of action is built into a prima facie case, note how various causes of action can each be separated into a list of required elements, as noted in Chart C. "If the elements of a cause of action like private nuisance are proved by the plaintiff, then the burden turns to the defendant to rebut the plaintiff's allegations of the prima facie case, or provide affirmative legal defenses to trump liability. If liability is established, damages will automatically be granted, and the question will turn to whether an injunction will be granted." Note for the students that virtually the entire discussion in *Boomer* is focused only upon questions at the end of this process — will Boomer get an injunction of some sort, or only damages in this case?

What are the elements of private nuisance when it is brought as an intentional tort? The elements can be seen in the cause of action block set out in the NLS text page 112, and in Chart C, and in Chart 3.1 set out in the main teachers manual (page 68, in the bottom linear box). You may ask students to list the facts that would have to be proved to show each of the elements: 1) plaintiff has suffered unreasonable injury to self or property; 2) defendant's use of defendant's land caused the injury (the *sic utere ... maxim* that you can find in the back of the book, at page 1011, at footnote 29); and 3) that the defendant acted knowingly, with "civil intention." When the students recognize that the existence of the petition proves civil intention, the proof of each of these elements becomes quite easy. The majority of the court, at the top of page 104, therefore quite matter-of-factly accepted the fact that the trial court "accordingly found defendant maintained a nuisance...." In this particular case the defendant Atlantic Cement Company was not able to interpose factual denials or any affirmative defense. (You may want to note for the students that possible defenses will be studied in depth in the next class, but that possible examples would have been if Boomer had moved to the community *after* the cement company began the "coming to the nuisance" defense might apply; if a statute had said that state regulation was the exclusive remedy, a very rare statutory situation, there would have been a statutory override of the common law. Failing these, no defenses were apparently available to avoid a finding of liability.) But of course the whole point of the *Boomer* case is that there is an argument against an injunction shutting down the plant. The cement company apparently wanted to pay permanent damages, and not face a shutdown. Note for the students that these issues will be discussed at greater length in regard to remedies issues three classes hence, so that for the moment it's important to focus upon the question of the plaintiffs' choice of private nuisance as an intentional tort as their prime cause of action.

If time remains, it might be useful to show students the tactical and strategic differences between different choices of cause of action. Note for the students that the most common tort is based on *negligence*, not intentional tort. What would have been the consequences if this had been brought as a negligence action? You may want to set out a facsimile of Chart 3.1 in the main teachers manual on the board page 68, because this provides a vivid example of how the intentional nuisance action offers advantages. Circling the words "unreasonable" and "balance" in that chart, you can show that in intentional private nuisance, the only "unreasonableness" that has to be shown is as to *the plaintiffs'* own suffering, not the very much more economically and politically freighted question of whether the *corporate defendant* acted "unreasonably" in all the circumstances. Similarly, the shift from negligence to intentional tort moves the overt balance of utilities from the defendant's defenses — where the defendant might argue that its manufacturing enterprise was so important to the community that it should not be subjected to any tort liability when compared to the limited utility of plaintiffs' interest — to a mere question of remedy *after* the imposition of liability. When it is an intentional tort, the balance of utility does not prevent a finding of liability and damages, but only the further *Ducktown* question (text at 115) whether the balance of equities and utilities should lead to an injunction.

As less important background, you can give students, as a handout, the facsimile of the *Boomer* case as reported in the West Reporter system reproduced as "Chart D" in Part III of this Manual, to show the various parts of a reported case, and what students would see if they looked up *Boomer* in its reported version.

• ***For the next class:*** Tell students to focus on the variety of **defenses** that defendants like the Atlantic Cement Company might possibly have raised in situations like *Boomer* and what they mean.

Class 4. Defenses — Chapter 3

This material is short in text and quite straightforward in the teaching. The main teachers manual suggests that you take the defenses offered in the *Schenectedy Chemical* case, NLS text pages 117-118, and analyze each of the laundry list as it arises, continuing into the affirmative defenses offered in the Comments and Questions, pages 118-121.

In teaching NLS as a first law course, much of this catalogue of defenses will be definitional. You may ask the students to imagine how the Atlantic Cement Company would have raised these defenses in *Boomer*, or how other defendants might do so in other settings. In each case, the purpose is to show the mechanics of the defense, and then to step back and analyze the economic and political arguments and consequences that underlie the defenses.

•***For next class*** The materials on other tort theories assigned for the next class should be read with an eye to comparing them with intentional private nuisance, noting the technical differences between the elements required to be shown for each, and even more importantly the consequences, advantages, and disadvantages of choosing each of the different alternatives.

If your class is using the first printing of NLS, you can supply them with the *Spur* map, missing from page 129, which can be found in the main teachers manual at 289-290.

Class 5. A Compendium of Tort Causes of Action — Chapter 3

To give the students the full import of environmental law's choice of alternative theories of action, it is useful to assign the trespass, negligence, and strict liabilities materials, page 131-142, as at least a skim assignment. Teaching this material as a first law course, the teacher must do a great deal more in familiarizing the students with the fact that the same set of facts may produce a variety of causes of action, some of them in the alternative — as when a defendant's action is alleged to be intentional for one cause of action, and negligent in another. The point can be made most vividly by asking the class whether there is any reason why

Boomer did not file his lawsuit under all of the theories set out in this section of the reading? With the exception of strict liability, each was, in fact, a realistic possibility, although Boomer's attorney stuck with private nuisance as an intentional tort because that was a well-known precedent in the case law which appeared to be fully sufficient to achieve the remedies that Boomer desired.

The discussion of these various alternative tort causes of action can be keyed back to Chart C discussed above, in each case showing how different elements of the tort would require proof, and the possibility of multiple causes of action and multiple prima facie cases thus presented.

Public Nuisance. The first and most interesting alternative is the public nuisance tort action. You can begin by asking what advantages public nuisance would have offered to Boomer, focusing on the direct rejoinder it would provide to Judge Bergan who tried to keep questions of public interest out of this "private" litigation in the first page of the *Boomer* case. Furthermore, besides making the discussion of public interest relevant to the question whether an injunction would be issued, public nuisance brings in a great deal of past precedent on the relevance of public health, quality of life, and aesthetics that would help to weight the balance in favor of Mr. Boomer's claims.

Note that the primary public nuisance remedy is some form of injunction. If damages are awarded under a public nuisance theory, they probably are equivalent to those awarded for the private nuisance damages subsumed therein. Plaintiffs are not likely to be able to recover for injuries to the public, even through some sort of common fund or fluid class damage recovery. Recovery of public nuisance damages by a governmental plaintiff may be more likely, but again, this has been rare. In reading the *Schenectedy Chemical* and *Spur* excerpts, the class should be asked why public nuisance offered those two very different plaintiffs a substantial advantage over the alternative causes of action that they might have brought. The state of New York obviously wanted a strong restoration remedy without having to go through the rigamarole of its own administrative procedure; Del Webb Company clearly faced an equitable estoppel under private nuisance, which it could avoid by filing in public nuisance, as well as capturing the intangible injuries to quality of life better in public nuisance than it could in private nuisance. Actions filed in public nuisance, furthermore, tend to have less of an estoppel effect when they are unsuccessful than a plaintiff's class action in private nuisance would in those same circumstances.

[You may wish to make a civil procedure note here: that this appellate decision is the first in the readings which is being heard on the pleadings alone, on defendant's motion to dismiss, prior to any trial being held on the merits. (The *Anderson* toxics decision in Chapter 4 is another.) Thus the paragraph in brackets at the bottom of page 124 is explaining what happened thereafter, on remand, when the parties decided to settle prior to trial on the merits. This civil procedure note is useful in explaining the different avenues litigation can follow, and in emphasizing the role of out-of-court negotiation that is a constant backdrop of legal process studied further in Chapter 24.]

The technical problems presented by public nuisance arise predominately in the definition of "public rights," and in the restricted standing doctrines of public nuisance law, noted in NLS text at page 130. The traditional rule is that private plaintiffs have to have injury that is different in kind from the public as a whole, because the district attorney or other public prosecutor is held to be the proper advocate of public interests generally. In many cases, of course, the public officials are not interested in litigating against clear public nuisances, so that it is important that the law of public nuisance standing allowing individual citizens to bring public nuisance actions is currently in evolution.

Trespass. The *Borland* case includes a set of difficult technicalities concerning the Alabama requirement for substantial injury. For purposes of a first law course, however, it is more important to note that this case could have been litigated in private, or public nuisance, but the trespass action offers advantages. The primary advantage is probably that the statute of limitations reaches back further for trespass, often six years, rather than the shorter one or two year statutes of limitation for damages under the nuisance actions. *See* page 133-134. There is also an advantage in getting injunctive relief under trespass actions, because of courts' gut reactions against unconsented physical invasions of private property. *Id.*

The important thing to note for the students is that the trespass cause of action uses basically the same facts as the intentional nuisance actions, but adds the requirement of a specific allegation of physical entry or penetration of the private property by defendant or defendant's instrumentality. This may give you an opportunity to talk about ancient forms of action, "trespass quaere clausum fregit," etc., and the extensive legal history that lies behind even the most modern common law actions. (*See* the nutshell E on "Forms of Action" in Part Three herein.) Also, because of historical peculiarity, trespass can only be brought as an "intentional" tort, unlike nuisance. There is no such thing as a "negligent" trespass action.

Negligence Torts. The most common negligence action is the personal injury action, typically trespass on the case. The empire of negligence, however, spreads far through tort law, and often can invade other areas, including intentional tort, unless attorneys understand the distinction well. For our purposes it is useful to note negligent private nuisance in *Dillon*, showing clearly the difficulties in bringing such an action successfully. Because the balance of utilities is so fundamental to the negligence cause of action, most modern environmental tort cases have been brought under intentional private nuisance.

Strict Liability. The advantages to strict liability are typically that the plaintiff does not have to prove fault, and that liability can be found despite defenses otherwise available, as against the independent contractor defense. Strict liability is sufficiently well-known and powerful in legal and policy terms that courts and attorneys tend toward strict liability theories even where intentional public or private nuisance action would accomplish virtually the same ends, *i.e.*, eliminating notions of "fault." In the *Branch* case it is not clear that strict liability was properly applied. *See* NLS text pages 141 at Comments 1 and 2. A good way to end this class is to note that there are several other kinds of common law actions that may be applicable in environmental cases. *See* NLS text 141-142.

•***For next class:*** Tell students to survey the different generic categories of damages that might be awarded in a case like *Boomer* or in other environmental lawsuits, and figure out how they, as plaintiff's attorneys, would try to justify and prove the different amounts of damages to a court.

Class 6. Remedies: Civil Damages, Natural Resources Damages — Chapter 3

We suggest you go to damage remedies before equitable remedies because in the chronology of a typical private law case, a finding of liability ordinarily results in automatic award of compensatory damages; and the subsequent question of whether an injunction will issue is a more complicated question.

Past Compensatory Damages. The text, at pages 148-149, very briefly discusses the fundamental category of recovery — compensation for past damages. Although this is by far the most common category, it does not offer as many fascinating wrinkles as permanent, punitive, and natural resources damages. Nevertheless for students in a first law course, a discussion of past compensatory damages is important — certainly more important than permanent damages. Going through an imagined catalogue of property and personal damages that could be pleaded and proved shows students how the reckoning in a private action can be cumulated. The main teachers manual, at pages 75-77, discusses broader ways of assessing compensatory damages in environmental cases, including natural resources damages, and you may wish to add that topic at this point. If you get into the question of recovery for the loss of "existence value" of various fauna and flora, or the cost of restoration as a further measure of damages for what has been lost, you will get deeply into philosophical questions of the value of non-human resources, proportionality between environmental ethics and human economics, etc.

Permanent Damages. You may want to take the lead from the main teachers manual and make this a minor discussion, interesting mostly for its substitution of permanent recovery for the injunction remedy in *Boomer*.

Punitive Damages. This can be a fascinating section of class discussion. Many students have never before heard of punitive damages, as distinct from criminal fines. The potency and problems posed by punitive damages can be developed in a discussion drawing upon the material in the text and the main teachers manual, pages 78-79.

If you assign pages 159-163 (the *Pruitt* case discussing long distance indirect economic damages from Kepone in Chesapeake Bay) you may use a schematic drawing of the bay to show the various categories of plaintiffs and the court's cut-off of liability, as noted in the main teachers manual, pages 79-81.

•*For the next class:* Tell students to think of questions which have developed in their minds about legal mechanics to date, as well as focusing on the variety of equitable remedies that they might have asked the court to order in *Boomer* and the subsequent cases they have read.

Class 7. Equity and Injunctions — Chapter 3

The range of available equitable remedies is often disregarded by most members of the bar, whose instinct is to think only of injunctions shut-down orders. The wider possibility are set out simply in the text and comments in the main teachers manual at page 77. In a first law course, however, students should be given more background on this material.

As to the nature of equitable orders, students must realize that equitable remedies are not set out in rigid form, but are wide open to the discretion of the equitable court. An advantage to their effectiveness is that, although these environmental torts are all civil actions, a defendant's violation of an injunction is contempt of court, which is a *crime* readily punishable by fine and/or imprisonment. The latter is an interesting legal process point for the class that highlights issues regarding the institutional competence of the court system.

Students may wonder when equitable remedies will be ordered, and why. The balance of equities, including a balance of the private and public interests implicated in the remedy decision, comes from the equity courts' derivation from British chancery, based on the role of the church and canon law in the British equity system. Your students will want to rush to the conclusion that asking a court to issue an equitable order is a guarantee that "fairness" will become the bottom line test of what will happen in the case. They must be disabused of this notion. "Equity" does not mean that the fairest result will always win. Under the canon of "in pari delicto," for instance, an injunction may be denied plaintiffs who are somewhat at fault, but at a low level, against defendants who are egregiously at fault.

Part of the nature of the equitable remedy that also is not obvious to your students is that juries theoretically have no role in the grant of an injunction; equitable remedies are issued by the discretionary decision of the judge alone.

A discussion of equitable remedies might introduce a discussion of the role of a court vis à vis public law bodies. A judge issuing injunctions begins to look very much like an administrative or legislative decisionmaker, even though the parameters of the equitable order are limited to the facts properly raised in the judicial case. Using the Alaska oil spill or some other such vivid case, your students may come up with an imaginative array of potential equitable remedies. Part of the exercise should be to show them that they must bear a heavy burden in persuading an equitable court to grant the equitable remedy — often arguably duplicating public law — on top of damages. Equitable relief still is often more or less "extraordinary."

Toward the end of this class looking back at *Boomer* you may wish to ask the students to assess the extent to which the common law system had been able to provide a comprehensive accounting of externalized cost from the cement company, to what extent the damages accounting was insufficient, and whether equitable remedies could have played a role in achieving a more rational overall accounting of externalized costs.

•***For the next class :*** Tell students to read the *Woburn Chemicals* case, pages 199-210, with an eye to the realistic obstacles that attend a group of low-income neighbors attempting to carry on a sophisticated toxic contamination tort case.

Class 8. Toxic Torts — Chapter 4

Toxic torts can be astonishingly complex. The questions of epidemiological proof where there is long-term latency between exposure and the onset of physical disabilities or death makes this an area where the law is sometimes in conflict with the glacial pace of scientific proof. The range of areas for which plaintiffs can recover has been growing beyond direct physical disease to include new kinds of emotional distress, cancer-phobia, medical surveillance and treatment for illnesses not evident at the time of decision, and so on.

Much of the material that is skipped over in this selection is scientific material on epidemiological proof by statistics and otherwise, and questions of burdens of proof, in addition to the special *Ayers* medical surveillance remedy. Although you may not assign any of these materials, it would be useful to read through them yourself on the side to get a sense of what further comments you might wish to make in the course of the toxic tort discussion.

Rather than getting deeply into the science, economics, and attenuated policy questions posed by toxic torts, the proposed assignment here focuses primarily on one particular case, the Woburn, Massachusetts chemical contamination case, leaving the teacher to add side-bar comments on a variety of issues that arise as the discussion progresses.

The optional assignment on problems of multiplicity, pages 171-176, may be raised after the *Woburn* case or before. In cases like Agent Orange, DES, asbestos, and the like, the difficulties of managing huge classes of defendants as well as plaintiffs poses a staggering problem for the judicial system, raising the question whether the whole field should be transferred into another forum. This discussion is of course extremely current, and allows the class to take a legal process question and transmute it into a timely question of current national policy.

As to class actions, you can teach the students a great deal about the phenomenon of a class action by giving them the handout from Part III herein of the class-action notice published by the court in the case of Biechele v. Norfolk & Western Ry., 309 F.Supp. 360-361 (in Part III of this manual). The students will recognize quickly that the notice is intended to encourage legal representation of all similarly-situated pollution victims in the delineated area, and gives these people the opt-out opportunity, without which their interest will automatically be represented and foreclosed by the lawsuit being litigated by the certified class. You should note, however, that the Burger Court substantially increased the procedural burdens of maintaining a federal class action. Today this chart might be appropriate in a state court certified class action, but probably would not be in federal litigation. (If the defendant could show that it's feasible for plaintiffs to give "better" service by going door-to-door, finding address lists and mailing individualized notices, etc., the Burger Court's construction of FRCP 23 requires them to do so. Jacquelin & Eisen v. Carlisle, 417 U.S. 156 (1974). In some cases (typically cases where many diffuse potential plaintiffs each has a relatively small claim), this holding creates a situation where, to protect the due process rights of citizens who would be included within a class action, the burden of notification is increased so much that those citizens' only feasible judicial remedy — a class action — becomes, in fact, altogether impractical.

The material on joint and several liability, pages 176-180, is clearly adjectival to the questions raised in the *Woburn* case where there were three possible defendants, one whose early settlement helped fund the litigation; joint and several liability can be made a side-bar comment in the course of the discussion of that case.

This is also an opportune time to introduce the students to litigation strategies. With the threat of joint and several liability hanging over it in the *Woburn* case, a small uniform company (NLS at 203) settled out early, its insurer recognizing that it would do well to settle out all potential liabilities by paying $1 million. If it can be shown that each defendant contributed toxic contamination to the ground water, the doctrine of joint and several liability, if applicable, means that the plaintiffs do not have to prove which defendant caused which injury, unless the injuries are clearly severable. In the case of severable injuries, each defendant is liable only for those damages that it caused. The Velsicol v. Rowe case, NLS at 176, provides a primer for the law of joint and several liability, if you wish to use it.

The *Woburn* case is dramatically set out by Schlichtmann. The students should be able by this time to be put through an exercise scoping out the range of issues involved in litigating all of the human health consequences of the Woburn case. You can start with the facts that are apparently known, and the large array of facts that will have to be proved ultimately at trial. Note that it was the cancer cases that were the ones that were litigated, but that a variety of other health injuries apparently were caused by the contamination. Beyond actual onset of disease, the students should recognize that future disease has often been made more likely, with attendant emotional consequences to the plaintiffs, and that these are highly conjectural areas of recovery. The cause of action of the *Woburn* case is not specified (and in our modern fact-pleading system, of course, does not have to be specified in the plaintiff's pleadings); Schlichtmann himself has characterized the case as private nuisance, public nuisance, negligence, and strict liability.

Students should recognize the immense difficulties in getting information from recalcitrant defendants, and in proving scientifically not only the causation of a particular disease, but even the fundamental question in the first stage of the trial, which was just how fast the pollutants might have traveled from the sources of contamination to the subject wells G and H. We ourselves are rather shocked by the sharp limitations imposed upon the plaintiffs' case by the trial court (*see* NLS text at page 209, comment 2 and page 210, comment 4).

This may be the point to talk about **juries**. The American Lawyer article on the *Woburn* case cited at the top of page 210 offers a fascinating view of the problems raised when a jury made up of regular, cross-section-of-society laypersons, is handed immensely difficult questions. (The article's view of plaintiff's lawyer seems like 20-20 hindsight to us.) The American jury system will give you much to talk about.

In reviewing the *Woburn* case, you can emphasize the immense amount of work and luck necessary to getting a case to trial, given the enormous constraints plaintiffs can face. The practical, scientific, and financial constraints that plaintiffs face, and the ultimate denouement — where Beatrice was able to avoid liability completely — is a cautionary note for the students.

The material also can be used to raise other troubling questions. If plaintiffs in toxic torts can recover for the (undeniably real) fear that they feel knowing that they and their children have been contaminated by carcinogens, the jury value of that item of damages is sufficiently large to bankrupt most corporations, and drive chemical companies out of business. Also, what happens when a jury awards compensation where the epidemiological proof shows that a significant portion of a community's illnesses, *but not all,* were caused by a particular defendant? The legal system is not well designed to apportion damages according to probability; it tends to be all or nothing, with consequent over-compensation or total frustration for plaintiffs. If plaintiffs recover for risk of future cancer, do they get a further recovery when the cancer actually occurs? These questions and others are raised in the text and the main teachers manual and will allow you to tie knots in your student's thought processes for well more than a class hour.

The *Ayers* case is not included in the suggested readings, because of its length. You may well wish, however, to note for students the remedy invented in that case, where the court ordered defendants to set up a $4 million medical surveillance fund to pay for the plaintiff community's medical care for the foreseeable future, to diagnose and provide for the unknown consequences of benzene pollution. The case also discusses recovery for fear of cancer from a proved carcinogen exposure.

Another legal process issue that deserves attention is the question of sovereign immunity: in *Ayers*, the fact that the defendant was a municipal dump shielded it from immunity except within the narrow terms of the New Jersey statute, which did not allow recovery, for instance, for pain and suffering. See `NLS text at page 204.

The brief discussion of sovereign immunity, NLS text at pages 220-221, is easy to bring into class discussion as a side-note, raising interesting legal process questions for the class. Most of the students will be shocked at the notion that governmental defendants can in some cases recklessly cause harm to citizens and the environment with impunity from common law actions. In this regard you should note as well that Justice Rehnquist firmly closed the door on tort recoveries in many environmental cases by persuading the Supreme Court that the Federal Tort Claims Act, waiving sovereign immunity, applied only to negligence torts, not to intentional torts. *Nelms v. Laird*, 407 U.S. 797 (1972).

(As to sovereign immunity, however, you can continue that discussion in the chapter 9 airport cases (NLS at 436-442), where the inverse condemnation constitutional claim is applied to avoid the serious problems attending governmental sovereign immunity for nuisance-like torts.)

•*For the next class:* Ask students to attempt a quick "scoping-out" legal analysis of the property and contract law strip-mining cases, and/or the corporate law problem case, asking questions similar to the tort analyses they have made.

Class 9. Environmental Remedies From Other Fields Of Law — Chapter 5

Although this Chapter is often skipped in the law school syllabus as duplicative of other elective and basic law school courses, in a first law course, Chapter 5 serves an especially important function, reminding the students that there is no delimited category called "environmental law," but rather that environmental lawyers draw actionable legal doctrines from wherever they can find them, common law or statutory.

The *Pacific Lumber* case tends to be quicker to cover. It details a depressing story, where students can discuss the long term short-comings of the corporate realm's quarterly-profits horizons, and the leveraged buyout binge that Wall Street produced in the late 1980s. The particular ideas by which the Pacific Lumber management could have resisted takeover, or by which plaintiffs could subsequently have constricted the Maxxam management's policies, are conjectural and not worth extended exploration in technical detail. The policy lessons are useful to discuss, and the fact that there are incipient untried corporate remedies is a useful legal process recognition.

First-time law students can wrestle far more deeply with the strip-mine broad form deed cases. The cases in the text tell enough of the story, which the class can recreate. The early 1900's documents conveyed purportedly broad extractive property rights, to the point of allowing destruction of the surface, but the parties to the original documents clearly had no conception that such drastic technologies as strip-mining might subsequently occur. To what extent can Judge Hill legitimately argue that public environmental policy should change the terms of deed and contract interpretation? Should he argue solely in terms of traditional doctrines of interpretation, which focus on the intent of the parties?

The vivid consequences of strip mining are chronicled in Harry Caudill's Night Comes To The Cumberlands, and his later book My Land Is Dying. Coupled with the photograph in the text, it should be clear to students that consequences of deed interpretation will determine the continued existence or destruction of the surface estate and the waters that flow from the surface. Note however that some cynics say the broad form deed litigation was only an attempt to give poor surface owners a stranglehold on the mineral rights holders, so that the strip miners would be forced to purchase the surface rights at an extortionate premium.

The teacher may want to skim through the unassigned pages at the end of this chapter for ideas about further sources of environmental law.

If you are going to use the RCRA-CERCLA toxics statutes as a special focus in the chapter 6 materials, emphasize that fact.

• ***For the next class:*** Tell students to read deeply through the Kepone narrative, and try to develop from it a catalogue of all the kinds of legal remedy that would apply, common law as well as statutory, state and local as well as federal.

Class 10. From Common Law To Public Law, The Kepone Case and Toxics Regulations — Chapter 6

This assignment requires a major decision. Will you just briefly introduce the idea of how statutes at every level of government, and regulations pursuant to them, supplement the pre-existing common law, or will you add a fairly intensive inquiry into one particular kind of statutory example, federal toxics regulation under the Resource Recovery and Conservation Act (RCRA) and the Superfund Statute (CERCLA)?

Over several years our past classes have tried both alignments. The NLS text and main teachers manual (at 96) provide the skeleton for discussion of different kinds of police power regulation at the state and local level, and their federal corollaries as they might apply in industrial chemical production. When the course is offered to first-time students of law, this catalogue may deserve more detail, exploring the kinds of state and local agencies (for this you may also want to read ahead quickly in Chapter 15, NLS pages 717-726). The overwhelming conclusion that comes through is that absent the incentive of private common law actions, public law remedies are extremely uncertain, subject to the vagaries of political and institutional motivation. Other than the fines paid by Allied Chemical (noted in Chapter 7) the vast majority of financial accountings deriving from the Kepone incident were the unreported settlements obtained by workers and neighbors of the factory, none of whose cases were allowed to come to judgment by Allied. Our obvious intent is to remind all concerned that the statutory systems designed to protect environmental quality remain a partial legal remedy to environmental problems, and that the common law continues to play an immensely important role.

This assignment is a good point to say something more about what the police power is. First-time students of law do not clearly distinguish between private law ordering and mandatory governmental imposition of restrictions and sanctions. The police power (discussed further in chapter 9's sections on eminent domain and regulatory restrictions on private property) is a basic necessary attribute of all governments, and raises fundamental issues of democracy fitting well into our legal process inquiry.

In discussing the different statutes, students should be asked how a piece of legislation comes to be passed. There is no abstract objective need which automatically results in legislative action: every statute is the product of a unique combination of motivations for imposing constraints on the private market-place and contains provisions and language that are the product of legislative happenstance.

In explaining the relationship of statutes and agencies to the Kepone scenario, you may wish to use Chart G, in Part III herein, which sets out a basic framework from eighth grade civics classes, showing the legislative, executive, and judicial branches, but giving prominent emphasis to a fourth branch of government, the civil service bureaucracy which does not exactly fit within the executive branch and has its own politics and dynamics. Chart G also shows the private sector marketplace which is the dominating substrate upon which these branches of government operate. Chart G, in other words, can be used as a review of the position of courts dealing with the statutory and regulatory litigation as well as the common law, and invites recognition of the pressures and tensions lying between and within the different branches of government.

At least some mention of the RCRA and CERCLA statutes is useful. NLS text 260-266 provides some basic statutory language from CERCLA; RCRA §7003 is in the *NEPACCO* case at 269-270. The statutory texts should be read to show how sweeping the statutory coverage is, in terms of who is liable for substantial responsibility for toxic waste, and how simple the basis for liability and the concurrent proof of violation are. As to joint and several liability, the *Monsanto* case, 287-292, emphasizes how the courts interpreted the statutory command to increase the breadth and severity of statutory coverage, using common law reasoning and common law antecedents.

A backdrop to this discussion, whether or not you assign the other materials in the draft assignment for this class, is that however drastic the statutory remedies, they and other statutes do not provide the compensatory damage remedies for people and resources in toxic contamination episodes, emphasizing again the concurrent utility of common law liability.

If you wish to get more deeply into the questions of statutory articulation in the judicial process, the *NEPACCO* case is a prime teaching tool; the main teachers manual (page 97 et seq.) sets out an extended series of comments on how to teach this material.

Finally, an interesting retrospective on the concurrent role of common law and statutory law is provided by the Karen Silkwood case (skim assignment, page 301-313). Most students will have some idea of the Karen Silkwood story, with its limits of corporate and governmental collusion in avoiding revelations about systematic sloppiness and hazards in the handling of plutonium materials. What the students will not instinctively know is that the area of radioactive pollution is almost entirely pre-empted from state and local police power regulation (*see* Chapter 10). The corporate defendants in *Silkwood* understandably supposed that state *courts* would be similarly prevented from constraining their actions or forcing legal remedies upon them. The Supreme Court makes it clear that common law remedies, even including punitive damages which sound much more like state legislative-type sanctions, co-exist with federal pre-emption of the regulatory role. (If this is so, some students may ask, then common law courts may even be able to issue *injunctions* in such cases, even though the state legislative police power cannot be applied. This latter proposition is *doubtful* based on the intentions of the court as expressed in the *Silkwood* case, and the logic of federal pre-emption, studied in Chapter 10.

• ***For the next class :*** Have the students read the short 1899 Refuse Act as an exercise in interpreting a (criminal) statute, a new kind of exercise for them. Ask them why the Refuse Act was so powerful when it was rediscovered as a tool to fight environmental pollution.

Or you may wish to have them focus on the *Film Recovery* case, to analyze the potency of criminal law, and to try to figure out why criminal law is not always the most desirable remedy for environmental pollution.

Class 11. Criminal Environmental Law — Chapter 7

This is another chapter where there are two very different ways to present the material:

Some classes have focused attention initially upon the 1899 Refuse Act, pages 322-327, as an introduction to the force of the words of the criminal statute (especially where the class has not spent a great deal of time on statutory interpretation in the preceding Chapter 6 material on RCRA and CERCLA). The notes in the text and main teachers manual are straightforward on this point. Students can be reminded that there are no common law crimes, and therefore this kind of enactment is very different from the common law causes of action they have seen previously as to the explicitness and enforceability of its commands, as well as other issues like the different burden of proof required in criminal prosecutions — beyond a reasonable doubt, rather than preponderance of the evidence.

Another issue you can raise is that the statute as written does not require that acts are "knowing," which sets up an issue discussed later in the chapter (but not in the proposed page block assignments), asking whether there is a constitutional due process requirement of proof of *knowledge* before serious criminal penalties are assessed (*see* NLS text, pages 351-354). Students can also be referred to the line in §407 which says that it covers "any refuse matter of any kind or description whatever *other than that flowing from streets and sewers and passing therefrom in a liquid state...,*" an accidental exception that encouraged a number of polluters like Allied Chemical to consider diverting their industrial pollution into public sewerage systems to by-pass the law. The last provision of §407 can also be referred to: by mentioning that the Chief of Engineers of the Army "may permit the deposit of any material above mentioned...," the act implicitly authorized the Corps to establish a Refuse Act Permit Program (RAP) discussed in the Goldfarb selection, at NLS text page 43.

Where classes discuss the latter *Kepone* narrative as part of the Refuse Act discussion, it proves natural to move directly to pages 336-343, which shows the difficulty of assigning criminal penalties to corporate actors in a situation like the Allied/LSP tolling arrangement. Students are usually angered by Goldfarb's narrative of the criminal trial in the *Kepone* case. They should be reminded that the heightened standards required for proof of criminal violations are ultimately linked to the civil rights of all, but it does seem to us that the judge bent over backwards to avoid assigning criminal stigma to the Allied management.

Note: In April, 1992, the U.S. Tax Court *denied* Allied's claim that the $8 million "environmental fund could be deducted as a normal business expense rather than a criminal fine. 63 TCM (CCH) 2672 (1992). Allied will appeal.

As to the problem of assessing criminal penalties against an entity like Allied and its officers, we note that when the Harvard Business School prepared a case study concerning Allied Chemical after the Kepone debacle, the tone of the business school exposition naturally was quite un-skeptical about the corporation's bona fides (*see* main teachers manual, pages 111-112).

Some classes skim over or skip the Refuse Act, and focus on *Film Recovery* and the questions about criminal prosecution that it raises, including the question of personal liability of corporate executives. This discussion is set out clearly in the text and the main teachers manual, and is the kind of narrative discussion where the teacher will find many opportunities to make side-bar comments on issues of criminal law and legal process.

•*For the next class :* Tell students that in the next class they will be exploring one of the unique legal doctrines brought into the legal system by environmental law: the public trust doctrine. Ask them to figure out where it came from, how it works, and where it might be going.

Class 12. A Quasi-Constitutional Environmental Right: The Public Trust — Chapter 8

The meat of this chapter is clearly the public trust doctrine. This being so, you may easily decide to skip the first section of this chapter. Nevertheless, you may want to put the public trust doctrine in the context of alleged federal constitutional rights:

The first section of the chapter quickly goes through the arguments against a federal environmental constitutional right, and can be summarized for students quite quickly. If you really wish to make something of the point, you could assign the *Tanner* case, pages 357-360, which would show the students how plaintiffs can try to get into federal court, and thereby hatch a whole catalogue of implied environmental constitutional claims.

The short answer, however, is that the claim of constitutional right seems quixotic at this point.

The public trust doctrine is commented on extensively in the main teachers manual, pages 116-125. You may wish to start the class with some dramatic example of how the public trust can be applied in a controversy and make a dramatic difference, as in *Illinois Central*, or *Florissant* (a case which is unreported, hence shaky, but which students love). You might use the Methuselah bristlecone pine hypothetical noted in the main teachers manual at page 119.

In pedagogical terms, doing the *Paepke* case in schematic diagram on the board is a useful way for showing how the court's tests, based on the Wisconsin cases, might apply to nibble away the park, in each case avoiding what was the logical question in weighing the public trust: is there a feasible and prudent alternative available, so that the public trust resource does not have to justify its continued existence in particular terms every time a new project is proposed?

Teaching this material as a first law course you probably will want to give special emphasis to the derivation of the public trust doctrine, coming from the Byzantine Holy Roman Empire, through continental law, to English law, then to the colonial U.S., the Northwest Ordinance, and implicitly into the national jurisprudence of the United States. The *Illinois Central* case is not excerpted in the materials, but the Sax discussion makes it clear that the U.S. Supreme Court matter-of-factly seized upon this old doctrine to override what all must have known was a corrupt land grant in the first place. The students should be reminded that the trust doctrine had not been generally known by lawyers and judges in the United States prior to 1970, and here is operating to override public law statutes. The wonder is that the public trust has generally been so matter-of-factly accepted as part of the American legal system once it is cited and applied to the facts of these particular cases. Note for the students also how the analogy of private trust law, which is well known to all members of the bar and the bench, likewise matter-of-factly has formed the definition and application of public trust elements in cases as they are raised. This process is a vivid exemplar of the Anglo-American legal system at work.

•***For the next class :*** The next class will probably continue the discussions that open up in this first public trust class. For the next class, you might tell students to focus upon the dramatic technical consequences of the public trust in *Mono Lake,* including the fact that it overrides private property rights. Tell students to read the *Gettysburg Tower* case, as a technical exercise in understanding the utility of state constitutional provisions.

Class 13. Public Trust — continued — Chapter 8

This class undoubtedly will have dangling ends left over from the prior class. In this second half of the unit on the public trust, the particular focus of the readings in the proposed syllabus are upon the details of how the public trust changes assumptions about private property rights. This of course was part of the *Florissant Fossil Beds* scenario, but is even more clearly presented in these readings. The *Mono Lake* case involves private property rights (although they are owned by the City of Los Angeles, which bought them on the private market) that had been unquestioned for more than 100 years. The assertion of the public trust doctrine by the environmental plaintiffs, however, produces this opinion in which the Supreme Court of California defines the public trust as concurrent with and potentially overriding such private property rights. The discussion continues through the Sax excerpts and the questions. It is clear that this is the aspect of the public trust doctrine that causes the greatest questions amongst the anti-environmentalist "privateers," members of the "wise-use" movement, and all who care about our own turf.

A number of other leads will undoubtedly open up in the course of discussions. We have found it useful to plug in the *Gettysburg Tower* case as rounding off this unit, because the public trust is clearly part of what is being litigated in the Pennsylvania case. The two technical questions being discussed in the Pennsylvania case are (1) whether the §27 constitutional provision is enforceable without further legislative enactments, and (2) whether the terms of §27 or of the public trust are violated by the Tower. As you parse carefully through the opinions and count them up, it is clear that a majority of the court believed that §27 did not require further legislation; the section was self-executing. (Note in the main teachers manual at page 125 that the first opinion in the case was written by O'Brien, joined by Pomeroy, *i.e.* only two justices. A different majority of the court, however, felt that the substantive law standard established by §27 and/or the public trust doctrine were not violated in these circumstances. This latter is an argument that the students may be invited to re-litigate. In terms of state constitutional law doctrine, however, we think that the trend is that such articles are indeed self-executing, (but students must be reminded that few attorneys know very much about their state constitutions). Students might find interesting things if they prowl around in their own state's constitutional provisions and the case law thereon.)

• *For the next class:* Tell students to look at the constitutional protections of private property rights in the governmental police power setting, and how difficult it is to apply property rights against governmental eminent domain actions (*Poletown*), and in the physical disruption circumstances of the airport cases.

Class 14. Property Rights and Environment — Eminent Domain and Inverse Condemnation — Chapter 9

The two topics of this class are not necessarily major in their national impact on environmental quality, but are extremely useful as legal process and environmental policy discussion points. Moreover the elements of our analysis of the police power — setting out the series of judicial tests of Authority, Proper Public Purpose, the Rationality of the Governmental Act and the Burden on the Individual — is presented fairly simply in the eminent domain setting, and thereafter carries through the subsequent two classes as a matrix for structuring the analysis and discussions.

Eminent Domain. The Columbia and Tellico Dam projects' scenario, NLS text at page 431, and the *Poletown* case, pages 432-433, lend themselves to being diagrammed on the board for brainstorming as legal cases. This process is set out in the text and the main teachers manual. What the students must be brought to recognize is that judicial deference to official governmental actions is extraordinarily strong in this setting. The *Berman v. Parker* case is given a garbled excerpt in the NLS text at page 429. A fuller series of quotations from that case:

> [In this condemnation case] we deal, in other words, with what traditionally has been known as the police power. An attempt to define its reach or trace its outer limits is fruitless, for each case must turn on its own facts.... Subject to specific constitutional limitations, when the legislature has spoken, the public interest has been declared in terms well-nigh conclusive. In such cases, the legislature, not the judiciary, is the main guardian of the public needs to be served by social legislation.... Once the object is within the authority of [the legislature], the right to realize it through the exercise of eminent domain is clear.... Once the object is within the authority of [the legislature], the means by which it will be attained is also for [the legislature] to determine.... The argument pressed on us is, indeed, a plea to substitute the landowner's standard of the public need for the standard prescribed by [the legislature].... It is not for the courts to oversee the choice of the boundary line, nor to sit in review on the size of a particular project area. Once the question of the public purpose has been decided, the amount and character of land to be taken for the project and the need for a particular tract to complete the integrated plan rests in the discretion of the legislative branch.... The rights of these property owners are satisfied when they receive that just compensation which the Fifth Amendment exacts as the price of the taking. 348 U.S. 32-33, 35-36. (Douglas, J.)

This passage from *Berman* was actually directed toward challenges to condemnation of particular tracts within an admittedly justified project area choice. ("It is the need of the area as a whole which Congress and its agencies are evaluating." 348 U.S. at 35.) But the strength of this statement has been interpreted by lower federal courts generally to override all meaningful question of the elements of eminent domain condemnations. Thus, the hints in the *Hawaii* case on page 435 for a stricter standard presage a possible change in this law.

The politics of these two eminent domain scenarios — involving pork-barrel federal agencies in the first instance and a huge industrial corporation manipulating state, local and federal governments in the *Poletown* case — undoubtedly will support some lively discussion in the class.

Inverse Condemnation Airport Cases. The airport cases similarly can be charted out, although the politics are less lively. Basically airport managers either did not foresee, or did not wish to compensate for, the substantial interferences that airports visit upon their nearest residential neighbors.

The heart of the airport cases is a wonderful legal process lesson for your students. Sovereign immunity is the triggering obstacle: you can explain to your students why in all likelihood tort actions could not be brought against the public authorities which were building these airports, nor therefore against the airlines which were legally required to follow the flight paths set up by the tort-immune public agencies. This is perhaps another good place to note that tort claims statutes waiving governmental immunity have sometimes been defined to cover only *negligent* actions, not intentional torts, which would be the most obviously applicable basis of tort claims in the airport setting. (*See* opinion by Rehnquist, J. in *Nelms v. Laird*, 407 U.S. 797 (1972), holding that sonic boom damage is an "intentional" tort because it was substantially foreseeable, hence is immune from tort liability despite the provisions of the Federal Tort Claims Act.) "Inverse" condemnation is brought by the landowners themselves against the government to force it to acknowledge that it was effectively condemning their property rights — in this case an easement of noise, vibrations, and sometimes aerial right of way. All the landowners had to prove was that the "defendant-condemnor" had the power of eminent domain, and was physically appropriating property rights from the land owner, but had failed to acknowledge, condemn and pay for the rights being taken. The courts (bemused and impressed by this logic) acknowledged the cause of action and granted the remedy requested, which was compensation for the property rights taken. Note that even the conservative judges, like Perry in *Thornburgh*, admit that the cause of action for inverse condemnation is good where there is a physical trespass through any tiny portion of the plaintiff landowners' air space.

You may ask the students whether, once landowners have established this precedent, it may extend to other areas, like the consequences of highway construction upon adjacent properties, and whether that might indeed bankrupt public authorities. The policy implications do not seem to be so devastating to us.

Analytically the four steps we discuss as the foundational elements of judicial scrutiny of the police power are, not coincidentally, also the four basic elements that a governmental entity has to set forth as its "cause of action" when it files a condemnation action against a piece of land. Students should be reminded that a condemnation action is a judicial process brought by the government as plaintiff against a piece of land and its landowner as defendants. If the government shows its statutory authority to condemn, the valid purpose for which it is condemning, an allegation that this land serves that purpose (although this element is often implied rather than expressed), and that just compensation will be paid into the court to be transferred to the defendant landowner, then the elements of a prima facie case of condemnation have been made, and the land "is liable" to the action. (Some states require a more stringent showing of "necessity" rationality.) The remedy is judicial issuance of a declaration of taking — in effect issuance of an involuntarily — granted deed from the landowner to the government of the particular interest in land that was sought to be condemned. Many different kinds of interest in land can be condemned — rental periods, partial condemnations, easements of right of way, and otherwise — but the most common eminent domain taking is a straight fee simple taking of an entire parcel.

•*For the next class:* Tell students that the next readings open up intensely political questions of legal process; they should read the materials to see the clash of powers and rights when government acts to regulate private property for environmental purposes. Ask them what kind of test they would propose for setting the limits of uncompensated government regulatory burdens on private property.

Class 15. Private Property Rights and Environment — Regulatory Takings Challenges — Chapter 9

This is indeed a central and immensely difficult question of environmental law, not to mention a fundamental question of justice and democracy. The approach of setting out a spectrum of different kinds of regulatory scenario (in the main teachers manual at 133 and following) is a useful way to show students the range of contested clashes between private and public interests. The manual and the text together also set out other ideas for covering this material. We remind you that the rather unclear "three-prong" test from *Penn Central* in the main teachers manual at 136 has been elaborated upon in the *Lucas* case. *Lucas* is excerpted in Part III of this manual for use by your students in association with the next assignment, Class 16, and is also discussed in the main teachers manual at 139-141 (written before the Supreme Court case came down — nevertheless, our analysis is surprisingly current as far as it goes).

The theme you probably will pull from this first class on regulatory takings is that the courts have not come up with a satisfactory bright line test of regulatory takings, and do not seem likely to do so any time soon. Nevertheless the explicit recognition of a balance of public and private harms — which we are pleased to see explicitly recognized, if begrudgingly, in Scalia's majority opinion in *Lucas* — is an important part of a rational constitutional balance.

•*For the next class:* This class undoubtedly spills over, given the wide variety of issues and political arguments it raises. You may tell students to focus on the *Lucas* case handout as an example of extreme cases where private property is completely wiped out in value by a regulation: in that extreme setting, what is the takings test? You might also ask them to look at the exaction and innocent landowner problems, NLS at 474-475.

Class 16. Regulatory Takings — continued — Chapter 9

This is the class that can tie together dangling loose ends from the prior two classes.

The primary issue presented in the readings suggested for Class 16 are the materials on the validity of environmental regulation where a piece of land is left with no remaining economic use. In part this picks up on the "baseline" discussions in the prior class period. In particular it focuses on the scenario set out in the recent *Lucas* case. The *Lucas* case, as noted above, was foreshadowed in the main teachers manual and appears in edited form in Part III of this manual as a handout. The important thing to note about *Lucas* is, first, that it purportedly deals only with the extraordinary case of a total *wipeout.* Second, it explicitly recognizes the "nuisance exception," and does not restrict the review in terms of traditional common law nuisance actions. Thus we are convinced that *First English Evangelical* would have been held a valid uncompensated regulation under Scalia's reasoning, and the reasoning of the NLS text on this point continues to be solid. (The alternative proposition, that a landowner has a constitutional right to put several hundred disabled children in a camp in the path of a flash flood, unless the government pays dollar-for-dollar the market value lost by the prohibition, is too extreme even for this Court to swallow; the logic of a public-private harm balance is unavoidable.)

The *Lucas* case and the comments after it are self-explanatory. (See Part III.)

The optional readings in this chapter are also fascinating: questions of remedies, amortization and offsets, exactions and *Nollan*, and due process and the innocent landowner. They are noted in the main teachers manual at 142-143.

• ***For the next class:***

(a) If assigning the optional Federal-State Environmental Issues class, you may have the students try to figure out what was happening in the note pre-emption case, *Mortier*, which appears in the first page assignments, 477-479. On dormant commerce clause, they should try to make sense out of the *Procter & Gamble* case.

(b) If skipping the optional Federal-State class, tell students to focus on chapter 11's *Overton Park* case, litigating it in their minds, and trying to figure out how administrative law judicial review is different from previous cases they have seen. (It involves a complex administrative process, and a court *reviewing* an administrative decision rather than making a final decision in the case.)

* Optional Class: Federal-State Environmental Issues: Pre-emption and Dormant Commerce Clause Cases

This optional class separates clearly into two doctrinal areas: pre-emption and the dormant commerce clause. In both cases students will be confronted with the peculiar problems of overlapping jurisdictions and/or line-drawing that arise in the division of authority between federal and state governments in various regulatory areas. You may want to give students a sense of the array of situations in which pre-emption arguments are made, surveying some of the materials not assigned in this chapter, and drawing upon your own experience. In testimony before the Alaska legislature advocating increased state regulation of the oil industry's preparedness to clean up oil spills along the Alaska Pipeline and in coastal waters, ZP was faced with insistent industry arguments that virtually anything the State wanted to do was pre-empted by Federal regulation in the field. At that point it seemed useful to remind the legislators of advice received from a mentor in practice two decades ago: "when you don't have any substantive arguments on your side, you can always wave around a pre-emption argument and it's usually good for at least 10 billable hours." The point is that the claim of preclusion by pre-emption is much more often successful in the political forum of state legislatures than when those claims are actually tested in court, given the traditionally strong presumption against pre-emption noted in the *Rice* quote at the bottom of page 478.

In going through the different kinds of pre-emption that might be argued, you can ask students to paraphrase how each such holding might be made. Further, it is important to stress the common sense reality that in many cases there is no contradiction ("physical contradiction" or "policy contradiction" as labeled in the NLS text at 479-480). A regulated party can comply with *both* systems of regulation by complying with the stricter of the two. Thus in *Mortier* if the local ordinance said that pesticide could not be sprayed within 100 feet of a residence and the federal regulation said pesticide could not be sprayed within 50 feet of a residence, the regulations are not in conflict because compliance with the State standard automatically incorporates compliance with the Federal standard. Only if the Federal regulation *required* that pesticides actually be sprayed up to the 50 foot line from residences would there be a conflict and contradiction between the two, and of course such scenarios are extremely unlikely.

PRE-EMPTION. Some teachers choose to use the fact situation of Huron Portland Cement Company v. Detroit, noted in the NLS text at 498, to set up both pre-emption and the dormant commerce clause arguments. In that case the court held that federal certification of boiler safety in the ships did not exempt them from a local smoke ordinance, and that seems logical. But the reason is not just because the *purposes* of the two regulatory regimes were different. As noted in the commentary, that is a nonsensical basis for validating or invalidating state regulation under federal supremacy theories. Rather it is clear that Congress did not *intend* its regulation of boilers to preclude other reasonable regulation by the states, for whatever purpose. Thus the intent of the legislature is the guiding principle. If, on the other hand, the burden of the state regulation was so great as to interfere with the application of the federal regulation, then there might be a form of contradiction pre-emption. (If the burden of the state regulation was such that although the ships could comply with both, the economic burden on the shipping industry was so great as to create substantial hardship in the continuation of that industry, then a dormant commerce clause burden on interstate commerce might be found likewise to void the regulation.) If the Court found that Congress intended *uniformity* of actual standards, then Detroit's ordinance might be voided for contradicting the policy of uniformity, although that is not likely to be made out in the *Huron Portland* setting.

You can remind students that in the *Silkwood* case, in Chapter 6, industry had argued that the existence of federal regulation precluded common law recoveries. The materials in this chapter are similar, in that it typically is regulated industrial polluters who are seeking to immunize themselves against (presumptively-stricter) state regulation by fleeing to the refuge of exclusive federal regulatory controls. Note what this says about the relative level of enforcement of federal and state agencies in cases in which the pre-emption argument is raised.

DORMANT COMMERCE CLAUSE. Philadelphia v. New Jersey is regarded by most law school teachers as the focal case in this field of environmental dormant commerce clause jurisprudence. Several of us, however, think *Procter & Gamble* is a case that goes much further as a teaching tool. In the dormant commerce clause cases like *Procter & Gamble,* a regulated industry is saying that a state or local police power enactment is void for a variety of different kinds of reasons that eerily track our four inquiries into regulatory validity, as noted in Comment 1, NLS text at 507.

Authority. In *Procter & Gamble* there are questions about authority: was the city given the power to regulate consumer products for extraterritorial purposes? (This is a simple question of delegation of police power via home rule to the city, and an echo of the argument made in the following inquiry into public purpose.)

Proper Public Purpose. There are several questions of proper public purpose: can Chicago exercise its police power, imposing heavy burdens on regulated parties, purely for the altruistic benefit of people who live *outside* the city? Remember that the reversed Chicago River carries all of Chicago's effluents down to the Mississippi drainage, not out into Lake Michigan from which the city gets its own water supply. Can a city regulate for "extraterritorial" purposes? An easy answer is to say that by this regulation Chicago may avoid tort litigation from polluted persons downriver, who now will get less phosphate in their water supply — but the argument that a city doesn't have the power to regulate for altruistic reasons is not likely anyway to be a winning attack on such an environmental relation.

A further argument on the purpose point, more commonly found in these cases, is the question whether or not the regulation is discriminatory. If a regulation discriminates in favor of the local market, it will be subjected to stricter scrutiny; "protectionism" is typically invalidated as an improper purpose under dormant commerce clause review. In this case, however, Chicago's regulation actually increases the burdens on the local market, so the protectionism claim is not successful. (Note also how the court uses the legislative purpose as the basis for much of its inquiry into the validity of the regulation.)

Rationality. There are arguments as to rationality that this court discusses at length: could a legislature rationally have believed that restricting phosphate dumped into the sewerage system could reduce eutrophication and algal blooms in the receiving waters? The court adopts a fairly deferential approach to judging the rationality of the action.

Burden. Fourth is the question of excessive burden (this time the burden on "interstate commerce" rather than on private property as in the regulatory takings area). The court apparently takes seriously the industry's argument of burdens upon Procter and Gamble; students can be asked to judge how substantial those economic burdens were. Ultimately the judge weighed the burdens on the industry against "the important and properly local objective" of the ordinance, and found that the burden did not outweigh the public interests advanced by the regulation.

•*For the next class:* Tell students to focus on the *Overton Park* case, litigating it in their minds and trying to figure out how this administrative law form of judicial review is different from previous cases they have seen. (It involves a complex administrative process, and a court *reviewing* an administrative decision rather than making a final decision in the case.)

Class 17. Environmental Administrative Law — *Overton Park* — Chapter 11

In getting into this administrative law material, it seems to us absolutely critical to begin with a factual case, so that students can get a sense of what is going on in the real world. *Overton Park* is a great case with which to do this. The setting and the story are set out fairly well in the text in the main teachers manual. In going through the various players in the story, it might be useful to use Chart G again, from Part III herein. In this case it is clear that the highway-building program is a beloved pork barrel for the state and federal agencies involved, as noted in the NLS text, as well as for local governments which are always pleased to see transportation corridors built in their jurisdictions. Thus the official decisionmakers are very much committed to building roads. The state legislature and the state's delegation in Congress typically echo these motivations. The underlying private sector marketplace includes the local Chamber of Commerce, construction and trade unions, and the like. In these circumstances it is easy to see how in general highway projects are politically virtually unstoppable, even when they target parkland for the reasons noted (in NLS text at 559), and in particular why this low income, unempowered community was perceived to pose no obstacle.

Alternatively, you can focus your initial analysis on how the legislative process (involving environmentalists at the national level and the fortuitous presence of Lady Bird Johnson, the amateur environmentalist with whom LBJ had to sleep at night) were able to place §4f, a small countervailing statutory obstacle, into the Highway Act. In no other industrial democracy could citizens with so little power bring a Cabinet-level Secretary into court for judicial review under the posture (implicitly) that his formal official finding may have been a fabrication — that the official is not telling the truth. It's the job of the judiciary to interpret §4f and to determine if the secretary truthfully had complied with it. In this case, of course, it turns out that the secretary *had* been fabricating when he had made his original finding, a lesson that vindicates some of the litigiousness of the American character.

As noted in the main teachers manual at 156 and following, in *Overton Park* you can illustrate step-by-step virtually all of the kinds of administrative process and judicial review elements set out in the "nutshell," NLS text, 539-544. The Secretary's initial decision was an informal adjudication, i.e., taking the words of a statute, interpreting and applying them to particular facts, and based thereon making a decision that federal funds could be released to go through Overton Park. There also was rulemaking, although it is not clearly set out in the case: DOT Order 5610.1 (NLS at 550) is an informal rulemaking published in the Federal Register requiring The Secretary to make formal findings, which he hadn't done in this case. But the rule wasn't retroactive, despite *Thorpe*. Students should be shown that the words of a statute may be fairly general and require clarification. The American administrative law system has pioneered the process of extensive substantive and procedural rules articulating the meaning and implementation of statutes. You can remind the students that rulemaking and agency adjudication both can be undertaken informally or formally according to the circumstances and legal requirements. Attorneys would almost always rather have formal proceedings — providing discovery, cross-examination, full reasoned decision on the record, etc. — but in cases like this, involving environmental citizen outsiders, typically the courts and the statutory provisions do not guarantee such formalized proceedings.

The focus of class discussion can be on the deference which the Court does or does not grant to the agency. Clearly the citizen plaintiffs were able to make the Court skeptical of the agency's claims of experience and rightful discretion. The administrative record was so thin, and the motivation to circumvent the purposes of Section §4f so obvious, that the Court was won to the uncharacteristic position of overturning an agency decision at the behest of a little group of outsiders. Nevertheless you can note for the students that the majority did not agree with Justice Black that the record was so corrupted that the case should be remanded directly back to the agency, but instead more delicately sent it back to the district court.

You might like to note to your students that the end of the Overton Park story is equally dramatic. As noted in Comment 6 in NLS text at 556-557, Secretary John Volpe ultimately took the case back into the agency. Some environmental activists were reportedly sitting in their low-rent offices in a basement in Washington, D.C. planning the next round of the inevitable fight against the agency's rehabilitated decision to go through the park, when a knock came at the door, and in walked Volpe. Sitting down with them he told them that they didn't have to fight the next round; he had just decided that the original facts had indeed been misrepresented by the Department, that he could not say there were no feasible and prudent alternatives, and that the road would not go through the park. As a sobering endnote, Volpe was shortly thereafter dismissed as Secretary of Transportation, sent to an exile that he probably preferred, the ambassadorship to Italy. (Republican Secretary of Transportation John Volpe, prior to appointment to government, was a major contractor in the State of Massachusetts with, unsurprisingly, extensive experience in building subsidized highways.)

One aspect of *Overton Park* that will not be obvious to the students is that in this case we are focusing on judicial review of a federal administrative agency that is involved with subsidized construction programs, rather than regulation, the more common locus of judicial review of agency action. In fact the only significant portion of the *Overton Park* case that is regulatory is §4f itself, in its restriction of the highway-building lobby's penchant for going through parks. In teaching this chapter it is probably useful to go back to the history of the development of administrative agencies (NLS at 537-539) noting that the highway-building program is a descendant of the more ancient administrative agencies, like the Corps of Engineers with its bridge and canal building, the Post Office, and the like. Regulatory agencies like the pollution regulatory agencies noted briefly in Chapter 6 came along much later in the game. The tools of citizen-initiated review of administrative agency decisions, however, remain basically the same in each setting. The next class picks up on the significant role played in American administrative law by citizen intervention and citizen enforcement.

You may in this class or the next wish to note also the "taxonomy" approach to statutes that we suggest and have followed, initially foreshadowed in chapter 6, described briefly at 535-536, and continuing in Chapters 12-23. There is an amazing range of regulatory approaches adopted by legislatures at the federal, state, and local level over the past forty years. Section 4f in the *Overton Park* case is, as we suggest in the main teachers manual, a roadblock statute; students should be reminded that the overall Department of Transportation and Federal Aid to Highways Acts are predominately concerned with government subsidy of the marketplace, a variant form of regulatory manipulation of economic incentives.

•***For the next class*** **:** The subject is citizen participation: Remind students of the critical role played by citizens in the *Overton Park* case, asking what would have happened to §4f if citizens had not enforced it. Ask them, in the reading for the next class, to focus on the continuing evolutionary role of citizens in the environmental governance process, and the counterpressures coming from the official players in industry and government.

Class 18: The Citizens' Role in Administrative Law — Chapter 11

The two major portions of this assignment are the evolution of citizen standing, including *Scenic Hudson*, and the U.S. Supreme Court's latest standing cases, *Lujan v. National Wildlife Federation* (text at 575), and *Lujan v. Defenders of Wildlife* (1992 case, excerpted in Part III herein as a handout). The first reading shows how in the two decades after 1966 there was a development of the legitimate role of citizens in the governing process, working within the agencies in rulemaking and adjudicatory participation and intervention, and subsequently in the judicial review of administrative agency actions that was the catalyst for the evolution.

Scenic Hudson is an opportunity to ask the students again what role citizens are attempting to play, as distinguished from the "official players" in an administrative proceeding. Typically there has been an official resentment against intervening outsiders, because the government regulators and industry participants in a decision have reached a happy consensus that is disrupted by the outsiders' perspective. In some cases the regulatory agency is overtly a proponent of a project or an opponent of the citizen regulatory argument; in other cases the agency purports to be a neutral decisionmaker, stepping back (as noted in Comment 3, page 567), acting like "an umpire blandly calling balls and strikes" between the mismatched marketplace and citizen forces. In either case the arguments for citizen intervention in the agency process, in the first instance, and access to judicial review thereafter, changed the cozy equilibrium that had prevailed through the 1950s. The Freedom of Information Act (FOIA), Comment 4, page 568, was a similar milestone that has attracted continued resistance since 1966.

Official congressional recognition of the role of citizens is an important emphasis, and the statutes cited in the text at 571 and footnote 44, and 565-566 (n.b. page 571 is not included in the draft reading assignment) vividly indicate the extent to which federal pollution law opens the door to direct citizen enforcement.

The page 571 material also emphasizes the greatly increased options for citizens' recovery of attorneys fees and expert witness fees where they have acted as private attorneys-general enforcing federal laws.

But the theme that you must also cover is that there was bound to be a major reaction against citizen outsiders being brought into the system. In the last decade views finding support in the opinions and writings of Justice Rehnquist have spearheaded efforts to keep citizens out of the governmental process.

The most important theater of this resistance is the standing doctrine. You may wish to review Supreme Court standing requirements under Article III, noted after *Scenic Hudson* at page 563, acknowledging that, sufficient constitutional injury for standing may be based upon "esthetic, conservational, and recreational, as well as economic values...." *Storm King* Case, Sierra Club v. Mort. 405 U.S. 727 (1972). The SCRAP Case, at NLS 564, showed the remarkable breadth that the Court then was willing to apply in granting standing to citizens. The *Lujan Cases* are vivid retrenchments upon this standing liberality. *Lujan v. NWF* (The BLM public lands case) is clearly a severe tightening of the standing rules, with an unconvincing distinction from *SCRAP* in insisting that plaintiffs allege that they actually use the particular tracts which are being opened to mining, rather than allege that their use of the area generally will be effected by the mining on those tracts, the majority is being far more insistent up on an actual physical linkage with the subject matter of the case. The majority shows an unwillingness to acknowledge the kinds of repercussive effect that extend throughout an area when mining comes into the wilderness as a sufficient interest for standing.

In *Lujan v. Defenders of Wildlfie* (International Endangered Species) the Court took the standing allegations of the parties — noted in the Teachers Manual pages 301-303 — and again required a remarkable particularity of fact linking plaintiffs' alleged interest to the particular locus and events being challenged. If for instance the plaintiffs had actually purchased tickets for future trips to the locales where overseas endangered species might be injured, that apparently would have improved their claim of standing in the eyes of the majority. If they had actually seen members of the species, or if they had contracts to study particular species, they would have been brought closer to the majority's somewhat pedantic insistence that there be a proven direct link between the plaintiff and the species that is being threatened. On balance, however, it is interesting to note that an actual majority of the Supreme Court does not buy the plurality's denigration of a claim of injury based on violation of law, the so-called "procedural injury" basis of standing. The two dissenters and all three concurring justices seem to accept that Congress can extend the scope of Article III standing by opening up statutes to citizen enforcement, and designating a violation of the statute as presumptive injury to potential plaintiffs.

Students may well be distressed by the tone of the current standing cases. The Court in both the *Lujan* cases implicitly or explicitly accepts the possibility that there may be violations of law that will never face enforcement actions because lack of standing will bar the only likely enforcers. The reality is that if citizens do not intervene and enforce the law, no one in government or in industry has any interest or likelihood of doing so. This clarifies the stakes in the standing controversy.

In coping with the standing jurisprudence of the Rehnquist court, citizen plaintiffs have become much more fastidious in constructing the standing argument for their cases. In most cases, this merely requires the time consuming irritation of constructing proof of particularized effects to the persons who are going to sign on to a complaint. In some cases, however — in a controversy that rekindles the dilemma underlying *Sierra Club v. Morton* — there may be few members of environmental organizations who actually suffer any direct impact from challenged government activity. In the Arctic National Wildlife Refuge, where until recently at least very few people ever had traveled, standing will require long distance trips by potential plaintiffs. Ultimately you may ask students whether the standing claim is a complete barrier, or merely a frustrating hurdle posed to citizens who are attempting to enforce federal law.

This chapter has other material that you may wish to assign, or include as sidebar commentary in the course of discussion, depending on the themes you choose to focus on, your radical discontent with current affairs, etc.

A proposed optional reading is the *Vermont Yankee* case, 581-589. This case is another example to the students of the waxing and possible waning of citizen efforts, focusing this time on citizen's attempts to expand agency procedures. The case can also be used to show agency maneuvering with administrative procedures, as indicated in Comment 1 page 587, where the NRC was clearly using the rulemaking to remove a highly-charged issue from future nuclear plant licensing adjudications. As to judicial expansion of the procedures required, the District of Columbia Court of Appeals had straightforwardly ordered expanded proceedings to "ventilate" the matter so as to produce a more revealing administrative record. The Supreme Court was unanimous in striking down the D.C. Circuit order, but judicial machismo and group psychology may be a better explanation for the 7-0 vote than the merits of the case: It appears to us that Justice Rehnquist may have persuaded his brethren that the D.C. Circuit was acting in an impertinent manner., and thereafter he justified the result by playing games with precedent and quotes out of context, as noted in the text and main teachers manual material.

It is important to remind your students that although the opinion's tone is scathing, *Vermont Yankee* resulted in a remand so that there could be an effective record produced for judicial review. (Comment 2, page 587.) There are other notes that are interesting in legal process terms, at 588-599.

As to the question of judicial review of agency interpretations of law, *Chevron* is a leading case (NLS text at 589), but we feel that the point can be adequately made in your discussions of the agency interpretation of the statute in *Overton Park*: where a court wishes to defer to an agency interpretation of law, it generally is able to do so, but when the definition of the statute is sufficiently clear, or the court sufficiently skeptical about the agency's good faith, judges ultimately can relegate to themselves (presumptively experts in interpreting the meaning of law), the ultimate decision on whose reading of a statute is accurate. In *Overton Park* the Supreme Court obviously felt that the agency's interpretation of the word "prudent" so as to import economic concerns would completely undercut the meaning and purpose of §4f, hence they overrode the agency's interpretation of the statutory term. Agency interpretations of the agency's own regulations, of course, tend to be deferred to in most instances.

•*For the next class:* The next two classes focus on NEPA. Tell students to read through the NEPA statute and the Chicod Creek Case, called NRDC v. Grant, asking how a vague short statute can move into the courts and become a tiger — or is it a paper tiger?

Class 19: NEPA — The National Environmental Policy Act — Chapter 12

In this and subsequent chapters, the text and main manual generally do a sufficient job in setting out coverage for a first law course offering as well.

In legal process terms, we would reemphasize that the *Chicod Creek* case, NRDC v. Grant, is a good vehicle for showing students how a relatively untried statute with unspecified terms can reach a court that, in environmental law terms, is completely inexperienced — and how through the American litigation process the issues are raised and processed so as to offer the opportunity for issues of fact, policy, and law to be contested at a fairly high level. The material also shows how a statute designed to force the on-rolling system to hesitate and ask questions about costs, benefits, and alternatives, became part of the federal decisionmaking system.

For this first class, however, a focus on what happened in Judge Larkin's court is a full and sufficient agenda for class discussion.

•*For the next class:* Tell students to figure out the generalized repercussions and consequences of this NEPA caselaw, in the lower courts and in the Supreme Court, where it meets three unfriendly majority opinions (*Kleppe*, *Marsh*, and *Robertson*).

(a) (if further optional class on NEPA is taught): If you choose to teach just one class on NEPA, you will want to draw some systemic conclusions from Judge Larkin's opinions in the *Chicod Creek* Case. Reading through the rest of the chapter (presumably unassigned to students) you can integrate much of the continuing controversy over NEPA back into their discussion of that case, so as to give a sense of how the EIS process poses real constraints upon agencies, and how there have been continual attempts to increase the deference courts give to agency decisions to do what the agency wanted to do in the first place.

(b) (if next class is on §7 of the Endangered Species Act): Tell students to focus on the explicit statutory language of §7 of the Endangered Species Act, asking themselves how easy that provision has been to apply to the passionate controversies noted in the text, the Snail Darter and Spotted Owl cases.

* Optional Second Class on NEPA — Chapter 12

There inevitably are a variety of fascinating avenues left open after the first class on NEPA, and the text and main teachers manual offer a variety of issues to be picked up and developed, breaking down into two different themes: First, what apparently is required to comply with NEPA today? (The substance of an EIS apparently must discuss impacts and alternatives to the proposed actions, as noted at 631-632. The bulk of the catalogue of requirements in §102(2)C seems to be duplicative prose, as noted in the first paragraph of subpart A, 631.)

Second, there are also NEPA procedural requirements, affecting when an EIS must be prepared, and a required interagency process which is often shortcut, but in most cases ends up with a purely formal reprinting of multiple agency comments in the back of each EIS.

The third theme is the counter attack against NEPA, part of which has already been seen in the limitation of standing represented in the *Lujan* cases in Chapter 11, but continuing in the NEPA context. Examples here include the ever-narrowing circumstances under which an agency must prepare a broad, early EIS,, as requested by the citizens in *Kleppe*, and general deference to agency determinations of the sufficiency of their compliance with statutory requirements. The Supreme Court's holdings can be characterized in many cases as reducing NEPA to a pure procedural formality, which may be tacked on at the end of an agency process, rather than an insistence on an organic reform in agency decisionmaking as the earlier federal cases had systematically required.

Lest students become too depressed by this process, some of the notes later in the chapter remind us that the potential for citizen suits remains, so the deterrent effect of NEPA remains as well, although often it may be substantially invisible. See Comment 5 in the main Teachers Manual at 176-177.

•*For the next class:* Tell students to focus on the explicit statutory language of §7 of the Endangered Species Act, asking themselves how easy that provision has been to apply to the passionate controversies noted in the text, the Snail Darter and Spotted Owl cases.

Class 20: Substantive Roadblocks: Section 7 of the Endangered Species Act of 1973 — Chapter 13

This material is probably quite topical in students' minds, and tends to get rolling fairly easily. You will have to decide whether you want to focus on the policy questions of endangered species protection as a metaphor (perhaps the best metaphor we have) for testing environmental ethics. Alternatively it is a fascinating exercise in, again, like NEPA, accidental statutory protections sneaking into enforceable federal law. Section 7 (and to a lesser extent §9's prohibition against "taking" any endangered species, noted at text Comment 13, page 673) were not recognized as containing prohibitions in the EPA's initial legislative passage. Subsequently, because of court enforcement, they have been taken seriously, and congressional amendments have blunted only some of their sharpest edges, rather than rolling the statute back to a nullity, as probably would have happened had the original Congress recognized what it was doing. The extensive parallels with NEPA are obvious.

The main teachers manual sets out a number of supplementary teaching ideas.

Several updates are necessary: on May 13th, 1992, the God Committee (foreshadowed in the text at page 680, footnote 26) decided to override the Act's protections, allegedly for economic reasons protecting timber cutters' jobs. That decision has led to no opening of forests to clearcutting, however, because due to multiple violations of other statutes, other outstanding injunctions have prevented the particular forest tracts from being clear-cut. The environmentalists are preparing an appellate court challenge to the God Committee decision, based in part on the fact that one of the God Committee members voting for the override admitted during the proceedings that the required statutory findings had not been made. In another case, *Seattle Audubon* (discussed at page 572 at footnote 50), the U.S. Supreme Court refused to overturn the noted appropriations rider for its alleged violations of the U.S. v. Klein rule prohibiting legislation that makes quasi-judicial findings. Justice Thomas could have characterized §318 of the Act challenged therein (again, see page 572) as a direct attempt to interpose a conclusion in the judicial proceeding, or could characterize it as an implied amendment of the underlying statute. He chose the latter, and so the appropriations rider was held valid. The significance of this precedent is more for its separation of powers consequences than for its effect on the spotted owl.

There is a continuing jousting in Congress over the Endangered Species Act. With Albert Gore raising important environmental issues, Dan Quayle and others on the resource exploitation side have been arguing for amendments of the Endangered Species Act. On August 10, Senator Symms of Idaho submitted "the Progressive Endangered Species Act Amendments," providing that the Act should protect only full species, and not endangered sub-species or populations of an endangered species. The terms of the controversy obviously are completely different in the two camps. One camp argues that the Endangered Species Act is a handle on a much larger problem of environmental diversity loss, and that the long-term and short-term economic consequences justify consistent accommodations between human activities and endangered species. The other camp argues that any substantive obstacle to business as usual (especially involving subsidized mining, grazing, and timber cutting) justifies an override of the intangible and rather frivolous concept of endangered species.

As usual the public press tends to superficial caricature. Our hope is that fuller economic analysis will become part of the process.

•*For the next class:*
(a) (if public lands optional material is assigned): Tell students to analyze the politics and economics of the public lands issues in somewhat the same terms as raised in the prior two chapters, asking them to analyze the difference between the multiple-use-sustained-yield principles applied on the public lands, and the more specialized statutes NEPA and the Endangered Species Act;

(b) (if following class is on the historical development of pollution regulation): Tell students to focus on the state-level origins of most pollution regulation, and the historical development of approaches to pollution regulation reflected in the reading. How could the *Utilex* case drag on so long?

* Optional Class: Public Lands and Resource Management — Chapter 14

This material has more than enough issues to take up more than one class. The approach you take might start with an inquiry into how legislation is written to change an existing industry/government alliance that has produced an exploitative "establishment" status quo derogating the long-term viability of a public resource. The linkages between the Department of Interior sub-agencies and the mining, grazing and logging industries on BLM lands is a vivid example of this well known phenomena. The statutory history set out in the readings (including Comment 4 at 696, where the drafters went out of their way to clarify that the statute's policies were not effective unless specifically re-enacted by subsequent legislation) shows the infighting and difficulties in this area.

Another approach is to ask policy questions about the public lands. Who has the right to determine their uses: the people who live in and around the resources and those who have developed industries to exploit the resources, or the vast amorphous population of the United States that theoretically owns both the land and the resources? Another take on this is the question of aesthetics and wilderness values. It is always good for an enlightening debate to ask whether the last 50,000 acres of sub-alpine forest in a particular region of the Northwest should be reserved for hikers, hunters, fishermen, and backpackers, or for a large copper mine or timber cutting operation that would keep a hundred local citizens off the dole for another 4 or 5 years. Is an appreciation of the outdoors an aristocratic elitism? Are questions of aesthetics fanciful? Should public lands be managed, as private lands almost never will be, for long-term biodiversity maintenance rather than for maximizing short-term financial gain? What about the loss of the world's oldest living thing (Comment 5, page 715)? The public trust discussions may resurface in your discussion of this class material.

•***For the next class:*** Tell students to focus on the state-level origins of most pollution regulation, and the historical development of approaches to pollution regulation reflected in the reading. How could the *Utilex* case drag on so long?

Class 21: Historical Development of Pollution regulation — Chapter 15

This class's material is useful as a general introduction to the field of statutory pollution regulation and the chapters that follow. The first section of the readings is designed to promote a historical understanding of state regulation as it existed in, say, 1970, when federal regulation began to increase exponentially. The second part of the readings indicates different ways that pollution statutes approach the problem of regulating pollution. We remind you that the statutory taxonomy set out at the beginning of chapter 11, pages 535-536, is also useful in approaching the overview question of how mass pollution problems can be approached.

Perhaps the easiest way to access the somewhat dry material is to ask the students what they can learn from the raw docket entry notations of the *Utilex* case file in the text, pages 723-726. The reality of that case file is a strong hesitation on the part of the professional staff of the state water resources commissions to enforce water pollution cleanup too strenuously. The political repercussions were likely to burn the fingers of the bureaucrat who was too militant in defense of water quality. Students may be asked to analyze the origin of most state pollution statutes and agencies — based in old public health codes, often enforced by departments of natural resources or conservation that had been reconstituted from fish and game departments — note also the limited character of the statutory authority (text pages 720-721). The make-up of the commission and the indefiniteness of the statutory language and political mandate, conspired to limit the strictness of water quality enforcement. Industry had a near monopoly on expertise, as well as the ability to push the agency into continuing spirals of administrative procedure leading to systematic ineffectiveness of the enforcement regime. (As an illustrative symptom, the sum total of administrative fines issued by the WRC had been for one calendar year in the late 1970's totaled less than $10,000 for all industries, state-wide.)

The invidious effect of competition between the states for industry deserves emphasis. If a state like Michigan did crack down on water pollution, industry would threaten to "go south." This problem — a regulatory analog of Hardin's tragedy of the commons led to the reformation of federal pollution laws chronicled at 727 and thereafter. The remainder of the chapter sets out a variety of different permit approaches and procedures. They can be used to foreshadow what regulatory schemes will be coming, particularly the Clean Air Act, with harm-based ambient standards, and Clean Water Act, with it's best-available-technology standards.

•***For the next class:***

(a) (If next class is regulation of market access-pesticides): Tell students to note the amazing contrast between the Les v. Reilly handout and Corrosion Proof Fittings handout case.

(b) (If next class is on auto emissions): Tell students to look at the problem of automobile air pollution, noting how the drastic provisions of the Clean Air Act's Title II attempted to roll back auto emissions — was it a wise attempt?

(c) (If next class is on the main Clean Air Act, Chapter 18) Tell students to analyze why a nationwide air pollution act was necessary to control air pollution, and ask them also to describe the means by which Congress directed that minimum federal quality levels be set and attained.

* Optional Class: Regulation of Market Access (Pesticides) — Chapter 16

If you choose to do this material on regulation of market access (a kind of "prior restraint" on toxins in the marketplace), we suggest you focus your class on the new handout cases — *Les v. Reilly* in Part III of this manual (on the Delaney Clause) and *Corrosion Proof Fittings* (on asbestos, in main teachers manual at page 279). These two cases beautifully set up the policy questions around risk assessment and regulatory prohibitions.

The Delaney Clause of the Federal Food, Drug and Cosmetic Act is noted on page 738 of the text; footnote 1 there says that "the Delaney Clause is such a crude regulatory device that the FDA has only applied it in a limited number of situations where certain explicit toxicological criteria have been satisfied, e.g., an increased risk of fatality of one in a million. The *Les v. Reilly* case, however, shows the D.C. Circuit enforcing the strict words of the Delaney Clause as they are written, in spite of a host of regulatory and economic commentators who have condemned its excessiveness. On the face of the Delaney Clause, any substance that is shown to be carcinogenic in animals is thereby banned from used as a food additive, despite the fact that the risk of one additional death may be one in a hundred million, or less, and the economic impact extraordinarily large. The D.C. Circuit's strict interpretation may actually be a backhand attempt to send the Delaney Clause back to Congress for modification. The decision offers a wonderful exercise in legal process.

The policy and judicial review questions in *Corrosion Proof Fittings* can be contrasted with *Les v. Reilly*, as noted in the comments that follow both of the cases as excerpted in these teachers manuals. The *Corrosions Proof Fittings* court, operating under a very different ToSCA statutory mandate for cases where a substances is not shown to be a carcinogen, was able to take on a balancing analysis that rolled back the strict EPA asbestos rule.

If you choose to focus on these two cases in your Chapter 16 coverage, you should recognize that they get you into policy issues, rather than a study of the strict "taxonomy" characteristics of ToSCA and FIFRA. You therefore should probably supply a quick sidebar summary of ToSCA's procedures gleaned from the text of Chapter 16, focusing on the theme raised in the main teachers manual commentary at page 194, of contrasting burdens of proof. FIFRA puts the burden of establishing that a product is safe initially on the applicant, subject to the strictures of accuracy of reporting under federal law. ToSCA puts the burden on EPA to establish by substantial evidence that chemical testing is necessary for a particular substance, and then to set testing protocols — a two step chain of hurdles that has made stringent ToSCA implementation extremely difficult.

Alternatively you could focus your classes exclusively on the structure of these two market-access regulatory systems.

The Chapter 16 text material shows two different attempts to regulate potentially toxic materials prior to their certification for use in the marketplace — ToSCA and FIFRA. A backdrop on this material is the current discussion about FDA delay in registering a variety of pharmaceutical products for use in the American market, including AIDS experimental vaccines, RU-486, etc. The approach you might take in viewing the practicalities of FIFRA compared to ToSCA is set out in the main teachers manual.

---

* Optional Class: Stark Statutory Pollution Standards (Auto Emissions — Clean Air Act Title II) — Chapter 17

The auto emissions chapter is based on one idea — the advantages and disadvantages of simple direct congressional pollution limits — and usually teaches in lively fashion. Students can be asked to characterize the prior situation in auto emissions: what would be the auto emissions story if it had been left to the marketplace, or to state air pollution agencies acting as 51 fractured jurisdictions, or left to an embattled EPA with some vague health protection standard weighing against national economic competitive burdens? Ask the students if they recognize what is truly revolutionary about Title II of the 1970 Clean Air Act? In little more than one paragraph of text, Congress almost literally dictated the actual precise parts per million emissions standard to be applied to all automobiles across the nation. By setting tail pipe standards at a strict 90% roll back from the 1970 production models, Congress almost totally eliminated agency enforcement discretion. EPA was effectively reduced to the role of a technician implementing a strict objective standard. The effectiveness of the federal auto pollution roll back, backed up by its potential prohibition on sales of particular auto models, created an immense industry effort to achieve the standards, an effort that has on balance been quite successful.

Students should also be asked whether the starkness of the regulatory approach has not cost a great deal as well. As noted in the text and the main teachers manual, there is some question whether the strictness has allowed sufficient flexibility and innovation in the industry, and whether it makes sense when applied in nationwide terms. The legal process implications, particularly those that focus on institutional competence, are obvious and can be entertaining.

•***For the next class:*** Tell students to analyze why a nationwide air pollution act was necessary to control air pollution, and ask them also to describe the means by which Congress directed that minimum federal quality levels be set and attained.

Class 22: The Clean Air Act, Harm-Based Ambient Standards, The National Commons and Federalism — Chapter 18

This class introduces the first of the massive federal command and control regulatory systems. 1970 marks a milestone, because in the midst of the environmental explosion Congress basically threw out the prior primacy of states, each to regulate environmental quality as it wished, instead substituting a nationwide floor of federal minimum standards for air quality.

The job in teaching this and the subsequent regulatory structures is to keep the class deeply involved and alive in the face of sometimes mind-boggling complexity, coupled with the fact that it is getting late in the semester and (if this is spring semester) the weather is becoming more seductive than the classroom. In each class it is therefore useful to try to have a single focus which can be used to teach the broader range of structural, policy, and technical legal issues.

To begin, it is useful to identify the different divisions of the Clean Air Act, set out in the text at pages 773-774, adding another note for the 1990 Clean Air Act Title IV which added an economic-based incentive system supplementing the pre-existing sections of the Act. You may alert students to the different bases for the different regulatory systems — harm-based (§107-110, 112), technology-based (§111 and §112 as amended), and political fiat (Title II, noted earlier in Chapter 17, more taxonomically described as roadblock standards — meet this standard or sell no cars). For purposes of this class it is probably best to focus on the first program, the workhorse ambient air regulatory system for the criteria pollutants like sulfur dioxide, sulfates, suspended particulate, etc.

In this chapter, for instance, you could cast students in the role of the state air quality division of the state's Department of Environmental Protection in Ohio and ask the students what drops on their desk late in 1970 that requires them to do something? Using Ohio, you can lead ultimately to the *Cleveland Electric* case on page 801, which shows how the State of Ohio desperately tried to avoid instituting a rigorous state implementation plan (SIP).

Beginning in 1970, states were divided into air quality control regions, the geographic units that would form the basis for most regulation under the new CAA. The federal primary air pollution standards for the original six criteria pollutants were published by early 1971, in a form that can be summarized in the chart from *Cleveland Electric*, reprinted as a handout in the main teachers manual at page 311 (you may be able to get a better copy by Xeroxing it from the Federal Reporter, 572 F.2d at 1154). And how did the states react, you may ask the students? Obviously, the State of Ohio already knew basically where its pollution sources were. Under the old Federal Clean Air Act there had been information-gathering as well as establishment of air quality districts. Now it was clear there would be federal teeth applied, because each state would have to put together a detailed SIP. The instinct of some states, like Ohio, was to try to minimize the existing problems, (including some strategies like placing air pollution monitoring stations upwind of major pollution sources, so as not to get the full brunt of a local source before it was diffused in the ambient air). Students should also note that industry on the downwind edge of a state was of less concern to the state, because its pollution traveled across the state boundary into somebody else's jurisdiction, *e.g.*, Kentucky, which was in violation of the Clean Air Act for some pollutants which were not even produced in any significant quantities within Kentucky.

The chronology set forth in *Cleveland Electric* shows how the state administration colluded with industry in attempting to delay as long as possible the promulgation of a strict SIP for sulfur dioxide. The clear implication was that if Ohio were to achieve the federal minimum standards for air quality, it would be greatly increasing the cost of power generated by old, dirty coal-fired power plants that had helped give Ohio a competitive position vis à vis other states. Similarly, much of the high-sulfur coal being burned in the state's power plants was being mined in Ohio, thereby benefiting the state economy in a second way. But as that case shows, even if a state is genuinely interested in implementing the federal standards as they are promulgated, the job of acting as a state broker, trying to figure out how much of a pollution roll back was necessary at all existing or potential air pollution sources in order to achieve the numerical federal goal, is hellish. Computer models are helpful, but this is an imprecise science.

Furthermore, students should be reminded that the state had to produce an acceptable SIP not only for sulfur dioxides, but also for every other criteria pollutant listed, now including lead. No wonder EPA was so reluctant to list lead and subsequently any other criteria pollutant, since every such listing added 51 cantankerous SIP problems to its already over-committed docket. Note, moreover, that ambient standards standing alone provided virtually no means to take account of transboundary pollution. This material is picked up at the end of the chapter and could be a side-bar comment for you. Where there is transboundary pollution, the downwind state merely has procedural opportunities to attempt to trigger conversations with EPA and the offending state; there is no substantive provision that empowers the downwind state to enforce pollution rollbacks so as to achieve air quality standards in its ambient atmosphere.

Behind every draft SIP is a potential FIP. You can note for students that the threat that the federal government held was on one hand a cut back on federal subsidies to the state, and on the other the EPA's power to "FIP" the state's SIP by imposing a federal implementation plan upon recalcitrant states.

At some point tracking through the political and technological complexity, students will wonder whether there isn't a better alternative. You can note that the pressure for environmental improvement came through to Congress in 1970 with many stories of harms caused by air pollution, so it was inevitable that Congress chose a harm-based standard for its national air pollution control efforts. Moreover, as Congress has been repeatedly told by industry, different parts of the country had very different air pollution characteristics, so accordingly the statute was drafted to allow the states to have different arrangements for achieving the minimum federal standards. By way of contrast, the new source performance standard program under §111 imposed technology-based standards (best available technology), which do not vary from location to location. Every new source of air pollution must put in the best technology that exists for controlling air pollution in that industry, whatever the cost, whatever the rate of diffusion of the surrounding environment, whatever the degree of harm or lack of harm imposed to human health and the environment by the emissions. After exploring the rationales that might support this NSPS strategy, you can use this opportunity to set up some of the major alternatives to harm-based ambient standards, noting that there is no obvious best solution.

Optional readings in this assignment include the lead cases, pages 780-787. The first case shows a court overriding EPA's attempts to avoid regulating lead, once the EPA had made studies that showed drastic human health consequences from ambient lead (particularly felt in injury to urban children's brain tissues), and the second case, *Lead Industries*, shows that once an agency has taken on a matter and studied it, the resulting regulations tend to be upheld by judicial deference to agency discretion.

There is also an interesting issue of safety and risk assessment presented in the toxic pollutants question, page 790-793. Judge Bork's initial opinion was particularly interesting for making a pragmatic compromise with the statutory language, using a law and economics balancing system. In reversing himself, Judge Bork for the Circuit Court en banc acknowledged that the threshold determination had to be based solely on the risk to health. This is another opportunity to raise the "how safe is safe?" question.

•***For the next class:*** Tell students to focus on the *Rybachek* case, for the technical functioning of the Clean Water Act as it applies to Alaska placer mines, and for some of the economic and political arguments that attend it. Alternatively you may hand out the "Average River" study problem and tell them to try to figure out from the reading the variety of different issues that it raises, with some sense of how they will be resolved.

Class 23: The Clean Water Act and Technology-Based Regulation — Chapter 19

If you are using the "Average River" study problem (main teachers manual at page 313, to be handed out) then you may organize the class as an overview class, using the Teachers Guide to the "Average River" problem as a point of departure for cataloging how the Clean Water Act would apply to the various problems set out. (The Teachers Guide is reprinted in the main manual at pages 314-315.)

In approaching this material, please refer to the overview essay on the Act prepared by Professor Goldfarb and inadvertently left out of the main teachers manual, reprinted in Part III of this Manual.

The initial reading in this selection is intended to introduce the federal National Pollution Discharge Elimination System (NPDES) as an overlay on the state water pollution standards, all of which had been based on ambient water quality in the various water bodies in each state. Although, unlike the Clean Air Act, not every state had to join the NPDES program, nevertheless an NPDES permit would be required for every point source in the United States. Note that the only way the federal government could hope to do this in a system that included more than a dozen states that chose not to help in the federal anti-pollution effort was to have a basis for setting point source standards that did not require sophisticated measuring and modeling of each point source and its receiving waters. The whole approach of the Clean Water Act was to forget the harm-based method of setting standards, at least initially, instead focusing on industry-by-industry categorization, and uniform nationwide imposition of those best technology standards on each category of industrial point source.

The *Rybachek* case: The various arguments made by the miners offer an opportunity either to become overwhelmed by acronyms (BPT, BAT, BCT, BMP, etc.) or an opportunity to see a serious battle going on. Though it may have seemed hypertechnical, for instance, the legal fight about whether EPA should categorize certain suspended solids as conventional pollutants or toxic pollutant discharges determined whether the stricter and more expensive BAT standards would apply rather than BCT. In making sense of this, we urge you to work through the different sets of requirements as set out in the overview of the Act and the text.

• You can make the *Rybachek* presentation clearer by using the TBELs chart on page 312 of the main manual.

A variety of other issues are raised in the surrounding text. Students should be reminded that in many cases point source discharges are not the main problem, but that non-point sources of pollution, which often involve the construction industry and agriculture, had such political fire-power attached to them that they were, in effect, left unregulated by the Clean Water Act. You may also mention that the Clean Water Act contains an echo of the old water pollution control system: water quality standards (WQSs) have been resurrected as backups to the best technology standards, where particular water bodies have continued to be so polluted that reliance on the technology standards is insufficient.

Students may be asked to draw conclusions about the relative enforceability and efficacy of the two approaches, Clean Air Act versus Clean Water Act. We don't commit ourselves, noting that there are necessities involved in both approaches, and expressing great academic interest in the continued development of these regulatory provisions, in addition to various ongoing experiments with economic incentive statutes exemplified in Chapter 20's material (the following optional class).

•For the next class:

(a) (If teaching the economic incentive chapter): Tell students to analyze the novel experiments of the Clean Air Act's 1990 amendments, asking whether they are the answer to avoid the vast complexities of the command and control pollution statutes.

(b) (If going straight to the toxic regulation classes): Tell students that they will be picking up again on toxic wastes; ask them to consider the two main regulatory apparatuses being constructed to handle this problem, RCRA and CERCLA, asking them what the statutes are doing, at what administrative and industrial cost.

---

* Optional Class: Economic Incentives and Artificial Pollution Market Statutes — Chapter 20

This material looks at the fascinating question of bringing environmental regulations into the market system, not in the traditional cynical view, by giving regulated industry a determinative say in how much regulations they face, but rather by making pollution credits and abatement credits tradable between industrial and emissions sources.

A very simple version of the process, showing the common sense advantages of trading in pollution rollbacks, is presented in the water pollution setting in the Colorado case noted in the main teachers manual at pages 212-213.

The fundamental theory of this statutory strategy is set out in the first two pages of the reading. The complex policy debate about whether marketplace efficiency incentives should be imported into the regulatory world is set out in the Latin/Ackerman-Stewart debates. You may not need to assign those excerpts, although they are both sophisticated and fascinating. The material from pages 870-881 sets out the structure of how economic incentive systems can work under bubbles, offsets, netting, and banking, or under the new 1990 CAA sulfur dioxide emissions trading program. Working through the details of this experimental program, you can note why the potential trading that was possible under the CAA prior to 1990 was so rarely used; we will observe with interest the degree to which the post-1990 trading picture will be better.

Economic trading systems require enormous sophistication in specifying the amounts of emissions credits that are allowed, and contain questions about long-term certainty (because a change in public attitude, a change in technology, a change in scientific knowledge can change the amount of pollution credit "currency" in the marketplace). Other fascinating questions arise. If an environmental group bought up a significant portfolio of pollution credits and simply retired them, without using them, might the government be tempted to issue more pollution credits to represent the permissible industrial pollution available in a particular airshed? The bottom line is that this economic approach to regulation is by no means simpler in its effectuation, although its incentives for action on the part of industry may indeed be built-in and greater.

The text in the main teachers manual examines in some detail the different structural and policy issues raised by the materials.

•***For next class:*** Tell students that they will be picking up again on toxic wastes; ask them to consider the two main regulatory apparatuses being constructed to handle this problem, RCRA and CERCLA, asking them what the statutes are doing, at what administrative and industrial cost.

Class 24: Regulation of Toxics — Chapters [6], 21, 22

In this and the subsequent class, students will be exploring the structures of the RCRA and CERCLA (Superfund) statutes. It's hard to know which statute should be studied first. Taxonomically, CERCLA is much simpler (which is why we put it first in the book) because it essentially is a system to provide for repayment of toxic waste dump cleanups. But chronologically, RCRA should precede CERCLA, because RCRA is the regulatory predecessor in the life cycle of toxic wastes, regulating from the moment of their creation to the moment of their disposal in a properly certified disposal cite (and if RCRA is complied with, the toxic wastes need never come under the terms of CERCLA).

To orient this process, you may wish to return to the beginning of Chapter 6, noting for students that governmental regulation of toxics includes pre-market certification (in ToSCA, FIFRA, etc.), collateral regulation of chemical manufacturing conditions under OSHA, CAA, and CWA, and the waste disposal statutory provisions of RCRA and/or CERCLA, the latter when a disposal site turns out to pose a risk of serious toxic contamination.

The approach to these classes will depend in great part upon how much discussion of these toxic statutes was included in the Chapter 6 coverage. You may find that the assignments you decide to make differ from the proposed class assignments because of prior coverage.

If looking for a good introductory tool to open up this area, we suggest the *NEPACCO* case at NLS text 266-269. The case offers liability under both CERCLA and RCRA, tells an all-too-common tale of sloppy disposal, and provides a jumping off point for bringing the rather complex and sometimes dry structures of both statutes into the narrative. The assignment as proposed includes a basic introduction to RCRA and a basic introduction to CERCLA drawn from all three relevant chapters. Additional themes in this first class could bring out some of the issues noted in the optional readings: more of the explicit structure of RCRA, 928-940; the draconian terms of EPA's burden of proof of causation — the *Wade* case — 285-287; joint and several liability — *Monsanto* — 287-292.

The *NEPACCO* case is discussed in the main teachers manual, 99-101.

If liability issues under the toxic statutes have already been covered sufficiently in your Chapter 6 classes, Alternate Assignment No. 24 focuses in greater depth upon the administrative structures of the two statutes.

•*For next class:* Tell students to focus on EPA's strategies for getting the most bang from its regulatory buck, using the *Cannons Engineering* case as the focal point of their attention.

Class 25: More Issues in Toxics Regulation — Chapters 21, 22, [23]

There will undoubtedly be issues dangling over from the prior toxics regulation class. In this class the focus may be on the draconian nature of EPA's enforcement strategies. The *Cannons Engineering* case, 911-923, shows how the simple burden of proof the EPA bears, the stringent joint and several liability it can assess, coupled with its wide administrative discretion to make settlement consent decrees with different classes of PRPs — all combine to put PRPs over a barrel.

Other background material is the optional assignment, 898-903, a fascinating view of how attorneys' fees can be far greater than the full cleanup cost of a site, (*Mobay Chemicals*); questions of fairness where a PRP is jointly and severally liable for waste dumped by dozens or even hundreds of other culpable PRPs, 903-908 (*Monsanto*); and the fascinating question of where RCRA hazardous waste facility sites will end up being located, 954-960 (This latter is from Chapter 23 on land use, but provides a necessary reminder of the NIMBY Syndrome, unless you are teaching the Optional Class on land use issues).

At some point you may wish to ask overarching questions about the amount of hazardous waste that actually is excluded from RCRA regulation (930-931, and the Dernbach quotation, 937-938); and the sobering message of the chart reprinted on page 885, showing the truly mind-boggling amounts of time required for administrative processing of a site. You may also want to mention EPA's latest enforcement strategy, shifting actual cleanup responsibility to private PRPs, an approach noted at 924-925.

•*For the next class:*
(a) (if teaching the optional land use chapter): Tell students to skim the entire assignment for different modes of land use issues that arise in environmental cases, and focus on the hazardous waste facility siting statutes: If they are in a hypothetical state that must identify and develop hazardous waste facility sites, what should be considered, and what procedures should be followed in order to locate a hazardous waste site in the village of New Wilsonville?

(b) (If next assignment is ADR): Tell students to focus on the Hudson River power controversy, which followed the Storm King case noted in Chapter 11 on page 562, asking whether it was an exception or a good example for the resolution of future environmental controversies.

---

* Optional Class — Land Use Issues In Environmental Law — Chapter 23

This chapter is just a glimpse at the interrelationship between land use and environmental law. Of course, you can remind students that land use issues were intimately involved in this course from the beginning, in the designation of the *Wilsonville* toxic site, in the zoning or non-zoning of the *Boomer* community so as to have residences located adjacent to cement plants, in wetlands regulation and flood plain zoning, and so on. Some of the examples in this chapter focus on federal forms of land use as in CZMA and the CWA §404 regulations. The vast majority of land use processes and regulations, however, are created and applied at the state and local level. For this reason we suggest the most accessible block of land use material for class coverage might be the section on locating hazardous waste facility sites, 954-960. This material involves state or local land use law. It is intimately linked to issues that the students have previously studied in the toxic tort and the toxic regulation assignments, and it is suitably open-ended.

You might do a simulation as suggested in the prior class tag line, casting some students as various citizens of New Wilsonville, and others as state officials who are under serious constraint of federal law (RCRA) or interstate compact obligation (main teachers manual Comment 4 at page 153-154) to find and develop adequate hazardous waste disposal facilities in their state. The students will very quickly come upon the NIMBY Syndrome. In asking them what objective criteria (as well as psychological and legal constraints) will be imposed on the process, you can encourage them to tie together a number of issues beginning with the *Wilsonville* case and private common law tort issues, questions perhaps of inverse condemnation, citizen challenges of administrative agency decisions, and requirements of federal toxic regulatory systems. The main teachers manual provides specific suggestions for this approach, at 237-238, and also provides suggestions on the variety of other materials in this chapter.

•*For the next class:* Tell students to focus on the Hudson River power controversy, which followed the Storm King case noted in Chapter 11 on page 562, asking whether it was an exception or a good example for the resolution of future environmental controversies.

Class 26: ADR — Alternate Dispute Resolution — Chapter 24

[You may wish to do a classroom simulation exercise, actively involving all students in pre-assigned roles, to show students vividly what ADR is and can do. Exercises are available from the Harvard Program on Negotiation, 617-495-1684. (Their "Jefferson Landfill" case is a good state policy/NIMBY simulation; there are several others.)]

[You can hand out the map of the Hudson River controversy reprinted in the main teachers manual at page 316 to illustrate the setting of that ADR case.]

This is a very important chapter in legal process terms, too often shortchanged in environmental law courses. One thing you can emphasize to students is that negotiation is a fundamental part of all lawyering: the vast majority of cases are settled out of court, once the probable outcome has been brainstormed by respective attorneys on either side testing each other's case hypothetically.

This chapter introduces several negotiations-based non-courtroom resolution processes, in two different settings. First is ADR between parties seeking to resolve particular disputes (sort of quasi-adjudication of particular cases). Second is "REG-NEG," negotiated rulemaking where the determinative party is a government agency which is promulgating a regulation, and invites in all seriously disputatious parties to help draft the proposed rules so as to minimize subsequent court challenges.

Of these two settings, the most lively one to get the students into probably is the Hudson River controversy, because we know so much about the ADR involved there. There are further notes on this controversy in the main teachers manual at 242-244.

The various notes and questions and text and the main teachers manual raise a variety of technical and philosophical spin-offs for class discussion.

•*For the next class:*
(a) (if doing an optional class on race, poverty and the environment): Ask students whether environmental law has been ignoring serious questions of how poor and discriminated-against minorities become the targets both of pollution and of systemic disregard, including the national environmental organizations. (Is the environmental movement just for yuppie white folks?)

(b) (if the next class goes to international environmental law): Ask students to analyze the problems posed by environmental cases that cross sovereign boundaries: Is it possible to have mandatory global environmental law? Does international law even deserve to be called law?

* Optional Class: Race, Poverty, and the Environment — Main Manual, 342-353

This unit is a short piece intended to get students into a serious and difficult area of the social and political consequences of the legal structures discussed throughout the course. The bibliography set out on page 353 will allow further background, or provide further handouts if desired.

Issues that can be developed also can be found in other areas of the text, as for instance in the public trust materials questioning how environmental balances should be undertaken (see text and comments after *Paepke* at Comment 2, NLS text, page 381; the tag line on the Chicod Creek case, Comment 3 at page 630; the conflict between endangered species and timber cutters and their families, 680-681; management theories for public lands, 715-716; etc.

Asking students to what extent they think environmentalism is a yuppie phenomenon that disregards economic realities for the poor guarantees a lively debate.

•*For the next class:* Ask students to analyze the problems posed by environmental cases that cross sovereign boundaries: is it possible to have mandatory global environmental law? Does international law even deserve to be called law?

Class 27: International Environmental Law — Chapter 25

As noted in the main teachers manual, this chapter is our unsatisfying nod at a huge and growing field. The materials on the Sandoz toxic spill case, and the problem of whaling regulation, are designed to offer a handle to students for diagnosing some of the fundamental obstacles lying between sound global environmental policy and its effective international implementation. The book was published before the Rio summit, but you may hand out the materials included in Part III herein (on the "Rio Declaration;" a summary of "Agenda 21," a 300-page document negotiated in Rio; and brief notes on the conventions produced by that "Earth Summit"). Many of us feared that the fact that Rio had become a summit, and such a grand one with more than 100 heads of states, condemned it to superficiality. In reality some significant steps were taken (as such things are measured in international law) and the emotional and political impact of Rio as a world-wide phenomenon has certainly seemed to be significant.

We advise you, however, to use those materials as a follow-up to the discussions of the materials in the text, since the text materials have specific legal structural details and identify specific problems in international environmental law which provide a context for the Rio materials and which the Rio materials are designed to address.

International environmental law offers wonderful opportunities to ask basic legal questions — what is "law" if it cannot be enforced? what is the role of precedent in international ordering? do analogies to common law have a place in international law? how do you define jurisdiction in a natural world where sovereignties and jurisdictions are artificial constraints? and so on. It is also a chance to pull together some policy principles — polluter pays cost internalization, public trust and intergenerational common heritage of humankind, strict liability without fault for hazardous behavior, requirements for forethought as in environmental impact assessment, the role of citizens in governance and decisionmaking, the individual versus the majority, and others. The policy issues of international environmentalism tend to be gloomy; perhaps after Rio, at least the Law side of it shows a faint gleam of hope.

PART THREE: SUPPLEMENTARY MATERIALS

• Syllabi

DRAFT SYLLABUS FOR TEACHING NATURE, LAW, AND SOCIETY AS A FIRST LAW COURSE

(Based on 3 class hours per week/ 13 weeks)

Class hour	Page assignment	Coverage	Chapter
1.	xxxiii-xxxvii	INTRODUCTION	1
	1-4	THE BREADTH & SCOPE OF ENVIRONMENTAL PROBLEMS	
	4-6, 6-7, 7-10	Ecology — Rachel Carson, Aldo Leopold, What on Earth Are We Doing?	
	11-15	Ethics — Leopold, and text	
	15-17,	The highway salting problem	
	17-27	Environmental analysis & legal strategies	
2.	33-40,	MORE ENVIRONMENTAL ANALYSIS — the tragedy of the commons — Hardin	2
		Traditional common law theories	
	102-112, HANDOUTS: legal process charts A, B	The *Boomer* case, to be read initially for facts and for analyzing the development of a law case	3
3.	Re-read 102-112,	*BOOMER*	3
	112-116 HANDOUTS: legal process charts C, D	A prima facie tort case: private nuisance, intentional	
4.	117-121	DEFENSES IN ENVIRONMENTAL TORT SUITS	3

5.	121-130,	A COMPENDIUM OF TORT CAUSES-OF-ACTION: Public nuisance — *Schenectady Chemicals,* *Spur Industries*	3
	131-142	Trespass, negligence, strict liability cases	
6.	148-159,	REMEDIES: civil damages available	3
	159-163,	Long-distance indirect economic damages — *Pruitt*: Kepone and Chesapeake Bay	
	163-170	Natural resources damages	
7.	142-148, 66-78	EQUITY AND INJUNCTIONS *Wilsonville*: a restoration injunction	3
8.	171-176,	NEW LESSONS FROM TOXIC TORTS Multiple parties, litigatability, class actions	4
	176-180, 196-198, comments 5 and 6, [epidemiological proof of causation]	Joint and several liability — *Velsicol*	
	199-210	A toxic tort case: logistics, theory, proof — *W.R. Grace*, the Woburn, Mass. chemicals case	
9.	224-232	ENVIRONMENTAL REMEDIES FROM OTHER FIELDS OF LAW: corporate law—*Pacific Lumber*;	5
	and/or 232-237	Property & contract law — stripmining cases	

10.	241-244,	FROM COMMON LAW TO PUBLIC LAW	6
	42-49,	The *Kepone* case — Goldfarb	
	244-258,	Statutes and *Kepone*	2
	260-266,	Statutory liability — Rich	
	266-279,	Parties liable under CERCLA and RCRA — *NEPACCO*	6
	301-313	The effect of environmental statutes on common law — *Silkwood*	
11.	322-327,	THE 1899 REFUSE ACT, ENVIRONMENTAL CRIMINAL LAW REDISCOVERED	7
	327-330,	*Film Recovery*	
	330-335,	Criminal prosecution	
	335-336,	Fifth amendment and the corporation	
	336-343	Difficulties in proving collective activity crimes — *Kepone* — Goldfarb	
12.	365-376,	THE PUBLIC TRUST AS QUASI-CONSTITUTIONAL ENVIRONMENTAL RIGHTS — Sax	8
	376-381,	Applying the modern public trust doctrine — *Paepke*	
	394-405	How far does the public trust go? — *Florissant*	
13.	381-393,	PUBLIC TRUST CONTINUED —*Mono Lake*	8
	405-412,	Public trust and private property rights — Sax	
	414-420	*National Gettysburg Tower*	

14.	425-429,	PROPERTY RIGHTS AND ENVIRONMENTAL LAW — EMINENT DOMAIN	9
	429-435,	Challenging an eminent domain condemnation — Poletown	
	436-442	Inverse condemnation —*Thornburg*	
15.	442-448,	PROPERTY RIGHTS CONTINUED — regulatory takings and the case of wetlands	9
	449-452,	*Johnson*	
	452-453,	*Sibson*	
	453-457,	Assorted tests — *Pennsylvania Coal*	
	457-464	Residuum test	
16.	465-472, Handout: *Lucas*	NO REMAINING ECONOMIC USE?	9
		Takings remedies	
	472-473,	Amortization and offsets	
	473,	Exactions and *Nollan*	
	474,	Due process and innocent landowners	
	474-475		
17.	476-482,	FEDERAL-STATE ENVIRONMENTAL ISSUES: preemption under the supremacy clause	10
		Basics of dormant commerce clause adjudication — Philadelphia v. N.J.	
	504-508,	Balancing burdens — *Procter & Gamble*	
	512-520		
		CONTINUED OPEN DISCUSSIONS, catch-up	
18.			
19.	544-561	ENVIRONMENTAL ADMINISTRATIVE LAW — *Overton Park*	11
		Administrative law in a nutshell	

20.	561-570,	THE CITIZEN'S ROLE IN ADMINISTRATIVE LAW —*Scenic Hudson* and citizen standing	11
	574-580, Handout: Lujan v. Defenders	Standing — Lujan v. NWF [BLM public lands]; Lujan v. Defenders of Wildlife [international endangered species]	
21.	596-603,	NEPA	12
	603-609,	The Chicod Creek case, NRDC v. Grant *Grant*, continued	
	609-624,	*Grant* (1972)	
	624-625,	*Grant* (1973)	
	625-630		
22.	630-636,	NEPA CONTINUED — Content of an EIS EIS process — *Kleppe* (Sierra Club)	12
	637-644,	*Marsh*	
	644-649,	*Robertson*	
	649-655		
23.		CONTINUED OPEN DISCUSSIONS, catch-up	
24.	656-659,	SUBSTANTIVE ROADBLOCKS: section 7 of the endangered species act of 1973, a stark prohibition statute	13
	659-665,	*Hill*, The Tellico Dam/snail darter case	
	674-684	The spotted owl and logging our old-growth national forests	
25.	685-686,	PUBLIC RESOURCE MANAGEMENT STATUTES	14
	686-688,	The public lands	
	688-700,	Multiple use mandate — Coggins	
	HANDOUT: MAP 707-716	Off-road vehicles	

26.	717-719,	HISTORICAL DEVELOPMENT OF POLLUTION REGULATION	15
	719-723,	Michigan's water pollution statute	
	723-726,	Utilex: water pollution case study	
	726-731,	Alternative approaches to standard setting	
	731-737	Modern permit processes	
27.	738-739,	REGULATION OF MARKET ACCESS — Pesticides	16
	739-741, Handouts: Les v. Reilly; skim *Corrosion-Proof Fittings*	Federal regulation of pesticides —Miller Les v. Reilly; skim *Corrosion-Proof Fittings*	
	747#8,	FIFRA licensing	
	748-750,	ToSCA — R. Druley	
28.	760-764, 766-772	STARK STATUTORY POLLUTION STANDARDS — Auto emissions — Clean Air Act — Title II excerpts Statutory overkill?	
			17
29.	774-780,	THE CLEAN AIR ACT, ambient standards, the national commons and federalism; Harm as the threshold of regulation	18
	787-790,	Commentary and question on the Clean Air Act	
	790-793, 800-811, Handout: Chart from *Cleveland Electric*	The perplex of safety and risk assessment *Cleveland Electric*	

30.	825-831,	THE CLEAN WATER ACT AND TECHNOLOGY-BASED REGULATION	19
		Conservation Foundation report	
	831-835,	*Rybachek*	
	835-848, Handouts: Chart and Average River problem,		
	856-859	CWA citizen suits	
31.		CONTINUED OPEN DISCUSSIONS, catch-up	
32.	859-860,	ECONOMIC INCENTIVES AND ARTIFICIAL POLLUTION MARKET STATUTES	20
	860-863,	Ideal versus real — Latin	
	863-866,	Reforming environmental law — Ackerman	
	866-870,	Effluent taxes	
	870-876,	Marketable permits — Hahn	
	876-881	EPA, Title IV acid deposition program	
33.	266-269,	TOXIC WASTE REGULATION — *NEPACCO*: a toxics case under RCRA and CERCLA	6
	926-928,	Introduction to RCRA	
	882-886,	Introduction to CERCLA	22
	260-266,	Statutory liability	21
	266-279,	Review *NEPACCO*	6
	928-924,	More on RCRA	
	285-287,	Proof of causation — *Wade* II	
	287-292	Joint and several liability — *Monsanto*	22 6

34.	911-923,	MORE ISSUES IN TOXICS REGULATION — EPA enforcement strategies — *Cannons Engineering*	21
	898-903,	The costs of CERCLA — *Conservation Chemical*	
	903-908,	Fairness — *Picillo*	
	924-925,	EPA CERCLA §106 orders — Shifting to private cleanups	
	954-960	State hazardous waste facility siting statutes	
			23
35.		CONTINUED OPEN DISCUSSIONS, catch-up	23
36.	954-960, 960-967, 967-971, 972-975	LAND USE IN ENVIRONMENTAL LAW State hazardous waste facility siting statutes §404 wetlands regulation *Bersani* Regional planning — *Wambat* Subdivision regulations and zoning	
37.	979-993,	ADR — ALTERNATIVE DISPUTE RESOLUTION A case study in EDR — Talbot	24
	skim 993-996	Negotiated rulemaking — Susskind	
38.	HANDOUTS	RACE, POVERTY, AND THE ENVIRONMENT	

39.	997-999,	INTERNATIONAL ENVIRONMENTAL LAW	25
	999-1006, 1013-1021, skim 1021-1033	The Sandoz spill — Schwabach Whaling — Birnie Extraterritorial municipal law, NGOs, Intergenerational equity, "Soft Law,"	
	Handouts: Rio Earth Summit materials	The North-South split, One world/One tribe?	
40.	1-1039	REVIEW	

A DRAFT SYLLABUS FOR AN EXTENDED COURSE

ENVIRONMENTAL LAW I AND II **FALL 1992-SPRING 1993**

Cook College, Rutgers University
(All NLS references are to Plater, Abrams, and Goldfarb, Environmental Law and Policy: Nature, Law, and Society ("NLS") (West, 1992) unless otherwise noted.)

[NOTE: The course comprises 56 class sessions, of 80 minutes each,taught over two semesters])

Environmental Law I

Class

1. Introductory lecture on Sources of Law
2. Lecture on Law and Science as contrasting problem-solving modes

3-6. The Legal Process, Law and Society, and Law and Scientific Uncertainty: *Village of Wilsonville v. SCA Services Inc.* (NLS, 66-79)

7. Private Nuisance: *Boomer v. Atlantic Cement Company* (NLS, 102-112)
8. Private Nuisance — Elements and Defenses: (NLS, 112-121)
9. Public Nuisance: (NLS, 121-130)
10. Trespass, Negligence, and Strict Liability: (NLS, 131-142)
11. Remedies: (NLS, 142-163)
12. Toxic Torts: (NLS, 171-198)
13. Toxic Torts: (NLS, 199-223)
14. Criminal Law: (NLS, 42-49, 336-343, 327-335, 343-348, 354-356 [#4, 5, 6])
15. Review Session
16. Midterm Examination
17. The Public Trust Doctrine: (NLS 365-381)
18. The Public Trust Doctrine: (NLS 381-393, 402-495 [#4, 5, 6])
19. State Environmental Protection Acts: (NLS 420-434 and New Jersey Environmental Rights Act — handout)
20. Constitutional Environmental Rights: (NLS, 357-365, 412-420)
21. Eminent Domain and Inverse Condemnation: (NLS, 425-442)
22. Regulatory Takings: (NLS 442-464)
23. Regulatory Takings: (NLS 465-475, and *Lucas v. South Carolina Coastal Commission* — handout)

23a [Possible third regulatory takings class, on *Lucas*]

24. Federal Preemption: (NLS, 476-490)
25. [optional] Federal Preemption: (NLS, 490-503)
26. Dormant Commerce Clause: (NLS, 503-523, 528-529)

27. Introduction to Environmental Statutes: (NLS, 244-258, 535-536)

28. Review Session

Final Examination, Environmental Law I

<u>Environmental Law II</u>

29-32. The Structure, Functions, and Politics of Administrative Agencies. Assignment: Sax, Defending the Environment, Chapters 2 and 3 (Handout).

33. 535-557; MEPA §§4 & 5

34. 557-595

35. 596-630

36. 630-655

37. 656-684

38. 685-716

39. 66-67, 78-99 [Material on Risk, from Chapter 2.]

40. 738-759 & *Corrosion Proof Fittings* handout

41. 717-737, 760-772

42. Midterm Examination

43. 773-800

44. 800-824

45. 825-848

46. 848-858

47. 859-881

48. 979-996

49. 258-300 [Material on CERCLA, from Chapter 6.]

50. 882-926

51. 927-946

52. 947-975

53. 997-1033

54. 1034-1039

55. Review Session

56. Final Examination, Environmental Law II

UNIVERSITY OF MICHIGAN SCHOOL OF NATURAL RESOURCES
WINTER 1992
ENVIRONMENTAL LAW ASSIGNMENT SHEET

The text for the course is Z. Plater, R. Abrams & W. Goldfarb, Environmental Law and Policy: Nature, Law & Society (1992). Handout material will be distributed free of charge from time-to-time during the semester. Handout readings are indicated on the assignment sheet by an "H."

Class Number	Pages	Topic
1	28-59	Externalities
2	78-99	Risk definition and management
3	101-142	Tort doctrines
4	142-170	Tort remedies
5	176-198, 204-223	Toxic torts
6	H-1	Proving toxic injury
7	241-277	Introduction to statutes
8	277-300	CERCLA litigation
9	301-320	Statutes' effect on the common law
10	327-356	Criminalizing environmental wrongs
11	First Examination	Coverage — through CERCLA
12	357-376, 381-393, 402n.4-412	Environmental rights & public trust
13	425-429, 442-475, H-2	Regulatory takings of private property
14	476-491, 508-512, H-3	Federalism
15	535-545, 567-580, H-4	Administrative law
16	596-631	NEPA
17	656-684, H-5	Endangered Species Act
18	717-741, 748-759, H-6	Statutory standards; market access control
19	Second Examination	Coverage — cumulative through ESA
20	760-772, 773-793, H-7	Legislated & harm-based standards
21	794-824	Ambient standards
22	825-858, H-8	Technology-based standards
23	859-881	Economic incentives
24	882-898	Site remediation laws
25	898-926	Allocating the cost of remediation
26	927-946	Control of waste materials
27	947-948, 954-975	Siting and land use
28	997-1033, H-9	International issues
29	Final Examination	Coverage — cumulative, all material

Handout List

Handout 1	Qualification of experts in toxic tort litigation
Handout 2	Lucas case and materials
Handout 3	Preemption, states' rights, and dormant commerce clause cases
Handout 4	Standing materials
Handout 5	Endangered species update materials
Handout 6	Corrosion Proof Fittings case
Handout 7	Chart of ambient air quality standards

Handout 8	Chart of CWA technology-based effluent standards
Handout 9	Account of June 1992 Earth Summit

• NATURE, LAW, AND SOCIETY: Raw Worksheet for Syllabus Design

	Author's Preface	xxvii-xxxi
	NLS Introduction	xxxiii-xxxvii
1	Chapter Introduction	1-2
1(A)	Breadth and Scope of Environmental Problems	2-4
1(B)	The Ecological and Ethical Bases of Environmental Law	4-6, Silent Spring — Rachel Carson 6-7, A Sand County Almanac — Aldo Leopold 7-10, What on Earth Are We Doing? — Sancton 10-11, C&Q 1-2 11-15, Thinking Like A Mountain — Leopold
1(C)	Environmental Analysis: Road Salt — A Paradigm	15-17, Highway salting 17-20, 21-23, 23-27, Environmental analysis & legal strategies
2(A)	Economic Analysis of Law and the Pursuit of Efficiency	29-33
2(B)	Environmental Law as a Response to the Problem of a Finite Commons	33-39, Tragedy of the Commons — Hardin 39-40, C&Q 1-5 40-41, Analyzing externalities 42-48, The *Kepone* case 48-49, C&Q 1-4
2(C)	Strategies for Reforming the Economics of Pollution	49-50, Market strategies 50-51, C&Q 1-6 51-53, Economics and government regulation 53-54, C&Q 1-2

2(D)	Measuring Project Benefits and Environmental Costs	54-56, Benefit/cost analysis 56-57, Measuring resource values 57-59, C&Q 1-4 59-61, Intergenerational justice & discount rates — Stiglitz 61-63, C&Q 1-5 63-65, The New Economics — Passell 65-66, C&Q 1-2
2(E)	Uncertainty, Risk and Environmental Law	66-76, Risk of future harm — the *Wilsonville* case 76-78, C&Q 1-7 78-81, Risk, safety, and outrage — Sandman 81, C&Q 1-2 81-86, Risk management by law — Huber 86-89, C&Q 1-8 89-90, Cancer risk and causation 90-91, C&Q 1-5
Part Two Introduction: Common Law Theories, Defenses, Remedies		101
3(A)	Private Nuisance, Intentional Tort and *Boomer*	102-108, *Boomer* 109-112, C&Q 1-5 112-116, Prima facie private nuisance case
3(B)	Defenses in Environmental Tort Suits	117-118, *Schenectady Chemical*
3(C)	Compendium of Tort Causes of Action	121-124, Public nuisance — *Schenectady Chem.* 124-125, C&Q 1-3 125-128, *Spur Industries* 128-130, C&Q 1-5 131-133, Trespass — *Borland* 133-134, C&Q 1-3 134-135, Negligence — *Dillon* 135-136, C&Q 1-3 137-140, Strict liability — *Branch* 141-142, C&Q 1-5

3(D)	Remedies in Environmental Litigation	142-144, Equity and injunctions — Plater 144-148, C&Q 1-5 148-149, Compensatory damage remedies 149-150, Permanent damages — *Boomer* 150-151, C&Q 1-4 151-156, Punitives, *Branch, Fischer* 156-159, C&Q 1-6 159-162, Remote/indirect damages, *Pruitt* 162-163, C&Q 1-2 163-166, Resource remedies — Alaska 166-170, C&Q 1-6
4(A)	Multiple Plaintiffs and Mass Toxic Tort Litigation	171-173, Multiplicity, litigatability 173-174, Class actions (*Biechele*) 175-176, C&Q 1-3
4(B)	Multiple Tortfeasors and Joint and Several Liability	176-180, *Velsicol Chemical* 180-181, C&Q 1-3
4(C)	Causation	182-192, Proof of causation — Allen 192-193, C&Q 1-5 193-195, *Chevron Chemical Company* 195-198, C&Q 1-6 199-203, Logistics, *W. R. Grace,* tthe Woburnchemicals case 203-204,C&Q 1-2
4(D)	New Remedies in Toxics Cases	204-208, Compensable items — *W.R. Grace* 208-210, C&Q 1-5 211-219, *Ayers* 219-223, C&Q 1-7
5(A)	A Corporate Law Retrospective	224-227, Pacific lumber — Anderberg 228-232, C&Q 1-3

5(B)	Property and Contract Law in Environmental Litigation	232-235, Strip mining — *Buchanan* 236, *Martin* 236-237, C&Q 1-2 237-238, Private agreements & warranties 238-240, C&Q 1-8
Part Three Introduction: From Common Law to Public Law		241-242
6	Chapter Introduction	243-244, The interplay of common law and statues
6(A)	Statutory Mosaic and *Kepone*	244-256, Statutes and *Kepone* 257-258, C&Q 1-3
6(B)	Role of Judges in Giving Meaning to Statutes	258-260 260-264, Statutory liability — Rich 264-266, C&Q 1-5 266-275, *NEPACCO* 275-277, C&Q 1-6 277-279, Parties liable under CERCLA 279-285, C&Q 1-7 285-287, *Wade II* 287, C&Q 1 287-291, Joint and several liability — *Monsanto* 291-292, C&Q 1-3 293-294, CERCLA private litigation 294-295, C&Q 1-4 295-299, Insurance and insolvency 299-300, C&Q 1-4
6(C)	The Effect of Environmental Statutes on Common law	301-302 302-306, C&Q 1-4 306-309, *Silkwood* 309-313, C&Q 1-5 313-315, Federal common law of interstate water pollution nuisance 316-320, C&Q 1-6
7	Chapter Introduction	321, The force of the criminal law in environmental cases

7(A)	The 1899 Refuse Act, Rediscovered in the 1960s	322 322-327, C&Q 1-10
7(B)	Recent Willingness to Prosecute Environmental Crimes	327-330, *Film Recovery* 330-333, Criminal prosecution — Ferrey 333-335, C&Q 1-3
7(C)	Problems in Corporate Prosecutions for Environmental Crimes	335-336, Fifth amendment and the corporation 336-342, Difficulties in proving collective activity crimes 342-343, C&Q 1-4 343-346, Executive liability for agents 346-348, C&Q 1-5
7(D)	Knowledge and Intent	348-349, *White Fuel Corporation* 349-351, C&Q 1-4 351-353, *Wulff* 353-356, C&Q 1-6
8(A)	A Federal Constitutional Right to Environmental Quality?	357-361, *Tanner* 361, NWF amendment to U.S. Constitution? 361-364, The Environment and the Constitution — Krier 364-365, C&Q 1-2
8(B)	The Public Trust Doctrine	365-366, Citizen action — Sax 366-374, Effective judicial intervention — Sax 374-376, C&Q 1-3 376-379, Applying the modern public trust doctrine — *Paepke* 379-381, C&Q 1-4 381-390, *Mono Lake* 391-393, C&Q 1-3 394-401, How far does the public trust go? — *Florissant* 401-405, C&Q 1-7 405-407, Public trust and private property rights — Sax 407-411, Liberating the public trust doctrine — Sax 411-412, C&Q 1-3

8(C)	State Constitutions and State Environmental Rights	412-414, Sample of state constitutions 414, C&Q 1-2 414-419, *National Gettysberg Tower* 419-420, C&Q 1-3 420-423, State statutory environmental rights — MEPA 423-424, C&Q 1-5
9	Chapter Introduction	425-428, Eminent domain — Plater 428-429, C&Q 1
9(A)	Eminent Domain Condemnations	429-430, Domain of deference 430-434, Challenging an eminent domain condemnation — Poletown 435, C&Q 1-3
9(B)	Inverse Condemnation: A Constitutional Tort	436-441, *Thornburg* 441-442, C&Q 1-2
9(C)	Challenges to Regulations as Unconstitutional Takings	442-448, The case of wetlands 449-452, *Johnson* 452-453, *Sibson* 453, C&Q 1 453-457, Assorted tests — *Pennsylvania Coal* 457-460, Residuum test 460-464, C&Q 1-7 465-468, No remaining economic use 468-472, C&Q 1-4 472-473, Takings remedies 473, Amoritization and offsets 474, Exactions and *Nollan* 474-475, Due process and innocents
10	Chapter Introduction	476, Environmental issues in the division of authority between federal and state governments

10(A)	PreEmption of State Authority by Federal Statutes	477-479, Supremacy clause
		479-482, C&Q 1-6
		482-488, State law preclusion — *Pacific Gas*
		488-490, C&Q 1-6
		490-497, Contradiction-based federal pre-emption — *Ray*
		497-498, C&Q 1-3
		498-500, Pre-empting state interference
		500-503, C&Q 1-6
10(B)	The "Dormant Commerce Clause" — Commerce Burdens	503-504
		504-507, Basics of dormant commerce clause adjudication — *Philadelphia*
		507-508, C&Q 1-4
		508-511, *Taylor*
		511-512, C&Q1-3
		512-519, Burdens — *Procter & Gamble*
		519-520, C&Q 1-3
		520-522, Market participant doctrine — *Swin*
		522-523, C&Q 1
		523-526, Differential fees — *Voinovich*
		526-528, C&Q 1-2
		528-529, Congressional Authorizaton Doctrine
		529-531, Quarantine of noxious material — *Bayh*
		531-532, Facial even-handedness — *Kettlewell*
		532-533, C&Q 1-4
Part Four Introduction:	Environmental Statutes and the Administrative State	535-536
11(A)	The Evolution of the Administrative Process	537-539
11(B)	Administrative Law in a Nutshell	539-544
11(C)	*Overton Park* — An Environmental Administrative Law Case	544-545, Introduction
		545-552, *Overton Park*
		552-557, C&Q 1-7

11(D)	Citizen Enforcement and Judicial Review	557-561, Reformation of administrative law — Stewart 561-566, *Scenic Hudson* 567-570, C&Q 1-6 570-572, Financing citizen enforcement 572, Removing courts' ability to grant relief to citizens 572-574, C&Q 1-2 574-580, Constricting standing — *Lujan* 580, C&Q 1-2 581-586, Expanding agency procedures —*Vermont Yankee* 587-589, C&Q 1-5
11(E)	Statutory Interpretations: How, By Whom?	589-590, Judicial review of agency interpretations — *Chevron* 590-593, C&Q 1-4 593-594, Judicial consideration of politics — Three Sisters 595, C&Q 1-3
12	Chapter Introduction	596, NEPA, The National Environmental Policy Act: A mandatory disclosure and stop and think statute
12(A)	NEPA	597-599, Public Law 91-190, Title I 599-603, C&Q 1-7
12(B)	NEPA Goes to Court	603-604 604-606, *Chicod Creek* 606-609, C&Q 1-4 609-614, *Grant* (continued) 614-624, C&Q 1-15 624-625, *Grant* (1972) 625-629, *Grant* (1973) 629-630, C&Q 1-3 630-636, Content of an EIS 637-642, EIS process —*Kleppe* (Sierra Club) 642-644, C&Q 1-7
12(C)	Further Issues in NEPA's Judicial Evolution	644-649, *Marsh* 649-652, *Robertson* 652-655, C&Q 1-7

13	Chapter Introduction	656, Substantive Roadblocks: Section 7 of the Endangered Species Act of 1973, a stark prohibition statute
13(A)	The Endangered Species Act	656-665, *Hill* 665-673, C&Q 1-14
13(B)	The Spotted Owl and Ancient Forests	674-680, *Seattle Audubon* 680-684, C&Q 1-7
14	Chapter Introduction	685-686, Public Resource Management Statutes
14(A)	The Public Lands	686-688
14(B)	The BLM, FLPMA, and Grazing on the Public Lands	688-694, Multiple use mandate — Coggins 694-700, C&Q 1-9
14(C)	Federal-State Issues on the Public Lands	700-703, *Kleppe* (New Mexico) 704-707, C&Q 1-7
14(D)	The BLM and Off-Road Vehicles: A Case Study	707-711, D. Sheridan 711-714, *Clark* 714-716, C&Q 1-5
15(A)	Early Public Agency Oversight of Health and Env.	717-719 719, C&Q 1
15(B)	A Case Study in Non-Enforcement Under A Typical Review and Permit Statute	719-721, Michigan's pollution statute 721-723, C&Q 1-5 723-726, Utilex: water pollution case study 726, C&Q 1-2
15(C)	Alternative Approaches to Standard Setting	726-731
15(D)	Modern Permit Processes	731-736 736-737, C&Q 1-3
16	Chapter Introduction	738-739

16(A)	Pesticides: FIFRA	739-741, Federal regulation of pesticides — Miller 742-744, *EDF* 744-748, C&Q 1-8
16(B)	Regulating Market Access of Toxics: ToSCA	748-750, ToSCA — R. Druley 750-755, *Chemical Manufacturers* 755-759, C&Q 1-9
17(A)	Automobile Air Pollution and the 1970 CAA's Title II	760-763, Title II excerpts 763-764, C&Q 1-5 764-766, Political context of Title II
17(B)	Statutory Overkill?	766-771 771-772, C&Q 1-3
18	Chapter Introduction	773-774, Administrative standard-setting statues: The Clean Air Act's harm-based ambient standards
18(A)	Ambient Standards, The Commons and American Federalism	774-777 777-779, C&Q 1-5
18(B)	Harm as a Threshold of Regulation	779-782, *Train* 782-783, C&Q 1-2 783-787, *Lead Industries* 787-790, C&Q 1-4
18(C)	Harm-Based Standards for Hazardous Air Pollutants	790-793 793, C&Q 1-2
18(D)	Technological Feasibility and the States as Brokers	794-799, *Union Electric Company* 799-800, C&Q 1-2
18(E)	Reverse Engineering to Achieve Ambient Quality Levels	800-808, *Cleveland Electric* 809-811, C&Q 1-7
18(F)	Assuring Attainment of Desired Quality Levels	811-815, *Citizens Against Refineries Effects* 815-818, C&Q 1-5

18(G)	Protecting Interstate and National Concerns in a Nationwide Ambient Standards Program	818-820 821, C&Q 1-2 821-823, Exporting pollution 824, C&Q 1-2
19	Chapter Introduction	825-827, *California* 827-831, C&Q 1-7
19(A)	Water Pollutants and Their Sources	831-834, State of Environment — Conservation Foundation 834-835, C&Q 1-2
19(B)	Development of Technology-Based Effluent Limitations	835-841, *Rybachek* 841-848, C&Q 1-12
19(C)	Harm-Based Elements in the Clean Water Act	848-851, NRDC v. EPA 851-858, C&Q 1-7
20	Chapter Introduction	859-860, Economic incentive and artificial polution market statutes
20(A)	Debating the Efficacy of Regulatory Strategies	860-863, Ideal versus real — Latin 863-866, Reforming environmental law — Ackerman 866, C&Q 1-2
20(B)	Effluent Taxes	866-868 868-870, C&Q 1-6
20(C)	Bubbles, Netting, Offsets and Banking	870-873, Marketable permits — Hahn 873-876, C&Q 1-6
20(D)	Using Tradable Emission Allowances to Reduce Acid Rain	876-877, EPA, Title IV acid deposition program 878-881, C&Q 1-10
21(A)	Identifying Sites, Funding and Setting the Standards	882-893, '90 National Contingency Plan — Starfield 893-898, C&Q 1-11

21(B)	EPA's Strategy for Cost Recovery and Loss Allocation	898-902, *Conservation Chemical*
		902-903, C&Q 1-4
		903-906, Fairness — *Picillo*
		906-908, C&Q 1-3
		908-909, Contribution
		909-910, C&Q 1-4
		911-918, Seeking settlements — *Cannons*
		918-923, C&Q 1-7
		924-925, Administrative orders
		925-926, C&Q 1-4
22	Chapter Introduction	927-928, A composite approach to preventing releases of hazardous wastes: The Resource Conservation and Recovery Act
22(A)	Tracking and Controlling the Life Cycle of Hazardous Waste	928-935
		935-940, C&Q 1-8
22(B)	The "Land Ban" and the Use of "Hammers" to Control	940-943
		943-946, C&Q 1-5
23	Chapter Introduction	947-948
23(A)	The Federal Coastal Zone Management Act	949-953, Secretary of Interior v. California
		953-954, C&Q 1-6
23(B)	State Hazardous Waste Facility Siting Statutes	954-956
		956-960, C&Q 1-5
23(C)	Critical Area Protection Statutes	960-965, *Bersani*
		965-967, C&Q 1-6
		967-970, Regional planning — *Wambat*
		971, C&Q 1-4
23(D)	Traditional Land Use Controls and the Environment	972-974, Subdivision regulations and zoning
		974-975, C&Q 1-3
Part Five Introduction: Trends in Environmental Law		977

24(A)	ADR: ADR Processes Environmental Cases	979-982, An Overview — Sander
24(B)	Environmental ADR	982-984, Array of ADR methods 984-992, Case study in EDR — Talbot 992-993, C&Q 1-4 993-995, Negotiated rulemaking — Susskind 996-996, C&Q 1-3
25	Chapter Introduction	997-999, International Environmental Law
25(A)	International Transboundary Pollution Cases	999-1006, The Sandoz spill — Schwabach 1006-1013, C&Q 1-8
25(B)	The Global Commons	1013-1017, Whaling — P. Birnie 1017-1021, C&Q 1-6
25(C)	Extraterritorial Municipal Law; Other Strategies	1021-1026 1026-1027, NGOs 1027-1029, Intergenerational equity — Weiss 1029-1030, "Soft Law" 1030-1031, The North-South split 1031-1033, One World/One Tribe?
Afterword		1034-1039

• A Course Prospectus and Legal Research Paper Assignements

Prospectus
Environmental Law

The course will meet three times a week, in Room 411, 10:00 to 10:50.

The major course text is Environmental Law and Policy: Nature, Law, and Society, by Plater, Abrams & Goldfarb (West Publishing Co. 1992)

The course structure and approach can be seen from the enclosed syllabus, and the coursebook's Table of Contents

Course credit— 3 credit hours

Midterm Exam: Takehome exam, one essay and ten objective questions. Exam averaged into course grade as 1/2 credit hour.

Final Exam: 1 1/2 hours, short essays, ten objective questions. Coverage: entire course. Exam averaged into course grade as 1 credit hour.

Paper: Research paper due Nov. 16 or at any time prior to then, at the office of my secretary Ms. Patricia Fazzone, Griswold 308, to be averaged into course grade as 1 credit hour.

Class participation: Averaged into course grade as 1/2 credit hour.

Research Paper Prospectus

Length five to six standard pages, double-spaced.

[FORMAT 1]

You will be assigned a role as plaintiff, defendant, or judicial clerk in one of the following fact patterns intended to set up a point of legal doctrine for argument and analysis. You will be assigned a particular jurisdiction (a trial court in one of the 50 states, or the District of Columbia or Puerto Rico) in which to do actual hands-on research in a law library, a project that will begin with a preliminary instruction session volunteered by a helpful law reference librarian. Your job will be to relate the facts of the case to actual legal case precedents and applicable statutes, if any, in your jurisdiction, and present a coherent, logical presentation of the case from your assigned perspective, anticipating all relevant arguments on point that will be raised by any party to the case, even if they undercut your position.

Your jurisdiction is: A trial court in ______________

Your fact pattern is:

___ **Fact Pattern 1:**

Mr. Greg Brown and Ms. Sarah White are neighbors, owners of oceanfront houses (in _____). They can walk out their doors straight onto the beach. Despite the closeness of the ocean, Mr. Brown has built an in-ground saltwater swimming pool in his front yard (on the opposite side of the house from the ocean). He complained to Ms. White that he bought the best model offered, with a high quality plastic vinyl liner, but he has to keep adding saltwater to the pool every day.

Ms. White is not sympathetic to his complaints. Her award-winning organic vegetable garden which grows in her own front yard, but only 20 feet from the Brown pool, has been mysteriously dying off, even though the garden was planted in a special ground-level greenhouse designed to permit agriculture in salt air coastal conditions. The local agricultural extension agent has told her that the symptoms of her garden are consistent with saltwater poisoning of the groundwater. Ms. White also swears that her wellwater tastes saltier than usual. Mr. Brown knows nothing about that because he gets his water from the town water supply.

Ms. White has threatened Mr. Brown with a lawsuit. You are contracted by one of them to serve as counselor. Counsel her/him.

___ **Fact Pattern 2:**

These proceedings relate to the complaint of residents of the town of Kerry, a mixed residential and rural community near a large metropolitan center. The Choctaw Quarry Company has been operating a granite quarry in the town continuously for two hundred and twenty five years. The quarry was originally on the outskirts of the metropolitan area, but over the years has been absorbed into the residential development. The homes are expensive single-family homes and mansions. The town has an unemployment reate of eighteen percent. However, Choctaw has been awarded a major federal contract to provide material for the Central Artery Project, which is expected to result in five hundred jobs.

The quarrying operations involve blasting with explosive charges set into the granite. The company has recently switched from conventional dynamite to a safer, more powerful plastic explosive. The new material reduces the risk to workers and is more efficient in quarrying the granite.

The Environmental Protection Agency and the International Climate Change Working Group have released a new report on the basis of new scientific research that blasting operations for granite sends shock waves in an area twenty times greater than prior research indicated, and that the granite formations suffer micro-fracturing as a direct result, which in turn releases radon gas into the adjacent soil and rock formations. Radon gas is a confirmed source of cancer in high concentrations. The public was warned a number of years ago about the risks of radon accummulation in the basements of buildings and homes. The town of Kerry is within the new danger zone established by the report and the soil and rock structure is the type associated with the release of radon gas. Various homes in the town have tested positive for radon concentrations above the safe levels. the residents of Kerry, like most others, ignored these warnings and did not install ventilation systems. The report does not differentiate between the amount of radon emissions caused by the different types of explosives.

For the sake of this hypothetical assume all the facts are true and do not assume any additional facts. The states of California, Washington, Massachusetts, and New Hampshire are available as jurisdictions under whose law the doctrine of "conming to the nuisance" should be analyzed. The paper may be written from the perspective of the plaintiffs/residents or the defendant/Choctaw.

___ **Fact Pattern 3:**

The Crystal Lake Environmental Action Reactors (CLEAR) is a group of neighbors living on and near the shores of Crystal Lake in your jurisdiction. Also on the shores of the lake is the microchip manufacturing plant of the Great Loads of Profit Corp. (GLOP). GLOP's plant regularly discharges wastewater into the lake, producing, according to CLEAR, bad smells and a major interference with their enjoyment of their properties.

GLOP counters that it's just a smell, and you cannot make microchips without the wastewater effluents.

CLEAR goes to court, where its complaint is answered with GLOP's motion to dismiss on grounds that "this matter is properly under the administrative jurisdiction of the state's Water Resources Commission (WRC). Under the primary jurisdiction doctrine, the court should dismiss this suit, shifting this alleged water pollution matter to the WRC, as the Legislature intended, for a full official agency opportunity to make findings and handle the matter to its ultimate administrative conclusion, however long that may take."

You are legal advisor to ___________. Based on the law of your jurisdiction, analyze the issue and predict the outcome of this motion.

[FORMAT 2] • [Many of the topics noted in the main teachers manual at page 263 can be adapted for use as first-time law research papers if held to narrow accessible terms.]

This paper should be an examination of an interesting legal question arising somewhere in the field of environmental law. It should not be a description of a fact situation or policy decision, but rather an analysis of a chosen legal issue; facts and policy discussions necessarily will be included, but only as required initially to set up the legal question (no more than a couple of paragraphs). The legal question chosen should be narrow so that you can make a searching inquiry and presentation within the confines of the space limitation. Your perspective may be that of environmental plaintiffs, or defendants, or neutral observer. (In each case you will have to anticipate all serious opposing arguments on point.) Presentation may be in the form of a brief, a legal commentary, or other paper format. Citations in any form you want. Topics should be checked initially with me. Please register your topic on the topic pre-emption list kept at the Reserve Desk under "Environmental Law."

In presentation, your analysis and argument must be succinct and to the point because of the shortened format. This form of legal research paper typically contains the equivalent substance of a 15-20-page "term paper"; the easiest way to do this is to make the paper a heavily-edited second or third draft. The page limit and paper deadline will be strictly adhered to so that everyone can rely on a level playing field.

[FORMAT 3]

Landmine Company owns some land near a national forest amid the Rocky Mountains. The company does a lot of logging, mining and resource refinement in a factory on that land. They also mine and log on the national forest land, for the Department of the Interior (DOI) granted them special mining and logging permits. Naturally, their operations create a considerable amount of pollution and inconvenience to the general area, which includes the National Forest and, Mudville, a fairly large town bordering the forest for which the company provides several hundred jobs and a large slice of the tax base. Founded in 1925, the company by far predates the town, and most residents have only moved to the area since 1960. Increasingly, however, the area is becoming a popular resort spot for Eastern tourists, who enjoy hiking, hunting and fishing in the area, especially the national forest. Many hotels and cafes now cater mainly to this tourist trade.

All is not well in paradise, however, for the local area is starting to feel a lot of environmental problems. In the neighborhood next to Landmine's land, many people complain of fumes that give them headaches and have led to the discoloration of their houses and cars as airborne chemicals react with the paint. Some people, those with asthma or other respiratory problems, have been forced to stay inside when the wind blows from the company (which is about 50% of the time), and a few have even moved. In addition, the resident's wells share a common aquifer with both the company and the national forest. These wells are becoming increasingly tainted with trace elements and chemicals that are common both to mining and the chemical processes used at the company. These pollutants have been proven to cause cancer and other ailments in animals when given in heavy doses. Coincidentally, there has been a rise in these ailments among citizens, especially those of a young age. Fearing for their health, some have taken to using expensive bottle water for both drinking and bathing. Naturally, a few of these citizens have, either by themselves or with others, complained to the company about these problems.

Local environmentalists are very upset at the logging and mining practices Landmine is carrying on in the National Forest. They claim that the forest is a treasure all should share, and the massive clearings cut by the company are unsightly and, due to increased mudslides and avalanches, dangerous. They also claim that the huge piles of tailings from the mines are leaching into the aquifer of the forest, poisoning streams and ponds. Additionally, they claim, the company, in an effort to stave off corporate raiders, is planning to launch a massive clear cutting program in the near future. These environmentalists, joined by large national organizations, have sued the Department of the Interior, claiming that the Department had no right to issue the logging and mining permits as it did. They are also planning to launch suit against the company.

Naturally, life is not simple. It turns out that Mudville is located in a basin in the mountains that traps automobile and industrial exhausts from the whole region, and that the air quality as a whole is generally fairly bad. Other companies in the area spew out many of the same pollutants as this company, and the winds, though blowing primarily from the company toward the town, do shift around quite a bit. Also, due to an increase in the use of fossil fuels nationwide, this town's rain and snowfall is very acidic, and often contains heavy metals and other toxic pollutants in solution. For years, this mild "toxic soup" has been falling on the whole watershed. Further, many of the mines on company and national forest land were run by independent prospectors and have been abandoned since the turn of the century.

Although Landmine does agree it should clean up its production, it lacks the space to do so. In fact, the company claims, the only space on which it could build an adequate treatment plant is on a 10 acre plot owned by Mrs. Johnson, whose family has owned this property next to the plant for generations. No other plot has the proximity to the plant, the level ground or the access to the street and town services. For the company to clean up, it is going to want to use that land, and if it can't, Landmine claims it will have to shut down all or some of its production, putting many people out of work.

Landmine is completely owned by Mr. Brooks, who regularly inspects all operations of the company, although he does not have much technical knowledge in any of the areas. The company has never been cited for any permit or safety violations, though some workers complain that the chemicals used in refining operations are often carelessly stored and handled, and that the supervisors don't seem to care that much about it.

Additional facts-

The Department of the Interior's Statute from Congress, giving it the authority to lease logging and mining permits, states in relevant part "The Secretary shall ensure that public lands are managed to best provide required resources while protecting the public lands from abuse"; this includes the leasing or selling of mineral, oil or logging rights.

The State Department of Environmental Quality (DEQ) has been given, through state statute, the responsibility to "ensure a safe and healthy environment for all residents, maintain healthy ecosystems needed for the development of tourist activities and promote economic development." DEQ has recently promulgated regulations that would severely limit the rights of the company to mine/timber both its land and the National Forest.

Logging practices in this part of the country regularly includes large clearcuts, as that's the only way companies can stay economically competitive.

INSTRUCTIONS

1. Inventory all the possible causes of action presented by these facts. Remember, parties that could appear in court may not have been specifically mentioned in the problem. Explain why you think each cause of action exists and what cases we have read support your belief.

2. Put yourself in the shoes of the plaintiffs. Decide whether you would rather sue Landmine or the Department of the Interior (you do not have enough room to thoroughly analyze all the issues pertaining to both). Explain your strategy as a plaintiff, what causes of actions you think will be successful and which ones are relevant but probably futile, what policy issues are important, what defenses and tactics the opposing side (either Landmine or Department of Interior) will probably use, and how you think a court will form its decision. Support your analysis by citing to factors and theories mentioned in any cases we read prior to break. You don't have to worry about proper citation form, but make sure we will recognize the cases to which you are referring.

Put all of your thoughts into an organized, reasoned paper (5 pages, double spaced, one inch margins). Feel free to call either of us if you have any questions, just remember that the later you wait to ask, the more likely we will be pressed for time.

• Fundamentals of Law — charts and diagrams

A. Diagram: The Life of a Law Case in the Judicial System
B. Chart: The Courts of the U.S., State & Federal
C. Diagram: The Design of a (Civil) Action
D. Reading a Reported Case: Annotated excerpts from *Boomer* as reported in the West Reporter System: syllabus, headnotes, attorneys, opinions
E. Nutshell: "Forms of Action"
F. Diagram: *Biechele* class action notice
G. Diagram: The Three (or Four, or Five, or Six) Branches of Government, State & Federal
H. Map: The Federal Circuits
I. Chart: Justices of the U.S. Supreme Court

A CHRONOLOGY OF A LAWSUIT

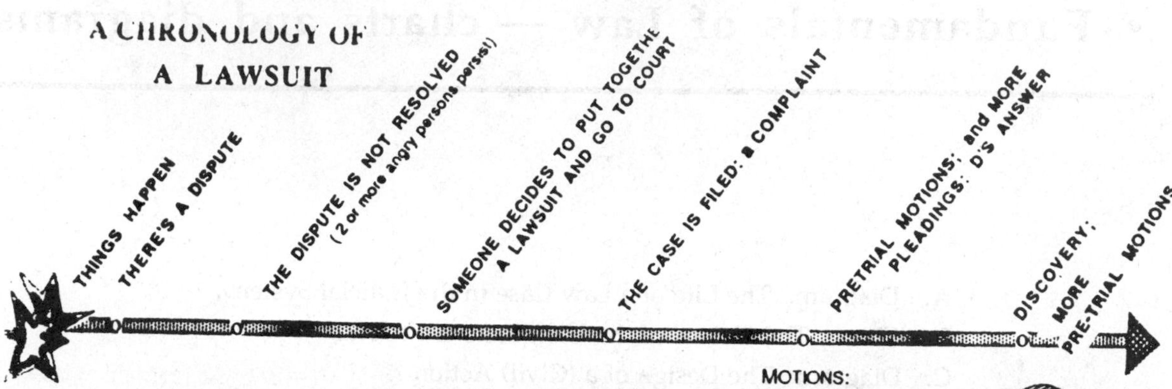

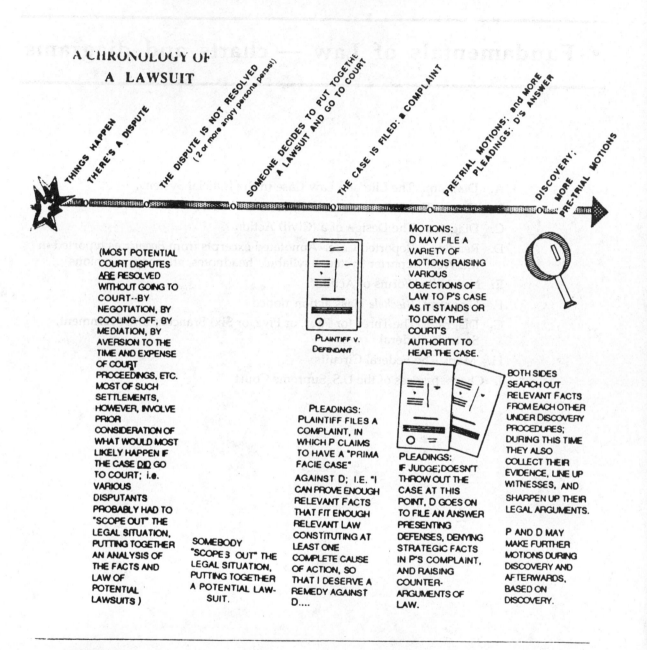

THINGS HAPPEN
THERE'S A DISPUTE
THE DISPUTE IS NOT RESOLVED
(2 or more angry persons persist)
SOMEONE DECIDES TO PUT TOGETHER A LAWSUIT AND GO TO COURT
THE CASE IS FILED: a COMPLAINT
PRETRIAL MOTIONS; and MORE PLEADINGS: D'S ANSWER
DISCOVERY; MORE PRE-TRIAL MOTIONS
(MOST POTENTIAL COURT DISPUTES ARE RESOLVED WITHOUT GOING TO COURT--BY NEGOTIATION, BY COOLING-OFF, BY MEDIATION, BY AVERSION TO THE TIME AND EXPENSE OF COURT PROCEEDINGS, ETC. MOST OF SUCH SETTLEMENTS, HOWEVER, INVOLVE PRIOR CONSIDERATION OF WHAT WOULD MOST LIKELY HAPPEN IF THE CASE DID GO TO COURT; i.e. VARIOUS DISPUTANTS PROBABLY HAD TO "SCOPE OUT" THE LEGAL SITUATION, PUTTING TOGETHER AN ANALYSIS OF THE FACTS AND LAW OF POTENTIAL LAWSUITS)
SOMEBODY "SCOPES OUT" THE LEGAL SITUATION, PUTTING TOGETHER A POTENTIAL LAW-SUIT.
PLAINTIFF V. DEFENDANT
PLEADINGS: PLAINTIFF FILES A COMPLAINT, IN WHICH P CLAIMS TO HAVE A "PRIMA FACIE CASE" AGAINST D; I.E. "I CAN PROVE ENOUGH RELEVANT FACTS THAT FIT ENOUGH RELEVANT LAW CONSTITUTING AT LEAST ONE COMPLETE CAUSE OF ACTION, SO THAT I DESERVE A REMEDY AGAINST D....
MOTIONS: D MAY FILE A VARIETY OF MOTIONS RAISING VARIOUS OBJECTIONS OF LAW TO P'S CASE AS IT STANDS OR TO DENY THE COURT'S AUTHORITY TO HEAR THE CASE.
PLEADINGS: IF JUDGE DOESN'T THROW OUT THE CASE AT THIS POINT, D GOES ON TO FILE AN ANSWER PRESENTING DEFENSES, DENYING STRATEGIC FACTS IN P'S COMPLAINT, AND RAISING COUNTER-ARGUMENTS OF LAW.
BOTH SIDES SEARCH OUT RELEVANT FACTS FROM EACH OTHER UNDER DISCOVERY PROCEDURES; DURING THIS TIME THEY ALSO COLLECT THEIR EVIDENCE, LINE UP WITNESSES, AND SHARPEN UP THEIR LEGAL ARGUMENTS.
P AND D MAY MAKE FURTHER MOTIONS DURING DISCOVERY AND AFTERWARDS, BASED ON DISCOVERY.

VARIOUS DETERMINATIVE MOTIONS WHICH CAN BE MADE PRIOR TO THE TRIAL COURT DECISION, (AND WHICH CAN BE IMMEDIATELY APPEALED, IF GRANTED, AS FINAL JUDGMENTS }

MOTION TO DISMISS

MOTION FOR SUMMARY JUDGMENT

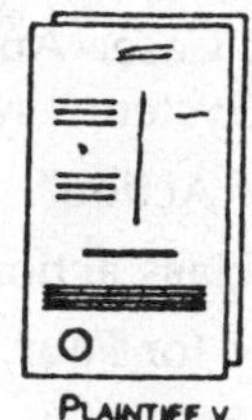

HIGHER APPEALS COURT(S)

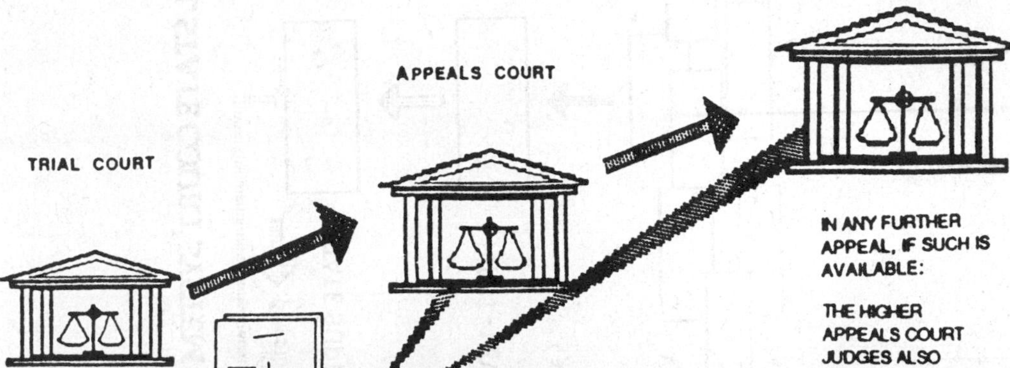

FACTS
LAW

AT THE TRIAL:

(THE TRIAL COURT JUDGE DECIDES VARIOUS MOTIONS THROUGHOUT TRIAL)

PLAINTIFF TRIES TO PRESENT AND PROVE SUFFICIENT FACTS, FITTING SUFFICIENT LAW, TO WIN.

DEFENDANT TRIES TO REBUT P'S FACTS AND/OR P'S ARGUMENTS OF LAW.

THE COURT: THE JUDGE OR JURY PINS DOWN THE FACTS. THE JUDGE FIGURES OUT THE APPLICABLE LAW. THE COURT MAKES THE DECISION.

IN THE DECISION, ESTABLISHED FACTS ARE APPLIED TO THE JUDGE'S RULINGS OF LAW, PRODUCING A REMEDY FOR THE DEFENDANT (DISMISSAL OF THE CASE),

OR FOR THE PLAINTIFF (MONEY DAMAGES and/or INJUNCTIVE ORDERS, ETC.)

THE APPEALS COURT JUDGES REVIEW ONLY THE OFFICIAL RECORD OF THE TRIAL COURT DECISION BELOW WHICH IS "SENT UP" TO THEM, TAKING NO EVIDENCE, LISTENING TO NO WITNESSES EXCEPT THE ATTORNEYS WHO ARE ARGUING THE CASE ON APPEAL. THEY REVIEW QUESTIONS OF LAW ONLY ("WAS ANY RELEVANT QUESTION OF LAW IMPROPERLY DEFINED, MISAPPLIED, OR WRONGLY DECIDED?"), ACCEPTING ALL THE FACTS AS THEY WERE FOUND TO BE BY THE TRIAL COURT.

SO THE PRIOR DECISION OF THE TRIAL COURT IS: AFFIRMED, REVERSED, DISMISSED, or REMANDED BACK TO THE TRIAL COURT.

IN ANY FURTHER APPEAL, IF SUCH IS AVAILABLE:

THE HIGHER APPEALS COURT JUDGES ALSO REVIEW QUESTIONS OF LAW ONLY ("WAS ANY RELEVANT QUESTION OF LAW IN THE PRIOR APPEALS COURT'S DECISION IMPROPERLY DEFINED, MISAPPLIED, OR WRONGLY DECIDED?")

SO THE PRIOR DECISION IS ULTIMATELY: AFFIRMED, REVERSED, DISMISSED, or REMANDED BACK TO A LOWER COURT.

MOTION FOR DIRECTED VERDICT

MOTION FOR J.N.O.V.

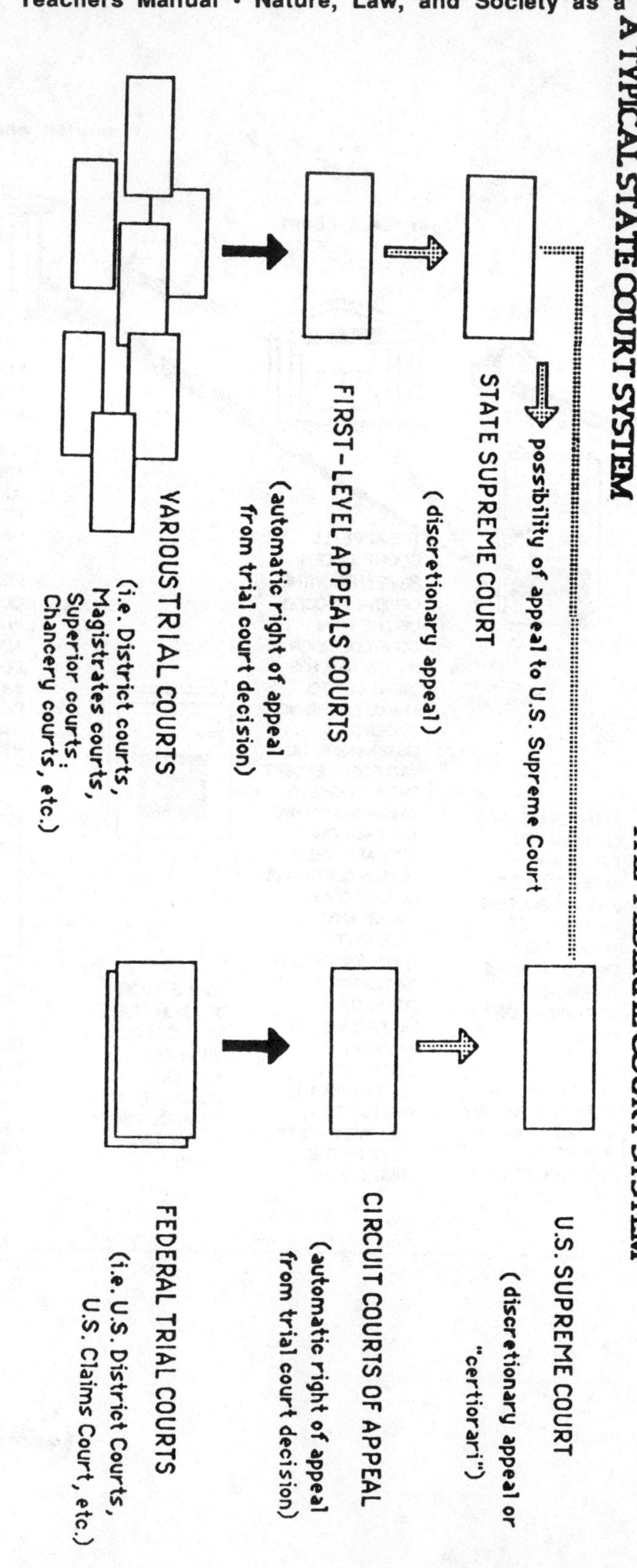
A TYPICAL STATE COURT SYSTEM
STATE SUPREME COURT
(discretionary appeal)
possibility of appeal to U.S. Supreme Court
FIRST-LEVEL APPEALS COURTS
(automatic right of appeal
from trial court decision)
VARIOUS TRIAL COURTS
(i.e. District courts,
Magistrates courts,
Superior courts,
Chancery courts, etc.)
THE FEDERAL COURT SYSTEM
U.S. SUPREME COURT
(discretionary appeal or
"certiorari")
CIRCUIT COURTS OF APPEAL
(automatic right of appeal
from trial court decision)
FEDERAL TRIAL COURTS
(i.e. U.S. District Courts,
U.S. Claims Court, etc.)

Following pages: Chart C

ANALYSIS OF THE MERITS
OF A CASE, ACTUAL OR HYPOTHETICAL

"PUTTING TOGETHER PLAINTIFF'S "PRIMA FACIE CASE"

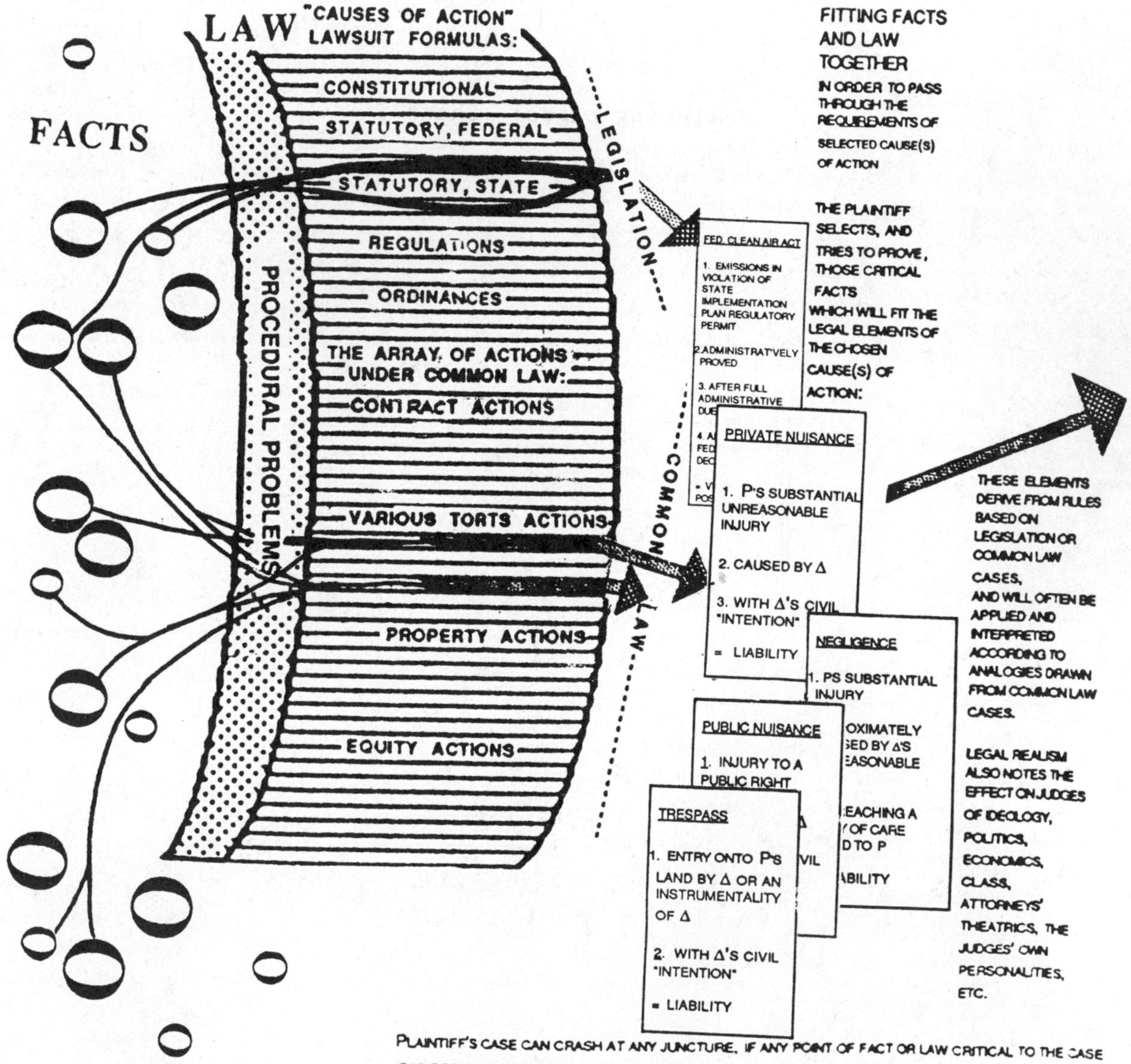

PLAINTIFF'S CASE CAN CRASH AT ANY JUNCTURE, IF ANY POINT OF FACT OR LAW CRITICAL TO THE CASE IS UNDERMINED, REBUTTED, OR THROWN OUT

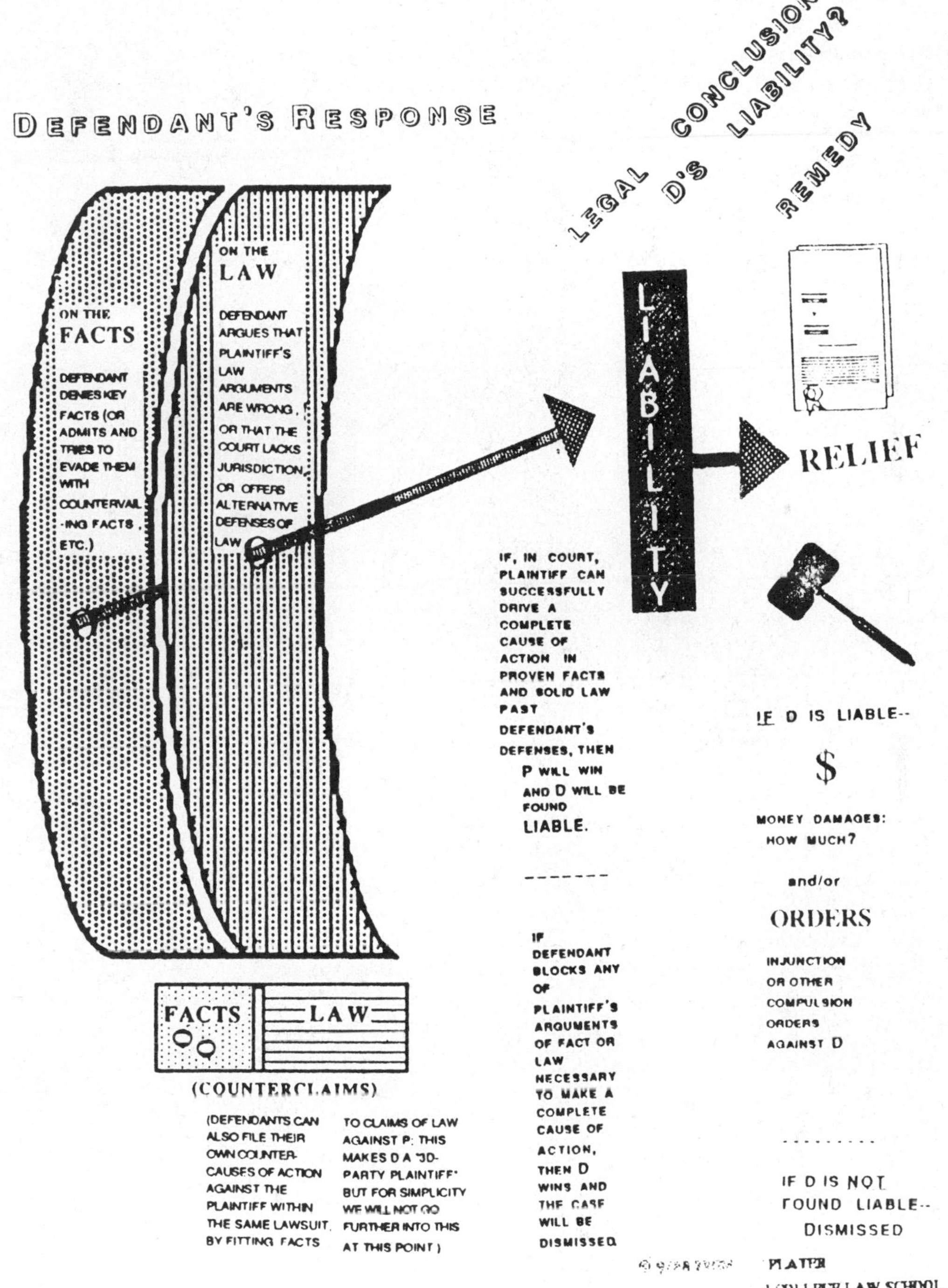

DEFENDANT'S RESPONSE
LEGAL CONCLUSION:
D'S LIABILITY?
REMEDY
ON THE FACTS
DEFENDANT DENIES KEY FACTS (OR ADMITS AND TRIES TO EVADE THEM WITH COUNTERVAIL-ING FACTS, ETC.)
ON THE LAW
DEFENDANT ARGUES THAT PLAINTIFF'S LAW ARGUMENTS ARE WRONG, OR THAT THE COURT LACKS JURISDICTION, OR OFFERS ALTERNATIVE DEFENSES OF LAW
LIABILITY
RELIEF
IF, IN COURT, PLAINTIFF CAN SUCCESSFULLY DRIVE A COMPLETE CAUSE OF ACTION IN PROVEN FACTS AND SOLID LAW PAST DEFENDANT'S DEFENSES, THEN P WILL WIN AND D WILL BE FOUND LIABLE.
IF DEFENDANT BLOCKS ANY OF PLAINTIFF'S ARGUMENTS OF FACT OR LAW NECESSARY TO MAKE A COMPLETE CAUSE OF ACTION, THEN D WINS AND THE CASE WILL BE DISMISSED.
IF D IS LIABLE--
$
MONEY DAMAGES: HOW MUCH?
and/or
ORDERS
INJUNCTION OR OTHER COMPULSION ORDERS AGAINST D
IF D IS NOT FOUND LIABLE-- DISMISSED
FACTS
LAW
(COUNTERCLAIMS)
(DEFENDANTS CAN ALSO FILE THEIR OWN COUNTER-CAUSES OF ACTION AGAINST THE PLAINTIFF WITHIN THE SAME LAWSUIT, BY FITTING FACTS TO CLAIMS OF LAW AGAINST P; THIS MAKES D A "3D-PARTY PLAINTIFF" BUT FOR SIMPLICITY WE WILL NOT GO FURTHER INTO THIS AT THIS POINT.)
PLATER
COLLEGE LAW SCHOOL

A FACSIMILE OF A REPORTED CASE

The following pages contain facsimiles of the actual West Reporter System case decision reported for the *Boomer* case, 257 N.E.2d 870 (1970), which is excerpted and reprinted in the coursebook at 102-108.

On the left-hand side are unannotated facsimiles of selected pages of the *Boomer* case opinions as you would find them in a law library within volume 257 of West's North Eastern Reporter, Second Series, with case heading and introductory material beginning on page 870.

On the right-hand side you will see annotated photo-reduced versions of the left-hand page, showing the different features of the case as reported. Note that the syllabus, headnotes, and other editorial features are unofficial. The only official text is the language of the court itself, speaking in its majority opinion and dissents (or in some cases in concurring opinions, which agree with the result rather than the reasoning of the majority).

The case name heading on the last page changes because a new case begins on that page at the end of the *Boomer* entry.

26 N.Y.2d 219

Oscar H. BOOMER et al., Appellants,

v.

ATLANTIC CEMENT COMPANY, Inc., Respondent. (And Five Other Actions.)

Charles J. MEILAK et al., Appellants,

v.

ATLANTIC CEMENT COMPANY, Inc., Respondent.

Court of Appeals of New York

March 4, 1970.

Actions by landowners for injunction restraining operator of cement plant from emitting dust and raw materials and conducting excessive blasting in operating its plant and for damages sustained as result of nuisance so created. The Supreme Court, Trial Term, Albany County, R. Waldron Herzberg, J., 55 Misc.2d 1023, 287 N.Y.S.2d 112, entered judgment for cement company which was affirmed by the Supreme Court, Appellate Division, 30 A.D.2d 480, 294 N.Y.S.2d 452. Judgment for cement company in second action was affirmed by the Supreme Court, Appellate Division, 31 A.D.2d 578, 295 N.Y.S.2d 622. From orders of the Appellate Division appeals were taken. The Court of Appeals, Bergan, J., held that where neighboring landowners sustained injury to property from dirt, smoke and vibration emanating from defendant's cement plant, and defendant's investment in plant was in excess of $45,000,000 and over 300 people were employed in the plant, and it appeared unlikely that techniques to eliminate annoying by-products of cement making were unlikely to be developed by any research defendant could undertake within any short period, injunction would be conditioned on payment by defendant and acceptance by landowners of permanent damages in compensation for servitude on the land.

Reversed and cases remitted with directions.

Jasen, J., dissented in part.

1. Health ⚷28

Court in resolving private litigation should not undertake to lay down and implement a policy for the elimination of air pollution.

2. Nuisance ⚷25(2)

Nuisance will be enjoined although marked disparity be shown in economic consequence between effect of injunction and effect of the nuisance.

3. Nuisance ⚷25(2)

Where neighboring landowners sustained injury to property from dirt, smoke and vibration emanating from defendant's cement plant, and defendant's investment in plant was in excess of $45,000,000 and over 300 people were employed in the plant, and it appeared unlikely that techniques to eliminate annoying by-products of cement making were unlikely to be developed by any research defendant could undertake within any short period, injunction would be conditioned on payment by defendant and acceptance by landowners of permanent damages in compensation for servitude on the land.

4. Judgment ⚷702

Limitation of relief granted landowners complaining of injury to property from dirt, smoke and vibration emanating from defendant's plant to an injunction conditioned on payment of permanent damages to landowners would not foreclose public health or other public agencies from seeking proper relief in a proper court.

5. Nuisance ⚷41

Where nuisance is of such permanent and unabatable character that a single recovery can be had, including the whole damage past and future resulting therefrom, there can be but one recovery.

6. Judgment ⚷606

Nuisance ⚷56

Judgment allowing permanent damages to landowners alleging injury to property

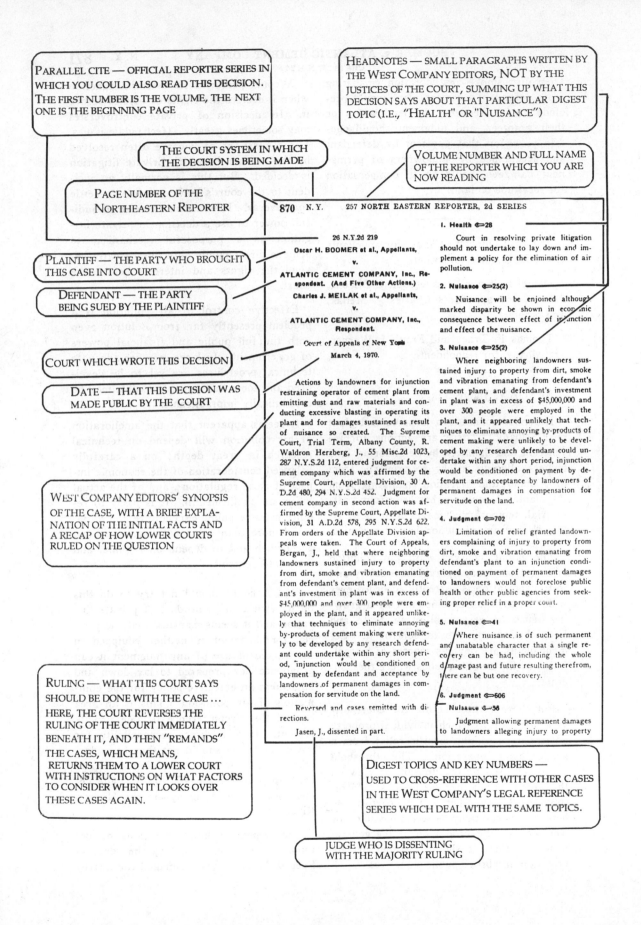

PARALLEL CITE — OFFICIAL REPORTER SERIES IN WHICH YOU COULD ALSO READ THIS DECISION. THE FIRST NUMBER IS THE VOLUME, THE NEXT ONE IS THE BEGINNING PAGE

HEADNOTES — SMALL PARAGRAPHS WRITTEN BY THE WEST COMPANY EDITORS, NOT BY THE JUSTICES OF THE COURT, SUMMING UP WHAT THIS DECISION SAYS ABOUT THAT PARTICULAR DIGEST TOPIC (I.E., "HEALTH" OR "NUISANCE")

THE COURT SYSTEM IN WHICH THE DECISION IS BEING MADE

VOLUME NUMBER AND FULL NAME OF THE REPORTER WHICH YOU ARE NOW READING

PAGE NUMBER OF THE NORTHEASTERN REPORTER

870 N.Y. 257 NORTH EASTERN REPORTER, 2d SERIES

26 N.Y.2d 219

Oscar H. BOOMER et al., Appellants,

v.

ATLANTIC CEMENT COMPANY, Inc., Respondent. (And Five Other Actions.)

Charles J. MEILAK et al., Appellants,

v.

ATLANTIC CEMENT COMPANY, Inc., Respondent.

Court of Appeals of New York.

March 4, 1970.

PLAINTIFF — THE PARTY WHO BROUGHT THIS CASE INTO COURT

DEFENDANT — THE PARTY BEING SUED BY THE PLAINTIFF

COURT WHICH WROTE THIS DECISION

DATE — THAT THIS DECISION WAS MADE PUBLIC BY THE COURT

Actions by landowners for injunction restraining operator of cement plant from emitting dust and raw materials and conducting excessive blasting in operating its plant and for damages sustained as result of nuisance so created. The Supreme Court, Trial Term, Albany County, R. Waldron Herzberg, J., 55 Misc.2d 1023, 287 N.Y.S.2d 112, entered judgment for cement company which was affirmed by the Supreme Court, Appellate Division, 30 A.D.2d 480, 294 N.Y.S.2d 452. Judgment for cement company in second action was affirmed by the Supreme Court, Appellate Division, 31 A.D.2d 578, 295 N.Y.S.2d 622. From orders of the Appellate Division appeals were taken. The Court of Appeals, Bergan, J., held that where neighboring landowners sustained injury to property from dirt, smoke and vibration emanating from defendant's cement plant, and defendant's investment in plant was in excess of $45,000,000 and over 300 people were employed in the plant, and it appeared unlikely that techniques to eliminate annoying by-products of cement making were unlikely to be developed by any research defendant could undertake within any short period, injunction would be conditioned on payment by defendant and acceptance by landowners of permanent damages in compensation for servitude on the land.

Reversed and cases remitted with directions.

Jasen, J., dissented in part.

1. Health ⚷28

Court in resolving private litigation should not undertake to lay down and implement a policy for the elimination of air pollution.

2. Nuisance ⚷25(2)

Nuisance will be enjoined although marked disparity be shown in economic consequence between effect of injunction and effect of the nuisance.

3. Nuisance ⚷25(2)

Where neighboring landowners sustained injury to property from dirt, smoke and vibration emanating from defendant's cement plant, and defendant's investment in plant was in excess of $45,000,000 and over 300 people were employed in the plant, and it appeared unlikely that techniques to eliminate annoying by-products of cement making were unlikely to be developed by any research defendant could undertake within any short period, injunction would be conditioned on payment by defendant and acceptance by landowners of permanent damages in compensation for servitude on the land.

4. Judgment ⚷702

Limitation of relief granted landowners complaining of injury to property from dirt, smoke and vibration emanating from defendant's plant to an injunction conditioned on payment of permanent damages to landowners would not foreclose public health or other public agencies from seeking proper relief in a proper court.

5. Nuisance ⚷41

Where nuisance is of such permanent and unabatable character that a single recovery can be had, including the whole damage past and future resulting therefrom, there can be but one recovery.

6. Judgment ⚷606

Nuisance ⚷56

Judgment allowing permanent damages to landowners alleging injury to property

WEST COMPANY EDITORS' SYNOPSIS OF THE CASE, WITH A BRIEF EXPLANATION OF THE INITIAL FACTS AND A RECAP OF HOW LOWER COURTS RULED ON THE QUESTION

RULING — WHAT THIS COURT SAYS SHOULD BE DONE WITH THE CASE … HERE, THE COURT REVERSES THE RULING OF THE COURT IMMEDIATELY BENEATH IT, AND THEN "REMANDS" THE CASES, WHICH MEANS, RETURNS THEM TO A LOWER COURT WITH INSTRUCTIONS ON WHAT FACTORS TO CONSIDER WHEN IT LOOKS OVER THESE CASES AGAIN.

DIGEST TOPICS AND KEY NUMBERS — USED TO CROSS-REFERENCE WITH OTHER CASES IN THE WEST COMPANY'S LEGAL REFERENCE SERIES WHICH DEAL WITH THE SAME TOPICS.

JUDGE WHO IS DISSENTING WITH THE MAJORITY RULING

from dirt, smoke and vibration emanating from defendant's cement plant would preclude future recovery by landowners or their grantees, and judgment should contain provision that payment by defendant and acceptance by landowners of permanent damages would be in compensation for servitude on land.

E. David Duncan, Albany, for appellants Oscar H. Boomer, and others.

Daniel H. Prior, Jr. and John J. Biscone, Albany, for appellants Charles J. Meilak, and others.

Thomas F. Tracy and Frank J. Warner, Jr., Albany, for respondent.

BERGAN, Judge.

Defendant operates a large cement plant near Albany. These are actions for injunction and damages by neighboring land owners alleging injury to property from dirt, smoke and vibration emanating from the plant. A nuisance has been found after trial, temporary damages have been allowed; but an injunction has been denied.

The public concern with air pollution arising from many sources in industry and in transportation is currently accorded ever wider recognition accompanied by a growing sense of responsibility in State and Federal Governments to control it. Cement plants are obvious sources of air pollution in the neighborhoods where they operate.

But there is now before the court private litigation in which individual property owners have sought specific relief from a single plant operation. The threshold question raised by the division of view on this appeal is whether the court should resolve the litigation between the parties now before it as equitably as seems possible; or whether, seeking promotion of the general public welfare, it should channel private litigation into broad public objectives.

A court performs its essential function when it decides the rights of parties before it. Its decision of private controversies may sometimes greatly affect public issues. Large questions of law are often resolved by the manner in which private litigation is decided. But this is normally an incident to the court's main function to settle controversy. It is a rare exercise of judicial power to use a decision in private litigation as a purposeful mechanism to achieve direct public objectives greatly beyond the rights and interests before the court.

Effective control of air pollution is a problem presently far from solution even with the full public and financial powers of government. In large measure adequate technical procedures are yet to be developed and some that appear possible may be economically impracticable.

It seems apparent that the amelioration of air pollution will depend on technical research in great depth; on a carefully balanced consideration of the economic impact of close regulation; and of the actual effect on public health. It is likely to require massive public expenditure and to demand more than any local community can accomplish and to depend on regional and interstate controls.

[1] A court should not try to do this on its own as a by-product of private litigation and it seems manifest that the judicial establishment is neither equipped in the limited nature of any judgment it can pronounce nor prepared to lay down and implement an effective policy for the elimination of air pollution. This is an area beyond the circumference of one private lawsuit. It is a direct responsibility for government and should not thus be undertaken as an incident to solving a dispute between property owners and a single cement plant—one of many—in the Hudson River valley.

The cement making operations of defendant have been found by the court at Special Term to have damaged the nearby

THE NAME BY WHICH THIS CASE IS KNOWN

from dirt, smoke and vibration emanating from defendant's cement plant would preclude future recovery by landowners or their grantees, and judgment should contain provision that payment by defendant and acceptance by landowners of permanent damages would be in compensation for servitude on land.

THE ATTORNEYS WHO REPRESENTED THE PARTIES IN THIS CASE

E. David Duncan, Albany, for appellants Oscar H. Boomer, and others.

Daniel H. Prior, Jr. and John J. Biscone, Albany, for appellants Charles J. Meilak, and others.

Thomas F. Tracy and Frank J. Warner, Jr., Albany, for respondent.

JUDGE WHO AUTHORED THE MAJORITY OPINION

BERGAN, Judge.

THE TEXT OF THE MAJORITY'S OPINION BEGINS HERE

Defendant operates a large cement plant near Albany. These are actions for injunction and damages by neighboring land owners alleging injury to property from dirt, smoke and vibration emanating from the plant. A nuisance has been found after trial, temporary damages have been allowed; but an injunction has been denied.

The public concern with air pollution arising from many sources in industry and in transportation is currently accorded ever wider recognition accompanied by a growing sense of responsibility in State and Federal Governments to control it. Cement plants are obvious sources of air pollution in the neighborhoods where they operate.

But there is now before the court private litigation in which individual property owners have sought specific relief from a single plant operation. The threshold question raised by the division of view on this appeal is whether the court should resolve the litigation between the parties now before it as equitably as seems possible; or whether, seeking promotion of the general public welfare, it should channel private litigation into broad public objectives.

A court performs its essential function when it decides the rights of parties before it. Its decision of private controversies may sometimes greatly affect public issues. Large questions of law are often resolved by the manner in which private litigation is decided. But this is normally an incident to the court's main function to settle controversy. It is a rare exercise of judicial power to use a decision in private litigation as a purposeful mechanism to achieve direct public objectives greatly beyond the rights and interests before the court.

Effective control of air pollution is a problem presently far from solution even with the full public and financial powers of government. In large measure adequate technical procedures are yet to be developed and some that appear possible may be economically impracticable.

It seems apparent that the amelioration of air pollution will depend on technical research in great depth; on a carefully balanced consideration of the economic impact of close regulation; and of the actual effect on public health. It is likely to require massive public expenditure and to demand more than any local community can accomplish and to depend on regional and interstate controls.

[1] A court should not try to do this on its own as a by-product of private litigation and it seems manifest that the judicial establishment is neither equipped in the limited nature of any judgment it can pronounce nor prepared to lay down and implement an effective policy for the elimination of air pollution. This is an area beyond the circumference of one private lawsuit. It is a direct responsibility for government and should not thus be undertaken as an incident to solving a dispute between property owners and a single cement plant—one of many—in the Hudson River valley.

The cement making operations of defendant have been found by the court at Special Term to have damaged the nearby

NUMBERS INSERTED BY WEST, CORRESPONDING TO HEADNOTE NUMBERS

Thus it seems fair to both sides to grant permanent damages to plaintiffs which will terminate this private litigation. The theory of damage is the "servitude on land" of plaintiffs imposed by defendant's nuisance. (See United States v. Causby, 328 U.S. 256, 261, 262, 267, 66 S.Ct. 1062, 90 L.Ed. 1206, where the term "servitude" addressed to the land was used by Justice Douglas relating to the effect of airplane noise on property near an airport.)

[6] The judgment, by allowance of permanent damages imposing a servitude on land, which is the basis of the actions, would preclude future recovery by plaintiffs or their grantees (see Northern Indiana Public Serv. Co. v. W. J. & M. S. Vesey, *supra*, p. 351, 200 N.E. 620).

This should be placed beyond debate by a provision of the judgment that the payment by defendant and the acceptance by plaintiffs of permanent damages found by the court shall be in compensation for a servitude on the land.

Although the Trial Term has found permanent damages as a possible basis of settlement of the litigation, on remission the court should be entirely free to re-examine this subject. It may again find the permanent damage already found; or make new findings.

The orders should be reversed, without costs, and the cases remitted to Supreme Court, Albany County to grant an injunction which shall be vacated upon payment by defendant of such amounts of permanent damage to the respective plaintiffs as shall for this purpose be determined by the court.

JASEN, Judge (dissenting).

I agree with the majority that a reversal is required here, but I do not subscribe to the newly enunciated doctrine of assessment of permanent damages, in lieu of an injunction, where substantial property rights have been impaired by the creation of a nuisance.

It has long been the rule in this State, as the majority acknowledges, that a nuisance which results in substantial continuing damage to neighbors must be enjoined. (Whalen v. Union Bag & Paper Co., 208 N.Y. 1, 101 N.E. 805; Campbell v. Seaman, 63 N.Y. 568; see, also, Kennedy v. Moog Servocontrols, 21 N.Y.2d 966, 290 N.Y.S.2d 193, 237 N.E.2d 356.) To now change the rule to permit the cement company to continue polluting the air indefinitely upon the payment of permanent damages is, in my opinion, compounding the magnitude of a very serious problem in our State and Nation today.

In recognition of this problem, the Legislature of this State has enacted the Air Pollution Control Act (Public Health Law, Consol.Laws, c. 45, §§ 1264 to 1299–m) declaring that it is the State policy to require the use of all available and reasonable methods to prevent and control air pollution (Public Health Law § 1265 [1]).

The harmful nature and widespread occurrence of air pollution have been extensively documented. Congressional hearings have revealed that air pollution causes substantial property damage, as well as being a contributing factor to a rising incidence of lung cancer, emphysema, bronchitis and asthma.[2]

The specific problem faced here is known as particulate contamination because of the fine dust particles emanating from defendant's cement plant. The particular type of nuisance is not new, having appeared in many cases for at least the past 60 years. (See Hulbert v. California Portland Cement Co., 161 Cal. 239, 118 P.

1. See, also, Air Quality Act of 1967, 81 U.S.Stat. 485 (1967).

2. See U.S.Cong., Senate Comm. on Public Works, Special Subcomm. on Air and Water Pollution, Air Pollution 1966, 89th Cong., 2d Sess., 1966, at pp. 22–24; U.S. Cong., Senate Comm. on Public Works, Special Subcomm. on Air and Water Pollution, Air Pollution 1968, 90th Cong., 2d Sess., 1968, at pp. 850, 1084.

Thus it seems fair to both sides to grant permanent damages to plaintiffs which will terminate this private litigation. The theory of damage is the "servitude on land" of plaintiffs imposed by defendant's nuisance. (See United States v. Causby, 328 U.S. 256, 261, 262, 267, 66 S.Ct. 1062, 90 L.Ed. 1206, where the term "servitude" addressed to the land was used by Justice Douglas relating to the effect of airplane noise on property near an airport.)

[6] The judgment, by allowance of permanent damages imposing a servitude on land, which is the basis of the actions, would preclude future recovery by plaintiffs or their grantees (see Northern Indiana Public Serv. Co. v. W. J. & M. S. Vesey, *supra*, p. 351, 200 N.E. 620).

This should be placed beyond debate by a provision of the judgment that the payment by defendant and the acceptance by plaintiffs of permanent damages found by the court shall be in compensation for a servitude on the land.

Although the Trial Term has found permanent damages as a possible basis of settlement of the litigation, on remission the court should be entirely free to re-examine this subject. It may again find the permanent damage already found; or make new findings.

The orders should be reversed, without costs, and the cases remitted to Supreme Court, Albany County to grant an injunction which shall be vacated upon payment by defendant of such amounts of permanent damage to the respective plaintiffs as shall for this purpose be determined by the court.

JASEN, Judge (dissenting).

I agree with the majority that a reversal is required here, but I do not subscribe to the newly enunciated doctrine of assessment of permanent damages, in lieu of an injunction, where substantial property rights have been impaired by the creation of a nuisance.

It has long been the rule in this State, as the majority acknowledges, that a nuisance which results in substantial continuing damage to neighbors must be enjoined. (Whalen v. Union Bag & Paper Co., 208 N.Y. 1, 101 N.E. 805; Campbell v. Seaman, 63 N.Y. 568; see, also, Kennedy v. Moog Servocontrols, 21 N.Y.2d 966, 290 N.Y.S.2d 193, 237 N.E.2d 356.) To now change the rule to permit the cement company to continue polluting the air indefinitely upon the payment of permanent damages is, in my opinion, compounding the magnitude of a very serious problem in our State and Nation today.

In recognition of this problem, the Legislature of this State has enacted the Air Pollution Control Act (Public Health Law, Consol.Laws, c. 45, §§ 1264 to 1299-m) declaring that it is the State policy to require the use of all available and reasonable methods to prevent and control air pollution (Public Health Law § 1265 [1]).

The harmful nature and widespread occurrence of air pollution have been extensively documented. Congressional hearings have revealed that air pollution causes substantial property damage, as well as being a contributing factor to a rising incidence of lung cancer, emphysema, bronchitis and asthma.[2]

The specific problem faced here is known as particulate contamination because of the fine dust particles emanating from defendant's cement plant. The particular type of nuisance is not new, having appeared in many cases for at least the past 60 years. (See Hulbert v. California Portland Cement Co., 161 Cal. 239, 118 P.

1. See, also, Air Quality Act of 1967, 81 U.S.Stat. 485 (1967)

2. See U.S.Cong., Senate Comm. on Public Works, Special Subcomm. on Air and Water Pollution, Air Pollution 1966, 89th Cong., 2d Sess., 1966, at pp. 22-24; U.S. Cong., Senate Comm. on Public Works, Special Subcomm. on Air and Water Pollution, Air Pollution 1968, 90th Cong., 2d Sess., 1968, at pp. 850, 1084.

RULING — WHAT THIS COURT SAYS SHOULD BE DONE WITH THE CASE … HERE, THE COURT REVERSES THE RULING OF THE COURT JUST BENEATH IT, AND THEN "REMANDS" THE CASES, WHICH MEANS, RETURNS THEM TO A LOWER COURT WITH INSTRUCTIONS ON WHAT FACTORS IT SHOULD CONSIDER WHEN IT LOOKS OVER THESE CASES AGAIN.

BEGINNING OF THE TEXT OF THE DISSENTING JUSTICE'S OPINION

FOOTNOTE — GIVES THE AUTHORITY USED TO SUPPORT THE STATEMENT ABOVE OR TO CLARIFY A POINT MADE WITHIN THE STATEMENT

In sum, then, by constitutional mandate as well as by judicial pronouncement, the permanent impairment of private property for private purposes is not authorized in the absence of clearly demonstrated public benefit and use.

I would enjoin the defendant cement company from continuing the discharge of dust particles upon its neighbors' properties unless, within 18 months, the cement company abated this nuisance.[7]

It is not my intention to cause the removal of the cement plant from the Albany area, but to recognize the urgency of the problem stemming from this stationary source of air pollution, and to allow the company a specified period of time to develop a means to alleviate this nuisance.

I am aware that the trial court found that the most modern dust control devices available have been installed in defendant's plant, but, I submit, this does not mean that *better* and more effective dust control devices could not be developed within the time allowed to abate the pollution.

Moreover, I believe it is incumbent upon the defendant to develop such devices, since the cement company, at the time the plant commenced production (1962), was well aware of the plaintiffs' presence in the area, as well as the probable consequences of its contemplated operation. Yet, it still chose to build and operate the plant at this site.

In a day when there is a growing concern for clean air, highly developed industry should not expect acquiescence by the courts, but should, instead, plan its operations to eliminate contamination of our air and damage to its neighbors.

Accordingly, the orders of the Appellate Division, insofar as they denied the injunction, should be reversed, and the actions remitted to Supreme Court, Albany County to grant an injunction to take effect 18 months hence, unless the nuisance is abated by improved techniques prior to said date.

FULD, C. J., and BURKE and SCILEPPI, JJ., concur with BERGAN, J.

JASEN, J., dissents in part and votes to reverse in a separate opinion.

BREITEL and GIBSON, JJ., taking no part.

In each action: Order reversed, without costs, and the case remitted to Supreme Court, Albany County, for further proceedings in accordance with the opinion herein.

26 N.Y.2d 232

Samuel RANHAND, Respondent,

v.

Irving SINOWITZ, Appellant.

Court of Appeals of New York.

March 5, 1970.

Action on notes. The Supreme Court, Special Term, New York County, Frederick Backer, J., entered a republished order denying defendant's motion for summary judgment, and defendant appealed. The Supreme Court, Appellate Division, First Judicial Department, by order entered April 17, 1969, 32 A.D.2d 519, 299 N.Y.S.2d 518, affirmed, and defendant appealed by permission of the Appellate Division, which certified the question whether the Supreme Court order, as affirmed, was properly made and certified that its deter-

7. The issuance of an injunction to become effective in the future is not an entirely new concept. For instance, in Schwarzenbach v. Oneonta Light & Power Co., 207 N.Y. 671, 100 N.E. 1134, an injunction against the maintenance of a dam spilling water on plaintiff's property was issued to become effective one year hence.

RANHAND v. SINOWITZ N.Y. **877**

Cite as 257 N.E.2d 877

In sum, then, by constitutional mandate as well as by judicial pronouncement, the permanent impairment of private property for private purposes is not authorized in the absence of clearly demonstrated public benefit and use.

I would enjoin the defendant cement company from continuing the discharge of dust particles upon its neighbors' properties unless, within 18 months, the cement company abated this nuisance.[7]

It is not my intention to cause the removal of the cement plant from the Albany area, but to recognize the urgency of the problem stemming from this stationary source of air pollution, and to allow the company a specified period of time to develop a means to alleviate this nuisance.

I am aware that the trial court found that the most modern dust control devices available have been installed in defendant's plant, but, I submit, this does not mean that *better* and more effective dust control devices could not be developed within the time allowed to abate the pollution.

Moreover, I believe it is incumbent upon the defendant to develop such devices, since the cement company, at the time the plant commenced production (1962), was well aware of the plaintiffs' presence in the area, as well as the probable consequences of its contemplated operation. Yet, it still chose to build and operate the plant at this site.

In a day when there is a growing concern for clean air, highly developed industry should not expect acquiescence by the courts, but should, instead, plan its operations to eliminate contamination of our air and damage to its neighbors.

Accordingly, the orders of the Appellate Division, insofar as they denied the injunction, should be reversed, and the actions remitted to Supreme Court, Albany County to grant an injunction to take effect 18 months hence, unless the nuisance is abated by improved techniques prior to said date.

FULD, C. J., and BURKE and SCILEPPI, JJ., concur with BERGAN, J.

JUSTICES WHO AGREED WITH THE MAJORITY OPINION, WHICH IS THE SAME THING AS THE COURT'S "RULING" IN THE CASE

JASEN, J., dissents in part and votes to reverse in a separate opinion.

DISSENTING JUDGES, OR THOSE WHO AGREE IN A SEPARATE OPINION

BREITEL and GIBSON, JJ., taking no part.

JUDGES WHO DID NOT HELP IN DECIDING THIS CASE

In each action: Order reversed, without costs, and the case remitted to Supreme Court, Albany County, for further proceedings in accordance with the opinion herein.

RULING — RECAPPED ONCE MORE AT THE END OF THE CASE.

26 N.Y.2d 232

Samuel RANHAND, Respondent,

v.

Irving SINOWITZ, Appellant.

Court of Appeals of New York.

March 5, 1970.

Action on notes. The Supreme Court, Special Term, New York County, Frederick Backer, J., entered a republished order denying defendant's motion for summary judgment, and defendant appealed. The Supreme Court, Appellate Division, First Judicial Department, by order entered April 17, 1969, 32 A.D.2d 519, 299 N.Y.S.2d 518, affirmed, and defendant appealed by permission of the Appellate Division, which certified the question whether the Supreme Court order, as affirmed, was properly made and certified that its deter-

7. The issuance of an injunction to become effective in the future is not an entirely new concept. For instance, in Schwarzenbach v. Oneonta Light & Power Co., 207 N.Y. 671, 100 N.E. 1134, an injunction against the maintenance of a dam spilling water on plaintiff's property was issued to become effective one year hence.

CHART E — NUTSHELL

SOME FORMS OF ACTION: TORT

Trespass.... The Writ of Trespass was early used for the purpose of summoning a defendant before the King's courts to compel him to respond in a civil proceeding for damages for injuries inflicted by him upon the plaintiff or his property under circumstances constituting a breach of the King's peace. In view of the fact that at the outset the King's courts were primarily interested in affairs involving title to and possession of land, Trespass, which dealt with more personal matters, did not develop until about the middle of the 13th century, and it did not come into common use until the middle of the 14th century. Up to that time the criminal remedy for breach of the King's peace seemed to suffice. Since the breach of the peace was an essential element in Trespass, the writ as well as the declaration alleged that the defendant's act had been committed vi et armis et contra pacem Domini Regis — with force and arms against the peace of the Lord King. However, as the action evolved, the requirement of proof of breach of peace was eliminated, and it became sufficient to show that the defendant had inflicted an injury by a direct and immediate application of force to the plaintiff's person or to his property, real or personal.

When the action of Trespass was used for the purpose of compelling the defendant to respond in damages for injury to the plaintiff's property, it took one of the following two forms:

Trespass to chattels (de bonis asportatis). This was the action brought by the plaintiff to recover damages for any forcible injury to a chattel, either by carrying it away, injuring or destroying it, or excluding the owner from the possession of it. The plaintiff was required to allege:

(1) Possession or immediate right to possession of the described chattel of stated value.
(2) Defendant's willful wrongful act interfering with that right.

Trespass to land (quare clausum fregit). An action to recover damages for a forcible interference with the plaintiff's possession of land. The plaintiff had to allege:

(1) Possession of described premises.
(2) Defendant's willful wrongful entry ("vi et armis").

It was not necessary to maintain this action that substantial damages were suffered; for in the absence thereof nominal damages could be recovered.

Trespass on the case. This action was created to provide a remedy for the invasion of personal or property interests not protected by the action of Trespass. For example, it lay where the defendant's acts were not immediately injurious, but only by consequence and collaterally, or where the defendant acted negligently rather than willfully or to a non-possessory interest. As the action developed it became the remedy for a wide variety of wrongs which were not covered by the other forms of action. The plaintiff's necessary allegations included the following:

(1) Facts giving rise to defendant's duty.
(2) Breach of that duty.
(3) Resulting substantial harm to the plaintiff. (Harm was the gist of this action; without it the action would not lie.)

Over the years the action was expanded to cover a wide variety of situations; for example, to permit the plaintiff to bring suit against a defendant who maintained a nuisance on his property; or to permit recovery for injuries to a reversionary interest, such as the interest of an owner of a chattel who had rented it for a period to a third person who was in possession when the defendant committed the wrongful act; or to furnish redress for injuries to incorporeal interests such as easements (for example, rights of way); or to be used in cases of libel, slander, malicious prosecution, fraud and deceit. Most importantly, it came into common use in cases of injuries occasioned by the defendant's negligence, where the essence of the wrongful act was the carelessness of the defendant rather than his direct and forcible act. Trespass on the case became one of the most widely used remedies in the common-law system.

Trover. By this action the plaintiff sought to recover the value of a chattel which had been "converted" by the defendant to his own use. Historically, the action originated as a special form of Trespass on the case. Originally the action lay against one who had found the chattel of the plaintiff and refused to deliver it on demand of the owner, but converted it to his own use. Later the action was permitted against any person who had in his possession, by any means, the personal property of another, and who sold or used it without the consent of the owner, or refused to deliver it on demand, the allegation of a finding by the defendant becoming purely fictional.

The plaintiff's allegations were as follows:

(1) That a designated chattel (or chattels) was (or were) the property of the plaintiff.
(2) The fictional loss by plaintiff and finding by defendant, not open to denial.
(3) Refusal of defendant to deliver the chattel (or chattels) to plaintiff on demand, or other conduct amounting to a conversion of the chattel (or chattels) by defendants to his own use.

The measure of damages, in Trover, was the full value of the chattel (or chattels) at the time when the conversion took place.

Detinue. In contrast to Trover, the plaintiff by this action sought to recover the possession of a chattel held by the defendant rather than its value, but damages could be recovered in the alternative. Originally the action lay only where the defendant had lawfully acquired the chattel but detained it unlawfully; but later the action was extended to include a wrongful taking. The necessary allegations were as follows:

(1) Possession or immediate right to possession of goods, so definitely described that the sheriff could identify them and of a stated value.
(2) Originally, a lawful taking by defendant, but later by extension any taking, lawful or unlawful.
(3) Demand and refusal or a wrongful detention continuing at the time of suit.

Eventually, this action was absorbed by the action of replevin and was rarely used.

Replevin. Here also the plaintiff sought to recover possession of a chattel from the defendant. Originally a wrongful taking was required, but this was later extended to include a wrongful detention following a lawful taking. The necessary allegations were as follows:

(1) Possession or immediate right to possession of a chattel described as in detinue.
(2) Originally a wrongful taking by defendant, but later only a wrongful detention.
(3) Detention continuing to time of suit.

The procedure in Replevin originally served to place the chattel (or chattels) in question in the possession of the plaintiff pending the outcome of the lawsuit. Later, by statute, provision was sometimes made for leaving the disputed chattel (or chattels) in defendant's possession if he posted a bond sufficient to cover the value thereof.

Ejectment. Originally this action was developed to protect a lessee's interest in the possession of leased land. It ultimately came, however, to be the principal method for trying title to real estate. Among the necessary allegations were these:

(1) Title and possession of land in the plaintiff.
(2) Entry by the defendant ousting the plaintiff.
(3) Defendant continuing in possession until suit.

Since this was the action by which "title," as distinguished from the mere right to possession, was tried, the description of the land had to be as exact and specific as that which would be written in a conveyance.

Adapted from:
O. Browder, R. Cunningham & J. Julin, Basic Property Law (2d ed. 1973).

Following pages: Diagram F

APPENDIX

LEGAL LEGAL LEGAL LEGAL

LEGAL NOTICE

TO ALL PERSONS CLAIMING TO BE AFFECTED BY COAL DUST FROM THE LOWER LAKE DOCKS OF THE NORFOLK & WESTERN RAILWAY COMPANY

IN THE UNITED STATES DISTRICT COURT FOR THE NORTHERN DISTRICT OF OHIO WESTERN DIVISION

Dallas Biechele, et al.,
Plaintiffs,
vs.
Norfolk & Western Railway Company,
Defendant.

No. C 68-139

TO ALL PERSONS LIVING OR OWNING REAL ESTATE WITHIN THE AREA OUTLINED ON THE MAP BELOW, AND THE BOUNDARIES SET FORTH IN THE BODY OF THIS NOTICE:

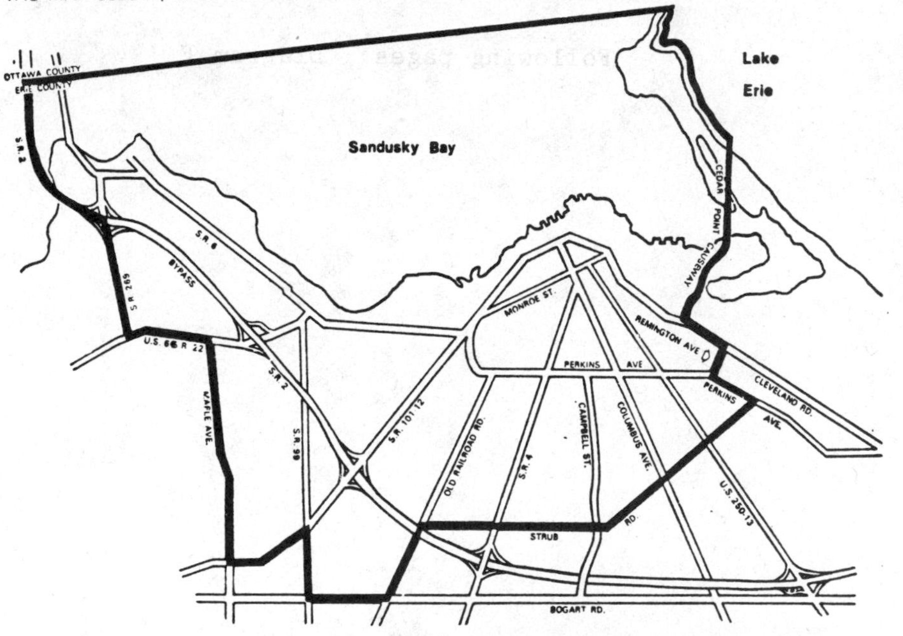

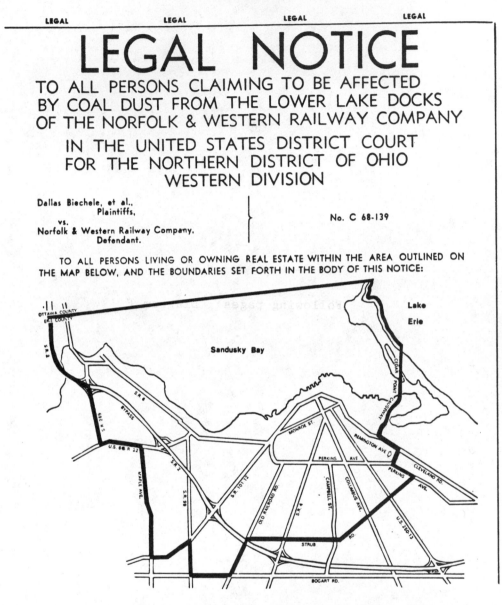

You are hereby notified that the District Court of the United States for the Northern District of Ohio, Western Division, has ordered that this action proceed as a class action, wherein all persons living or owning property within the following described boundaries are members of the class:

Commencing on the shore of Lake Erie at the northernmost point of Cedar Point; thence southeasterly along the shore of Lake Erie to the beginning of the Cedar Point Causeway; thence southerly along the center of the Cedar Point Causeway and Causeway Drive to the center of Cleveland Road; thence easterly along the center of Cleveland Road to Remington Avenue; thence southerly along the center of Remington Avenue to Perkins Avenue; thence easterly along the center of Perkins Avenue to Strub Road; thence southwesterly and westerly along the center of Strub Road to Old Railroad Road; thence southwesterly along the center of Old Railroad Road to Bogart Road; thence westerly along the center of Bogart road to State Route 99; thence northerly along the center of State Route 99 to State Routes 12 and 101; thence westerly along the center of State Routes 12 and 101 to Maple Avenue; thence northerly along the center of

Maple Avenue to U.S. Route 6 and State Route 22; thence westerly along the center of U.S. Route 6 and State Route 22 to State Route 269; thence northerly along the center of State Route 269 to State Route 2; thence northerly along the center line of State Route 2 to its point of intersection with the Erie-Ottawa County Line; thence easterly across Sandusky Bay to the place of beginning.

IF YOU LIVE OR OWN REAL ESTATE WITHIN THOSE BOUNDARIES, you are a member of the class, and unless you make a written request to be excluded. YOU WILL BE INCLUDED IN AND BOUND BY THE JUDGMENT RENDERED BY THE COURT, whether it is favorable or unfavorable to you.

IF YOU WANT TO BE EXCLUDED from membership in the class, you must complete and sign the form headed REQUEST FOR EXCLUSION at the bottom of this notice or write a letter requesting exclusion, and mail it to the Clerk of the United States District Court, 1716 Spielbusch Avenue, Toledo, Ohio, 43624, or have your lawyer do this for you.

IF YOU DO NOT WANT TO BE EXCLUDED, but want to have your own lawyer represent you, you should instruct him to enter your appearance.

This action involves two matters, a claim for an order of injunction restraining the defendant Norfolk & Western Railway Company from continuing the activities alleged to cause coal dust to be blown about, and claims for damages to person and property alleged to have been caused by coal dust.

As to the claim for injunction, all persons living or owning real estate within the boundaries described above will be bound by the judgment in this action whether it is favorable or unfavorable, unless they request exclusion. They need take no action of any kind to be assured of the protection of an order of injunction if one is ultimately issued.

As to claims for damages to person or property, regardless of the outcome of this lawsuit, all such claims will be barred unless the person asserting such claim enters his appearance in this action on or before November 8, 1968.

IF YOU WANT TO MAKE A CLAIM FOR DAMAGES, you may preserve your right to do so by completeing the form headed ENTRY OF APPEARANCE at the bottom of this notice, or by writing a letter saying that you enter your appearance in this lawsuit, and mailing the notice or letter to the Clerk of the United States District Court, 1716 Spielbusch Avenue, Toledo, Ohio, 43624, or by having your lawyer do this for you.

ALL REQUESTS FOR EXCLUSION OR ENTRIES OF APPEARANCE MUST BE FILED WITH THE CLERK OR POSTMARKED NO LATER THAN MIDNIGHT ON FRIDAY, NOVEMBER 8, 1968, OR THEY WILL BE INEFFECTUAL.

This action is presently at issue, and may be called for hearing by the Court at any time after November 8, 1968.

THE COURT'S ORDER THAT THIS ACTION SHALL PROCEED AS A CLASS ACTION IS NOT A DETERMINATION OF THE MERITS OF THE CLAIMS ASSERTED, AND IS ONLY A PRELIMINARY PROCEDURAL DETERMINATION AS TO THE POTENTIAL PARTIES INVOLVED. THE DECISION AS TO WHETHER ANY INJUNCTIVE RELIEF WILL BE GRANTED OR ANY DAMAGES AWARDED WILL FOLLOW A TRIAL ON THE MERITS OF THE ACTION.

DON J. YOUNG
United States District Judge

REQUEST FOR EXCLUSION

Dallas Biechele, et al.,
Plaintiffs,
v.
Norfolk & Western Railway Company,
Defendant.

No. C 68-139

The undersigned requests to be excluded from the class of parties plaintiff to the above captioned action.

Name ....

Address ....

....

ENTRY OF APPEARANCE

Dallas Biechele, et al.,
Plantiffs,
v.
Norfolk & Western Railway Company,
Defendant.

No. C 68-139

I hereby enter my appearance as a member of the class of parties plaintiff to the above action.

Name ....

Address ....

....

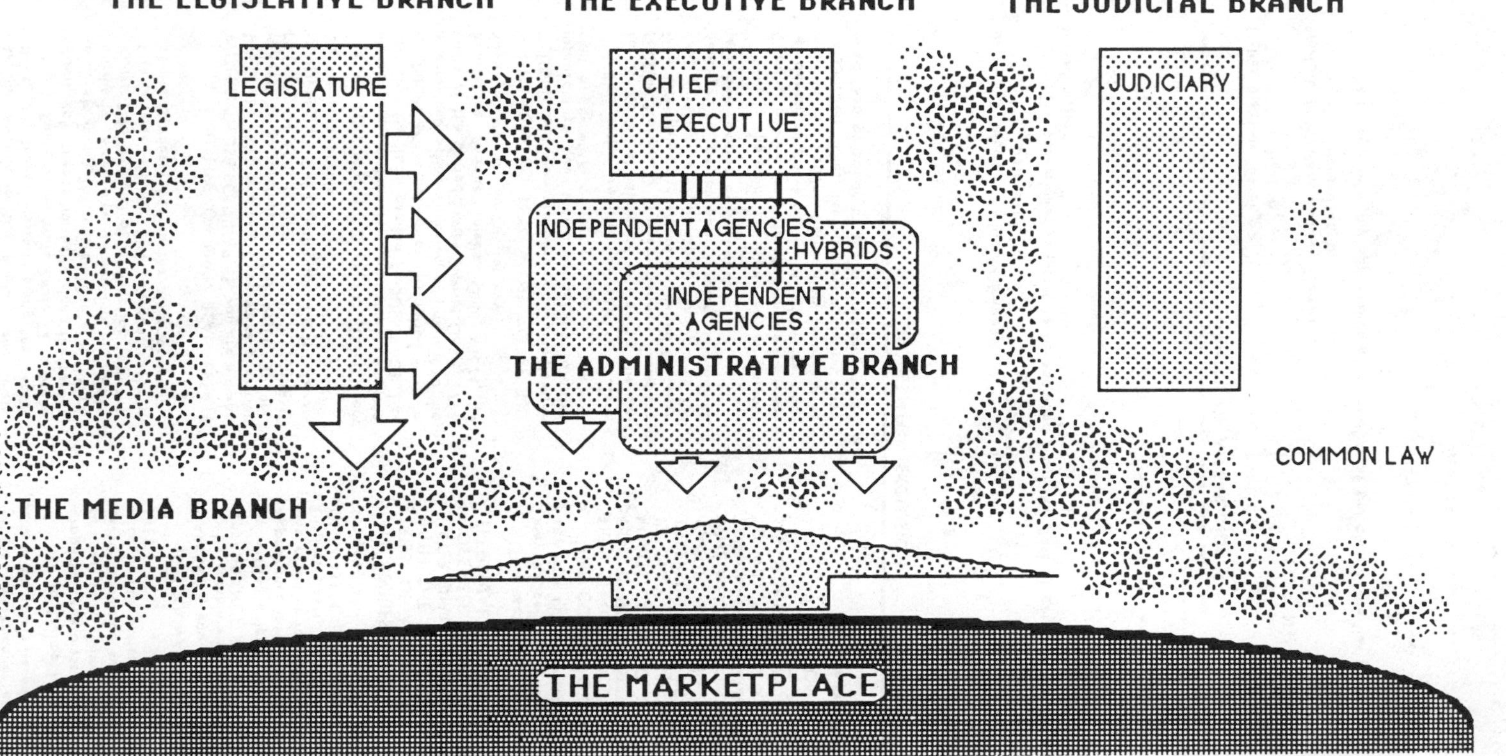

Chart G. THE THREE (or Four, or Five, or Six) BRANCHES OF GOVERNMENT IN THE UNITED STATES

This chart shows the legislative, executive, and judicial branches of government as they exist at the federal level and in each of the 50 states. The official active functions of daily government are the passing of statutes by the legislature, usually with approval of the chief executive; statutes are directed to the administrative agencies, the society at large, and in some cases to the chief executive. Agencies may issue subsidiary legislation (regulations) and adjudicate particular cases under statutes or regulations. Further adjudicative review, or original adjudication under statutes, regulations, and the common law, takes place in the court system. A fundamental point of this chart's version of 8th grade civics is to emphasize that most of the work of government is done by the administrative agencies, which are *not* predominantly under the direct political power of the chief executive. Independent agencies are resposible to the legislature. Even in Cabinet-level (dependent) agencies, the chief executive controls only the top echelon of political appointees; the civil service exists and rolls on relatively insulated from changes at the top. The Media and the Marketplace are two other unofficial but strategic instruments of governance.

Map H.

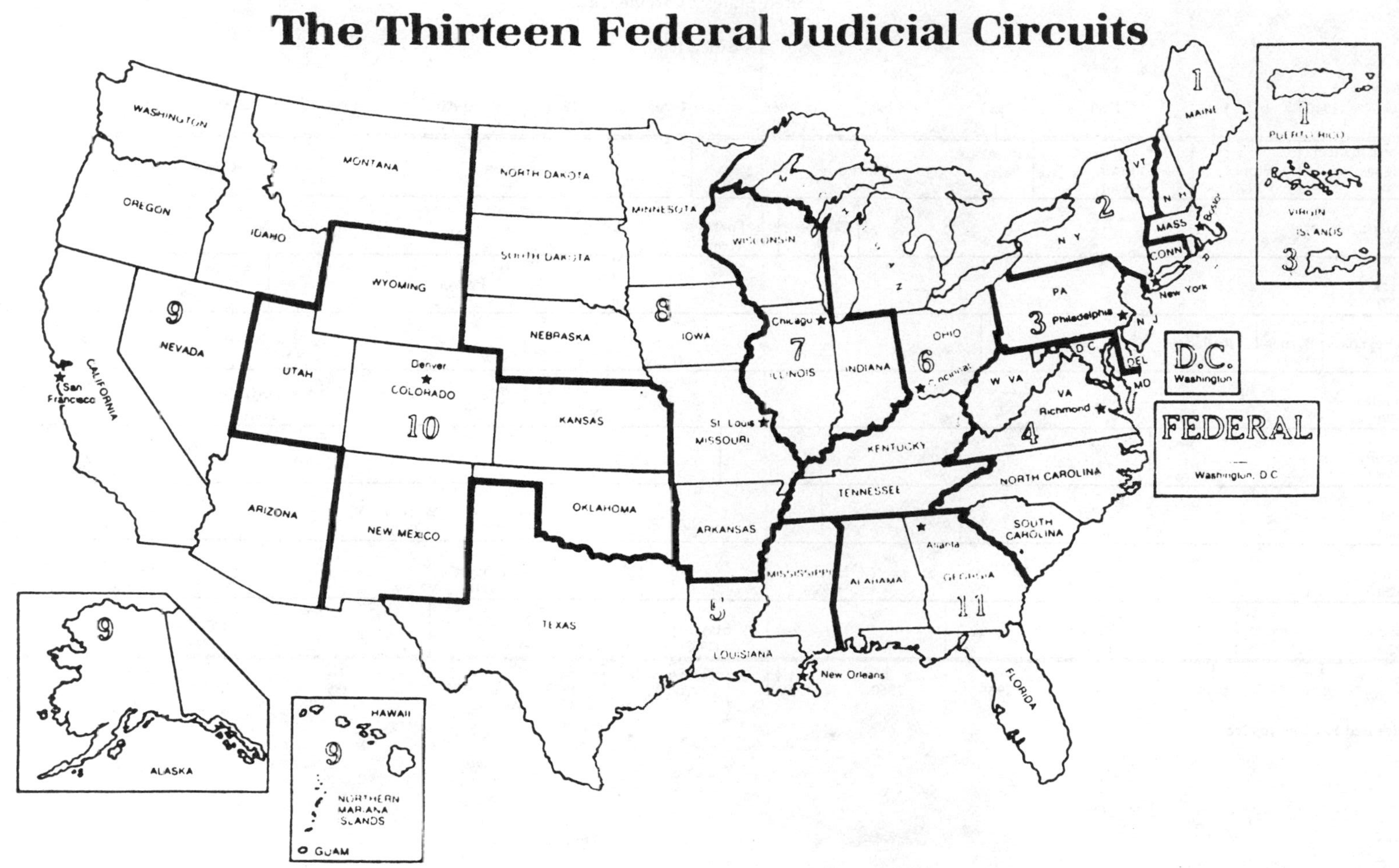
The Thirteen Federal Judicial Circuits
WASHINGTON
OREGON
IDAHO
MONTANA
NORTH DAKOTA
SOUTH DAKOTA
MINNESOTA
WYOMING
NEBRASKA
9
NEVADA
CALIFORNIA
San Francisco
UTAH
Denver
COLORADO
10
KANSAS
8
IOWA
WISCONSIN
Chicago
7
ILLINOIS
INDIANA
St Louis
MISSOURI
ARIZONA
NEW MEXICO
OKLAHOMA
ARKANSAS
TEXAS
5
LOUISIANA
New Orleans
MISSISSIPPI
ALABAMA
KENTUCKY
TENNESSEE
OHIO
6
Cincinnati
W VA
VA
Richmond
4
NORTH CAROLINA
SOUTH CAROLINA
Atlanta
GEORGIA
11
FLORIDA
PA
3
Philadelphia
D C
DEL
MD
N J
N Y
2
New York
CONN
MASS
Boston
VT
N H
MAINE
1
1
PUERTO RICO
VIRGIN ISLANDS
3
D.C.
Washington
FEDERAL
Washington, D.C.
9
ALASKA
HAWAII
9
NORTHERN MARIANA ISLANDS
GUAM

Chart I.

United States Supreme Court
Since 1940

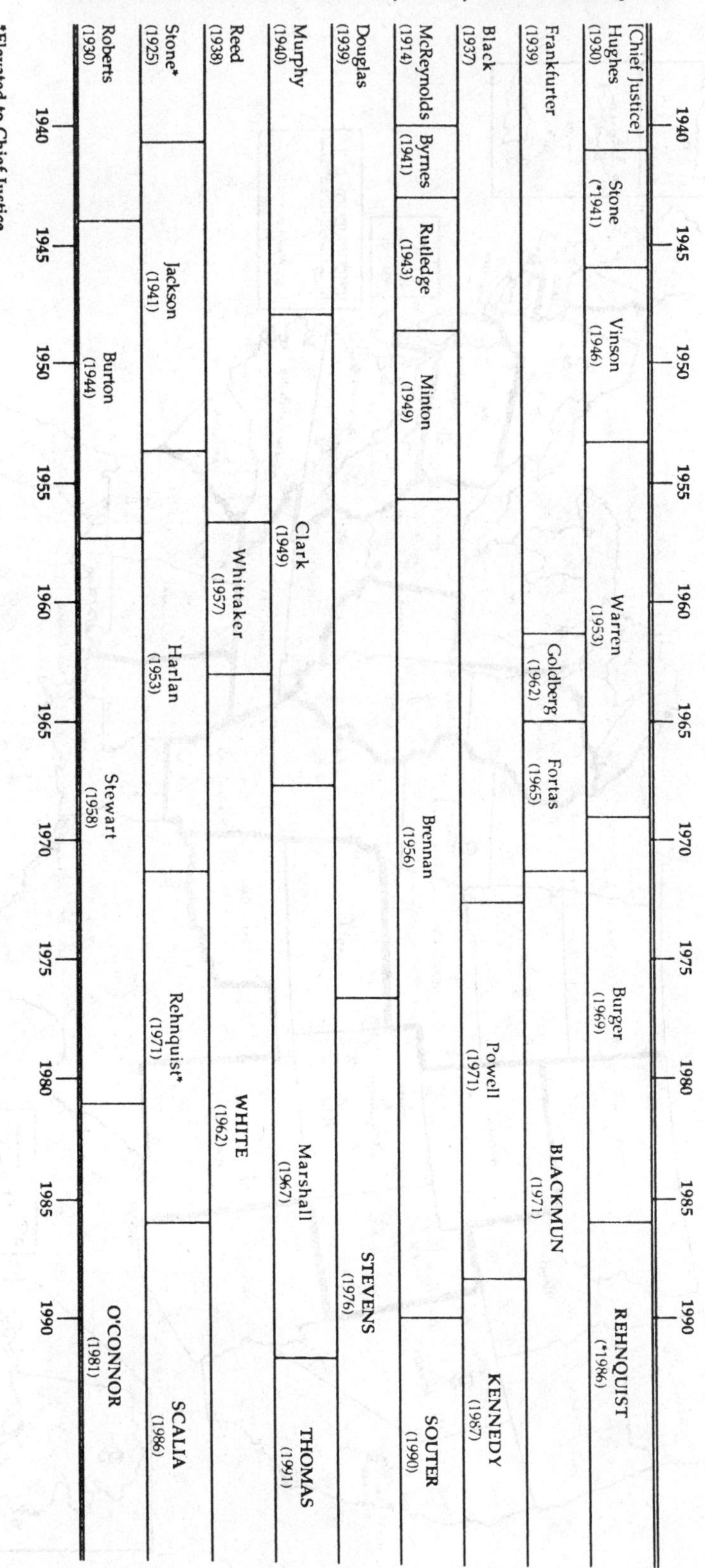

*Elevated to Chief Justice

Readings on How to Study Law — citations and excerpts

A. Publications on the Legal Process Itself
Meador, Daniel John, **American Courts**, West Publishing Company, St. Paul, MN (1991).
Mermin, Samuel, **Law and the Legal System: An Introduction**, 2nd Ed., Little, Brown and Company, Boston, MA (1982).

B. Publications on How One Should Study this Process:
Burton, Steven J., **An Introduction to Law and Legal Reasoning**, Little, Brown and Company, Boston, MA (1985).
LaRue, Lewis H., **A Student's Guide to the Study of the Law: An Introduction**, Matthew Bender & Co., New York, NY (1987).
Makdisi, Jon, **Introduction to the Study of the Law: Cases and Materials**, Anderson Publishing Co., Cincinnati, OH (1990).

C. Single Articles on Fundamentals:
Delaney, **How to Brief a Case: An Introduction to Jurisprudence**, Delaney Publications, (1983).
Llewellyn, Karl, **The Bramble Bush**, Oceana Publications, New York, NY (1951).

Stanley V. Kinyon, How to Study Law and Write Law Examinations
2nd Ed., West Publishing Company (1951)

The fundamental thing in reading cases is to know *what to look for*. Otherwise you may concentrate on the wrong thing or miss an important point.

Perhaps the best way to explain what to look for is to point out what you can normally expect to find in a case and what the judge normally puts or tries to put in his opinion.

1. The first thing you will usually find in a case is a brief statement of the kind of controversy involved. That is, whether it was a criminal prosecution, an action of tort for damages, an action for breach of contract, or to recover land, etc. This is usually accompanied by an explanation of how the case got to this particular court; whether it started there, or, if it is a matter on appeal (as it usually is), how and why it happened to get there, whether plaintiff or defendant appealed, and to just what action of the lower court the appealing party is objecting. For example: "This is an appeal by defendant from an adverse judgement," or "from an order of the lower court denying his motion for new trial," or "from an order of the lower court overruling his demurrer to the complaint," etc. These facts are frequently found in a

preliminary paragraph prepared by the clerk of the court and inserted before the judge's opinion. Nevertheless, since they tell you just how that particular court came to consider the controversy and just what it had to decide, they are extremely important and should not be overlooked or passed over lightly.

2. The next thing you will usually find is a statement of the facts of the controversy–who the parties were, what they did, what happened to them, who brought the action and what he wanted. Normally, the judge writing the opinion starts off with a complete statement of facts, but judges are not always careful to do this and you will frequently find the fact strewn throughout the opinion. Thus you can never be sure you know all about the controversy until you have read the whole opinion. Sometimes the statement of facts is made categorically on the basis of the court's or jury's *findings* of fact; sometimes it is made by stating what the plaintiff and defendant *alleged* in their pleadings; and sometimes it is in the form of a *resumé* of the *evidence* produced at trial. Wherever they may appear, however, and in whatever form they may be stated, every case contains some statement of the facts and circumstances, out of which the controversy arose.

3. Next comes a statement of the question or questions the court is called upon to decide –the various "issues" (either of law or fact) which must be settled before a decision on the controversy can be reached. Any of you who have done any debating understand "issues"– the breaking up of a general problem into specific sub-problems. Some judges are very careful to state the issue clearly; others will leave them to inference from the discussion, or else wander around from one thing to another and leave the precise questions they are deciding in doubt.

4. After the issues comes the argument on them – a discussion of the pros and cons. This is where logic comes into play. You'll recall that there are two main types of logical reasoning –inductive and deductive. Inductive reasoning involves the *formulation* of general propositions from a consideration of specific problems or observations; deductive reasoning involves the *application* of a general proposition already formulated to some specific situation or problem so that a conclusion can be drawn as to it. In each case the court, have these definite and specific issues or problems to decide, decides or purports to decide them by first concluding what the general rule or proposition of law is as to this type of issue, and then deducing the decision on that issue from the general rule. If there happens to be a statute or constitutional provision prescribing a general rule as to questions like those involved in the case, the judge has his major premise and will devote his argument to a consideration of its scope and applicability to the issues in the case. If there is no statute or other prescribed general rule, the judge will try by induction to derive one from the decisions and opinions in previous cases involving issues similar to those in the present case, or from general principles of fairness, policy and common sense, and then apply it to the issues at hand and deduce his conclusion.

5. Finally, after the argument on all the issues (and sometimes a good deal of irrelevant argument and discussion), the judge states the *general* conclusion to be drawn therefrom, and winds up the opinion with a statement of the court's decision. For example: "Judgment affirmed"; "Judgment reversed"; "Case remanded"; "New trial ordered"; etc.

It is to be remembered, of course, that legal opinions do not all follow the same order and are not all cut from the same pattern. They are written by many different judges, each of whom has his own style of writing and his own particular method of presenting a legal argument. Some opinions are not as easy to understand as others and it would be erroneous to assume in reading them that they are all perfect. Courts frequently disagree as to the principles that ought to be applied in certain types of controversy and occasionally the same court will change its view as to the law on a particular point. In reading these cases, you are not trying to find *the* ultimate and perfect rule, you are trying to learn by *inductive* reasoning from what various courts have actually decided in particular cases the rules and principles most frequently applied and most likely to be applied by them in future cases of that type.

Now, having in mind what you can expect to find in the cases, and also the fact that they are not necessarily perfect and seldom embody an unchanging principle or universal truth, you are in a position to read them intelligently. Its not a bad idea, however, to adopt a systematic method of reading them. The following has proved effective, and you might try it as a starter.

First, get a clear picture of the controversy involved. Get all the facts and issues straight. Consider the following:
What kind of an action it is.
Who the parties were,
What they did and what happened to them,
Who brought the action,
What s/he wanted,
What the defense was,
What happened in the lower court (if it's a case on appeal),
How the case got to this court,
Just what this court had to decide.

At this point stop for a moment. Look at the problem, first from the plaintiff's point of view, then from the defendant's. Ask yourself how *you* would decide it, what *you* think the decision ought to be. Compare this case with others you have studied on the same topic. What result do *they* indicate ought to be reached here? By doing this you put yourself in a better position to read the court's argument critically, and spot any fallacies in it. We are all somewhat prone to accept what we read in print as the Gospel, and this little device of considering the problem in your own mind *before* reading the court's argument is a rather effective means of keeping a critical attitude.

Now read the argument and the court's conclusions. Consider the various rules and propositions advanced on each issue and the reasons given for adopting them. See whether the conclusions drawn follow logically from the rules. Then ask yourself whether you agree with the court, and if not, why not. Consider also how the result in this case lines up with other similar cases you have studied.

In thus analysing the court's argument and conclusions it is important to distinguish carefully between the rules and propositions of law actually relied upon by the court in deciding the issues involved in the case (these are called "holdings") and other legal propositions and discussions which you may find in the opinion but which are not relevant nor applicable to the issues before the court (these are called "dicta"). When the case was before the court, counsel for the opposing parties probably availed themselves of the opportunity to prepare fully and present to the court their arguments pro and con upon the issues involved in it, and the court thus had the opportunity to consider all aspects of each issue, choose the better result and "hold" with that view. The *dicta*, however, not being relevant to the issues before the court, was probably not argued by counsel nor thoroughly considered by the court. It was not necessary to the decision of the case and the court may have stated it casually without considring all aspects of the problem. Courts in each jurisdiction regard their own prior "holdings" as creating *binding precedents* which they feel obliged to follow in later cases involving the same issues. This is called the doctrine of *stare decisis* and makes for stability and predictability in the law. *Dicta,* on the other hand, being casual and not a matter of *actual decision,* is not regarded as establishing law which will be binding on the court in a subsequent case. Thus, the former case containing the *dictum* is not a controlling "authority" on the question although it may be followed in later decisions.

You may find it very helpful, in picking out the important matters in the cases and in weeding out the irrelevant, to keep a pen or pencil handy and *underline,* all statements of pertinent facts, issues, rules, etc. as you read. (Do this only in your own casebooks, however. Do not deface books in the library or elsewhere which are for common use!!!)

Finally, study carefully the notes the author has appended to the case. They contain a good deal of valuable information about other similar cases and frequently suggest problems and criticisms which might not occur to you. There is an increasing tendency among the authors of casebooks to put in more collateral matter along with the cases in order to clarify their significance. This matter is there for your benefit; take advantage of it.

If you adopt some such method as the above in reading your cases and acquire the habit of following it, you are much more likely to get an accurate understanding of each case and are much less apt to overlook some important detail. Furthermore, if you get out of each case all the things mentioned above you can feel reasonably well prepared for class discussion or lecture.

CLASSWORK-TAKING NOTES

Class procedure under the case system varies considerably, depending upon the particular instructor. In some courses you'll find nearly all the time devoted to recitations and detailed discussion of the cases by the students. In others the instructor will spend most of the time lecturing. In many there will be some student recitation and discussion coupled with short lectures or summaries by the instructor. No matter what the method, however, the objective is the same, namely, to supplement and integrate your case reading and individual study. Class work affords you the opportunity to critically analyse and compare the cases you have read so as to determine their value as precedents more accurately. It furnishes information about other cases. In short, it helps you tie up the individual cases, fill in the gaps and get a better understanding of the rules of law and the situations in which they are applicable.

As to your work in class, it's absolutely essential that you take notes, unless you have a memory that never fades. The courses are relatively long, you are studying a number of them at the same time, and it's almost impossible to review adequately for your law school and bar exams unless you have a good set of notes in each course. Note-taking, of course, is not standardized. It's largely an individual problem, and each of you will have to work out the details of your own system. The object is to take the sort of notes that will be most helpful to *you,* and although there are no iron-clad rules, the following suggestions should be helpful.

In the first place, *don't try to write down everything that is said in class*! Someone defined a lecture as being "a process by which the lecturer's notes become the student's notes without going through the minds of either", and that is exactly what it is when you simply write down everything you hear. Pick out the important things – the rules, propositions, problems and explanations that you really want to remember – and let the rest go! For example: when you're starting a new Chapter or sub-division in your casebook, write the title or the sub-title in your notebook. If the instructor makes any general statements about the Chapter or sub-division, write a brief summary of them in your own words. That orients you for the things to come. When you come to a discussion of an assigned case, write down its name and *then stopand listen to what is being said about it.* Presumably you've read and briefed it, so compare what you hear with your own impressions and understanding of the case. Think about the questions that are asked and the answers given to them. If you disagree with what is said, or don't understand it, speak up as soon as there is an opportunity. When a hypothetical problem is suggested take it down if you can, but don't lose the thread of the argument. If the instructor makes some statement or explanation during the discussion of a case that seems to you to be important and worth remembering, write it down. Weigh his statements carefully and separate the grain from the chaff. Finally, when the discussion has proceeded to a point where a conclusion has been reached or a rule developed, get it clearly in mind and then write a concise, accurate statement of it in your own words together with any explanation of it you think is necessary. *Remember that the reasons for the rules are as important as the rules themselves.* Don't be too sketchy, however. Write complete sentences so that when you come to read your notes later on they'll be clear and understandable. Take down all citations to other cases, texts and law review material, and if the instructor is obviously *dictating* some quotation or statement try to copy it. If he thinks it's important enought to dictate, it's important enough to take down.

When you go from one problem to the next, indicate the transition if possible. Try to make your notes a condensed text, running along smoothly and weaving the cases together without puzzling gaps or a lot of irrelevant and distracting junk. Your whole objective in taking notes is to get a permanent, understandable and accurate record of the *important* things said in class about the cases and the rules and principles of law they exemplify. To accomplish this you have to concentrate all of the time and follow everything closely.

Nevertheless, you'll find, if you acquire the habit of doing it, that it pays big dividends and saves you hours of work later on trying to puzzle out something you missed when you were looking out the window.

On Briefing Cases

As a teacher, you may decide to have your students work at briefing cases during the first few weeks of class (although at least one of us never wrote a case brief in law school and shrinks from advising his students to prepare such formal annotations). Briefing cases provides students practice at close reading, breaking opinions into components, and clarifying ideas as learn legal analysis. It will also ensure more complete class participation. If nothing else, briefing cases teaches students one of many ways to analyze opinions.

Traditionally, briefs contain six sections:

1. (F) facts: the main legal facts which surround the cause of action.
2. (P) procedural history: whather the opinion is a trial court or appellate opinion and what happened prior.
3. (I) issue: the legal question presented by the case
4. (H) holding: the court's statement of the rule of law that controls the facts of the case
5. (J) judgment: the final one or two-word decision of the court, ie. for the plaintiff, etc.
6. (R) reasoning: the court's reaons for deciding the way it did.

The greatest value of briefing may be as practice in analyzing opinions.

For a more extended discussion of this process, see Delaney, **How to Brief a Case: An Introduction to Jurisprudence**, Delaney Publications, (1983).

• Glossary of Terms — as adapted from Black's Law Dictionary (West Publishing, 1991)

abate: to lessen, do away with, or nullify as in the case of pollution; to quash, beat down, or destroy, as in the case of a nuisance or an objectionable wit.

adjudication: the legal process of resolving a dispute; formal pronouncement of a judgment; the detemination of the issues in an action according to which judgment is rendered.

adversary system: legal system where two parties brought together by a dispute present their opposing cases to a judge or jury who deliberates over and decides the case.

affirm: to uphold, ratify, approve, establish, reassert; to state a matter of fact affirmatively.

affirmative defense: a response to a plaintiff's claim which attacks the plaintiff's legal right to bring an action, as opposed to attacking the truth of the claim; all affirmative defenses must be raised in the defendant's answer.

alternative dispute resolution: procedures for settling disputes by means other than litigation; e.g., by arbitration, mediation, negotiation.

answer: the response of a defendant to a plaintiff's complaint, denying in part or in whole the allegation made by the plaintiff; must include any affirmative defenses the defendant wishes to use.

appeal: resort to a superior court (i.e. appellate) to review the decision of an inferior court (i.e. trial) or administrative agency; generally regarded as a continuation of the original suit rather than as the inception.

appellant: party who appeals a decision by an inferior court to a superior court.

appellate court: court having a jurisdiction of appeal and review of decisions of lower courts; a court to which causes are removable by appeal, certiorari, error or report.

appellee: party against whom an appeal is brought, sometimes called a respondent; one who wins a lower decision.

battle of experts: each party in a suit brings her own expert witnesses to give testimony, each with a different rendition of scientific "fact."

breach of duty: action or failure to act that breaks or violates a duty.

burden of proof: the necessity or duty of affirmatively proving a fact or facts in dispute on an issue raised between parties, usually resting on one party or the other as a duty to prove the facts which support her claim.

"but for" test: negligence test which finds negligence as a causal factor if the incident had not happened "but for" the event in question; test used in determining tort liability by applying the causative criterion as to whether the plaintiff would not have suffered the wrong "but for" the action of the defendant.

causation: that which led directly or indirectly to the injury complained of in the suit.

cause of action: set of facts surrounding the dispute which allow a party to maintain a claim in court to seek remedy.

certiorari: process by which superior courts, typically the Supreme Court, grants review of a lower court's decision; latin for "to be informed of."

circuit: judicial divisions within the United States (there are 13) or a state.

civil action: action brought to enforce, redress, or protect a private right; an ordinary action as opposed to a criminal action.

civil procedure: body of law focusing on the methods, procedures, and practices of civil litigation.

claim: cause of action; demand for remedy, money, or property as of right.

class action: action brought by one or more plaintiffs on behalf of a class of persons; many plaintiffs bringing one suit.

common law: body of law that derives its authority from judgements and decrees of the courts, not from legislative enactment.

complaint: plaintiff's initial pleading or claim which sets out the jurisdiction of the court, the elements of the case, and the remedy requested.

concur: agree with a decision, but not necessarily for the same reasons.

cost internalization: forcing all of the costs of a process to be paid for by the producer or consumer; i,e., forcing a producer of air pollution to pay for all units of pollution that would otherwise be emitted into the commons at a cost to society in general.

criminal action: action, suit, or cause instituted to punish an infraction of the criminal laws.

damages: monitary compensation for injuries or pollution; these can be compensatory (based on actual loss) or punitive (as a punishment).

defendant: party against whom a suit is brought; the party accused of the wrongdoing.

deference: one decisionmaker's (usually a court's) refusal to overturn or uphold a decision by another decisionmaker because the other's authority is superior.

dicta: also obiter dicta; statements made by a court in an opinion which are not directly necessary to deciding the case before the court.

directed verdict: when the party with the burden of proof has failed to present a prima facie case for the jury, a judge may enter a directed verdict in favor of the other party because the case can only be decided that one way.

discovery: opportunity during a suit for each party to ask questions (interrogatories) of the other party or to request information from the other party in the form of internal documents, records, etc.

discretion: power granted by statute or equity to a court, legislature, or executive; not limited by objective standards; invites deference.

dismiss: send away, discharge, discontinue, dispose of; to dismiss an action or suit without further consideration.

dissent: disagree with a court's majority decision.

duty: legal or moral obligation to which the law gives effect.

effluent: liquid waste discharged into a body of water.

enjoin: require, command, postively direct; forbid; restrain by injunction; to order; to prohibit an activity or force an action.

equity: principle of deciding cases based on fairness rather than the strict guidelines of the common law.

estoppel: keeping a party from arguing out of a set of restrictions when that same party relied on those restrictions earlier in the proceedings; a bar which precludes a person from denying or asserting anything to the contrary of that which has, in contemplation of law, been established as the truth, either by the acts of judicial or legislative officers or by his own deed or representations, express or implied.

evidence: proof presented at a trial in the form of witnesses, records, documents, exhibits, concrete objects, etc., for the purpose of making a case.

externalities: private costs of manufacturing or consuming that are forced onto society as a whole.

foreseeability: reasonable anticipation that harm or injury is likely to result from an act or ommision.

grantee: person to whom a grant is made; the party in a deed to whom the conveyance is made.

grantor: person who makes a grant; the party to a deed who makes a conveyance.

holding: main legal principle to be taken/understood from an opinion.

indivisible harm: harm which has many sources, and which can not be separated into individual causations.

injunction: noun form of the verb enjoin; an order prohibiting or forcing an action.

intentional tort: injury cause of action where the defendant's intent to commit a causal action is at issue.

joint and several liability: responsible together and individually; the person who has been wronged can sue and recover from one or both of the parties.

judgment: final decision of a court resolving a dispute and detrmining the rights and obligations of the parties.

jurisdiction: power of a court to hear an action; the realm, geographical or topical, over which a court has power or authority to hear a case.

liability: obligation one is bound in law or justice to perform.

mediation: private, informal dispute resolution in which a neutral third person, the mediator, helps disputing parties to reach an agreement; the mediator has no power to enforce the decision on the parties.

motion: requests made during a suit; an application made to a court or a judge for purposes of obtaining a rule or order directing some act to be done in favor of the applicant.

motion for j.n.o.v.: motion that judgment be entered in accordance with the movant's earlier motion for a directed verdit and notwithstanding the contrary verdict actually returned by the jury.

motion for summary judgment: motion made after one party has set out her case so completely that there can be no other decision as a matter of law but to decide in her favor; that judgement be summarily entered for one party without futher deliberation.

motion to dismiss: motion to dismiss a case from trial because one of the parties has failed to set out the elements substantively or procedurally necessary to maintain a cause of action in court.

multiple tortfeasors: plural defendants in a tort action; persons who commit a tort.

negligence: breach of a duty owed by one party to another resulting in liability.

nuisance: anything that works hurt, inconvenience, or damage to another; anything done by one which annoys or disturbs another in the free use, possession or enjoyment of her property, or which renders its ordinary use or occupation uncomfortable.

obiter dicta: see dicta.

opinion: statement by a judge or a court of the decision reached in a suit, explaining the applicable law and the reasons for the decision.

party: person who is a plaintiff or a defendant.

plaintiff: party bringing suit against the defendant; the person who seeks relief for a wrong against her.

pleading: formal statement by a party to an action or proceeding of the operative facts, as distinguished from evidentiary facts, which constitute the respective claim or defense.

precedent: case or decision of a court with such similar facts to the case before the court that it supports a similar finding.

prima facie case: putting out the elements of the case to the degree that a decision can be made in your favor.

private nuisance: nuisance which threatens injury to one or a few persons.

procedural/substantive: process of the law as opposed to the substanceof the law; how-enforced versus what-enforced or why-enforced.

proximate cause: primary or moving cause of an injury; that which, in natural and continuous sequence, unbroken by an efficient intervening cause, produces the injury and without which the injury would not have happened.

public nuisance: violation of a public right either by a dirtect encroachment upon a public right or property or by doing some act which tends to a common injury, or by omitting to do some act which the common good requires, and which it is the duty of a person to do, which results in injury ot the public.

public trust: idea that certain common properties, such as rivers, the seashore and the air are held by the government in trusteeship for the free and unimpeded use of the general public.

question of fact: question for the jury in a trial by jury or for the court in a trial by jury or for the court in a trial to the court. A question of the truth to be decided upon conflicting evidence.

question of law: question for the court; a question arising in a cse in court as to the terms of the law by which the case is to be adjudicated.

rebut: in pleading and evidence, to defeat, refute, or take away the effect of something.

relief: assistance, redress, or benefit which a complainant seeks from a court, particularly in equity.

remand: when an appellate case is sent back to the lower court for another review, often with special instructions.

remedy: means by which a right is enforced or the violation of a right is prevented, redressed, or compensated.

remittitur: reducing of a verdict because of the excessiveness of the award; often required of a plaintiff as a condition of affirmance of the judgment entered upon the verdict.

res judicata: rule that a final judgement rendered by a court on the merits is conclusive as to the rights of the parties and constitutes an absolute bar to a subsequent action involving the same claim, demand or cause of action.

reverse: overthrow, vacate, set aside, repeal, revoke; as to reverse a judgment, sentence or decree of a lower court.

servitude: term of the civil law for easement; a right of one person to use another person's land via a right of ownership for a purpose not at odds with the first owner's use..

sovereign immunity: judicial doctrine which precludes bringing suit against the government without its consent; founded on the principle that "the King can do no wrong;" federal government generally waives its tort immunity in the Federal Tort Claims Act, 28 U.S.C.A. § 1346(b), 2674.

stare decisis: adhere to the precedents, and not to unsettle things which are established.

statute of limitations: statutory limitation on amount of time which may pass before a claim by a plaintiff expires and not to be heard; "speak now or forever hold your peace."

strict liability: concept of no-fault liability in tort law where a party is liable for all injuries resulting from the mechanism under the defendant's control.

summary judgment: decision by the court that given one party's evidence, no reasonable person could decide for the other party and the action can therefore be decided in favor of the party that has so convincingly proven its case; a motion made by one party that there is no genuine issue of material fact and therefore she is entitled to judgment as a matter of law.

tort: injury; that discipline of law that deals with injuries or harms done to people; a private or civil wrong or injury, other than breach of contract, for which the court will provide a remedy in the form of an action for damages.

trespass: tort cause of action for the physical invasion of a party's property.

trial court: trial court is the lowest court where a claim will first be heard.

witness: one who testifies to what she has seen, heard, or otherwise observed; person whose declaration under oath is received for evidence.

writ: order issued by a court requiring the performance of a specified act, or giving authority to have it done.

• THE CONSTITUTION OF THE UNITED STATES OF AMERICA

We the People of the United States, in order to form a more perfect Union, establish Justice, insure domestic Tranquillity, provide for the common defense, promote the general Welfare, and secure the Blessings of Liberty to ourselves and our Posterity, do ordain and establish this Constitution for the United States of America.

ARTICLE I

Section 1. All legislative Powers herein granted shall be vested in a Congress of the United States, which shall consist of a Senate and House of Representatives.

Section 2. [1] The House of Representatives shall be composed of Members chosen every second Year by the People of the several States, and the Electors in each State shall have the Qualifications requisite for Electors of the most numerous Branch of the State Legislature.

[2] No person shall be a Representative who shall not have attained to the Age of twenty five Years, and have been seven Years a Citizen of the United States, and who shall not, when elected, be an Inhabitant of that State in which he shall be chosen.

[3] Representatives and direct Taxes shall be apportioned among the several States which may be included within this Union, according to their respective Numbers, which shall be determined by adding to the Whole Number of free Persons, including those bound to Service for a Term of Years, and excluding Indians not taxed, three fifths of all other Persons. The actual Enumeration shall be made within three Years after the first Meeting of the Congress of the United States, and within every subsequent Term of ten years, in such Manner as they shall by Law direct. The Number of Representatives shall not exceed one for every thirty Thousand, but each State shall have at Least one Representative; and until such enumeration shall be made, the State of New Hampshire shall be entitled to chose three, Massachusetts eight, Rhode Island and Providence Plantations one, Connecticut five, New York six, New Jersey four, Pennsylvania eight, Delaware one, Maryland six, Virginia ten, North Carolina five, South Carolina five, and Georgia three.

[4] When vacancies happen in the Representation from any State, the Executive Authority thereof shall issue Writs of Election to fill such Vacancies.

[5] The House of Representatives shall choose their Speaker and other Officers; and shall have the sole Power of Impeachment.

Section 3. [1] The Senate of the United States shall be composed of two Senators from each State, chosen by the Legislature thereof, for six Years; and each Senator shall have one Vote.

[2] Immediately after they shall be assembled in Consequence of the first Election, they shall be divided as equally as may be into three Classes. The Seats of the Senators of the first Class shall be vacated at the Expiration of the second Year, of the second Class at the Expiration of the fourth Year, and of the third Class at the Expiration of the sixth Year, so that one third may be chosen every second Year; and if Vacancies happen by Resignation, or otherwise, during the Recess of the Legislature of any State, the Executive thereof may make temporary Appointments until the next Meeting of the Legislature, which shall then fill such Vacancies.

[3] No Person shall be a Senator who shall not have attained to the Age of thirty Years, and been nine Years a Citizen of the United States, and who shall not, when elected, be an Inhabitant of that State for which he shall be chosen.

[4] The Vice President of the United States shall be President of the Senate, but shall have no Vote, unless they be equally divided.

[5] The Senate shall chose their other Officers, and also a President pro tempore, in the Absence of the Vice President, or when he shall exercise the Office of President of the United States.

[6] The Senate shall have the sole Power to try all Impeachments. When siting for that Purpose, they shall be on Oath or Affirmation. When the President of the United States is tried, the Chief Justice shall preside: And no Person shall be convicted without the Concurrence of two thirds of the Members present.

[7] Judgment in Cases of Impeachment shall not extend further than to removal from Office, and disqualification to hold and enjoy any Office of honor, Trust, or Profit under the United States: but the Party convicted shall nevertheless be liable and subject to Indictment, Trial, Judgment, and Punishment, according to Law.

Section 4. [1] The Times, Places and Manner of holding Elections for Senators and Representatives, shall be prescribed in each State by the Legislature thereof; but the Congress may at any time by Law make or alter such Regulations, except as to the Places of choosing Senators.

[2] The Congress shall assemble at least once in every Year, and such Meeting shall be on the first Monday in December, unless they shall by Law appoint a different Day.

Section 5. [1] Each House shall be the Judge of the Elections, Returns, and Qualifications of its own Members, and a Majority of each shall constitute a Quorum to do Business; but a smaller Number may adjourn from day to day, and may be authorized to compel the Attendance of absent Members, in such Manner, and under such Penalties as each House may provide.

[2] Each House may determine the Rules of its Proceedings, punish its Members for disorderly Behavior, and, with the Concurrence of two thirds, expel a Member.

[3] Each House shall keep a Journal of its Proceedings, and from time to time publish the same, excepting such Parts as may in their Judgment require Secrecy; and the Yeas and Nays of the Members of either House on any question shall, at the Desire of one fifth of those Present, be

entered on the Journal.

[4] Neither House, during the Session of Congress, shall, without the Consent of the other, adjourn for more than three days, nor to any other Place than that in which the two Houses shall be sitting.

Section 6. [1] The Senators and Representatives shall receive a Compensation for their Services, to be ascertained by Law, and paid out of the Treasury of the United States. They shall in all Cases, except Treason, Felony and Breach of the Peach, be privileged from Arrest during their Attendance at the Session of their Respective Houses, and in going to and returning from the same; and for any Speech or Debate in either House, they shall not be questioned in any other Place.

[2] No Senator or Representative shall, during the Time for which he was elected, be appointed to any civil Office under the Authority of the United States, which shall have been created, or the Emoluments whereof shall have been increased during such time; and no Person holding any Office under the United States, shall be a Member of either House during his Continuance in Office.

Section 7. [1] All Bills for raising Revenue shall originate in the House of Representatives; but the Senate may propose or concur with Amendments as on other Bills.

[2] Every Bill which shall have passed the House of Representatives and the Senate, shall, before it become a Law, be presented to the President of the United States; If he approves he shall sign it, but if not he shall return it, with his Objections to that House in which it shall have originated, who shall enter the Objections at large on their Journal, and proceed to reconsider it. If after such Reconsideration two thirds of that House shall agree to pass the Bill, it shall be sent together with the Objections, to the other House, by which it shall likewise be reconsidered, and if approved by two thirds of that House, it shall become a Law. But in all such Cases the Votes of both Houses shall be determined by Yeas and Nays, and the Names of the Persons voting for and against the Bill shall be entered on the Journal of each House respectively. If any Bill shall not be returned by the President within ten Days (Sundays excepted)after it shall have been presented to him, the Same shall be a Law, in like Manner as if he had signed it, to him, the Same shall be a Law, in like Manner as if he had signed it, unless the Congress by their Adjournment prevent its Return in which Case it shall not be a Law.

[3] Every Order, Resolution, or Vote, to Which the Concurrence of the Senate and House of Representatives may be necessary (except on a question of Adjournment) shall be presented to the President of the United Stated; and before the Same shall take Effect, shall be approved by him, or being disapproved by him, shall be re-passed by two thirds of the Senate and House of Representatives, according the to the Rules and Limitations prescribed in the Case of a Bill.

Section 8. [1] The Congress shall have Power To lay and collect Taxes, Duties, Imposts and Excises, to pay the Debts and provide for the common Defense and general Welfare of the United States; but all Duties, Imposts and Excises shall be uniform throughout the United States;

[2] To borrow Money on the credit of the United States;

[3] To regulate Commerce with foreign Nations, and among the several States, and with the Indian Tribes;

[4] To establish an uniform Rule of Naturalization, and uniform Laws on the subject of Bankruptcies throughout the United States;

[5] To coin Money, regulate the Value thereof, and of foreign Coin, and fix the Standard of Weights and Measures;

[6] To provide for the Punishment of counterfeiting the Securities and current Coins of the United States;

[7] To Establish Post Offices and Post Roads;

[8] To promote the Progress of Science and useful Arts, by securing for limited Times to Authors and Inventors the exclusive Right to their respective Writings and Discoveries;

[9] To constitute Tribunals inferior to the Supreme Court;

[10] To define and punish Piracies and Felonies committed on the high Seas, and Offenses against the Law of Nations;

[11] To declare War, grant Letters of Marque and Reprisal, and make Rules concerning Captures on Land and Water;

[12] To raise and support Armies, but no Appropriation of Money to that Use shall be for a longer Term than two Years;

[13] To provide and maintain a Navy;

[14] To make Rules for the Government and Regulation of the land and naval Forces.

[15] To provide for calling forth the Militia to execute the Laws of the Union, suppress Insurrections and repeal Invasions;

[16] To provide for organizing, arming, and discipling, the Militia, and for governing such Part of them as may be employed in the Service of the United States, reserving to the States respectively, the Appointment of the Officers, and the Authority of training the Militia according to the discipline prescribed by Congress;

[17] To exercise exclusive Legislation in all Cases whatsoever, over such District (not exceeding ten Miles square as may, by Cession of particular States, and the Acceptance of Congress, become the Seat of the Government of the United States, and to Exercise like Authority over all Places purchased by the Consent of the Legislature of the State in which the Same shall be, for the Erection of Forts, Magazines, Arsenals, dock-yards, and other needful Buildings—And

[18] To make all Laws which shall be necessary and proper for carrying into Execution the foregoing Powers, and all other Powers vested by this Constitution in the Government of the

United States, or in any Department or Officer thereof.

Section 9. [1] The Migration or Importation of Such Persons as any of the States now existing shall think proper to admit, shall not be prohibited by the Congress prior to the Year one thousand eight hundred and eight, but a Tax or duty may be imposed on such Importation, not exceeding ten dollars for each Person.

[2] The Privilege of the Writ of Habeas Corpus shall not be suspended, unless when in Cases of Rebellion or Invasion the public Safety may require it.

[3] No Bill of Attainder or ex post facto Law shall be passed.

[4] No Capitation, or other direct, Tax shall be laid, unless in Proportion to the Census or Enumeration herein before directed to be taken.

[5] No Tax or Duty shall be laid on Articles exported from any State.

[6] No Preference shall be given by any Regulation of Commerce or Revenue to the Ports of one State over those of another: nor shall Vessels bound to, or from, one State be obliged to enter, clear, or pay Duties in another.

[7] No Money shall be drawn from the Treasury, but in Consequence of Appropriations made by Law; and a regular Statement and Account of the Receipts and Expenditures of all public Money shall be published from time to time.

[8] No Title of Nobility shall be granted by the United States: And no Person holding any Office of Profit or Trust under them, shall, without the Consent of the Congress, accept of any present, Emolument, Office, or Title, of any kind whatever, from any King, Prince, or foreign State.

Section 10. [1] No state shall enter into any Treaty, Alliance, or Confederation; grant Letters of Marque and Reprisal; coin Money; emit Bills of Credit; make any thing but gold and silver Coin a Tender in payment of Debts; pass any Bill of Attainder, ex post facto Law, or Law impairing the Obligation of Contracts, or grant any Title of Nobility.

[2] No State shall, without the Consent of the Congress, lay any Imposts or Duties on Imports or Exports, except what may be absolutely necessary for executing its inspection Laws: and the net Produce of all Duties and Imposts, laid by any State on Imports or Exports, shall be for the Use of the Treasury of the United States; and all such Laws shall be subject to the Revision and Control of the Congress.

[3] No State shall, without the Consent of Congress, lay any Duty of Tonnage, keep Troops, or Ships of War in time of Peace, enter into any Agreement or Compact with another State, or with a foreign Power, or engage in War, unless actually invaded, or in such imminent Danger as will not admit of delay.

ARTICLE II

Section 1. [1] The executive Power shall be vested in a President of the United States of

America. He shall hold his Office during the Term of four Years, and, together with the Vice President, chosen for the same Term, be elected, as follows:

[2] Each State shall appoint, in such Manner as the Legislature thereof may direct, a Number of Electors, equal to the whole Number of Senators and Representatives to which the State may be entitled in the Congress; but no Senator or Representative, or Person holding an Office of Trust or Profit under the United States, shall be appointed an Elector.

[3] The Electors shall meet in their respective States, and vote by Ballot for two Persons, of whom one at least shall not be an Inhabitant of the same State with themselves. And they shall make a List of all the Persons voted for, and of the Number of Votes for each; which List they shall sign and certify, and transmit sealed to the Seat of the Government of the United States, directed to the President of the Senate. The President of the Senate shall, in the Presence of the Senate and House of Representatives, open all the Certificates, and the Votes shall then be counted. The Person having the greatest Number of Votes shall be the President, if such Number be a Majority of the whole Number of Electors appointed; and if there be more than one who have such Majority, and have an equal Number of Votes, then the House of Representatives shall immediately chose by Ballot one of them for President; and if no Person have a Majority, then from the five highest on the List the said House shall in like Manner chose the President. But in choosing the President, the Votes shall be taken by States, the Representation from each State having one Vote; A quorum for this Purpose shall consist of a Member or Members from two thirds of the States, and a Majority of all the States shall be necessary to a Choice. In every Case, after the Choice of the President, the Person having the greater Number of Votes of the Electors shall be the Vice President. But if there should remain two or more who have equal Votes, the Senate shall chose from them by Ballot the Vice President.

[4] The Congress may determine the Time of choosing the Electors, and the Day on which they shall give their Votes; which Day shall be the same throughout the United States.

[5] No person except a natural born Citizen, or a Citizen of the United States, at the time of the Adoption of this Constitution, shall be eligible to the Office of President; neither shall any Person be eligible to that Office who shall not have attained to the Age of thirty five Years, and been fourteen Years a Resident within the Untied States.

[6] In case of the removal of the President from Office, or of his Death, Resignation or Inability to discharge the Powers and Duties of the same Office, the Same shall devolve on the Vice President, and the Congress may by Law provide for the Case of Removal, Death, Resignation or Inability both of the President and Vice President, declaring what Officer shall then act as President, and such Officer shall act accordingly, until the Disability be removed, or a President shall be elected.

[7] The President shall, at stated Times, receive for his Services, a Compensation, which shall neither be increased nor diminished during the Period for which he shall have been elected, and he shall not receive within that Period any other Emolument from the United States, or any of them.

[8] Before he enter on the Execution of his Office, he shall take the following Oath or Affirmation: "I do solemnly swear (or affirm) that I will faithfully execute the Office of

President of the United States, and will to the bet of my Ability, preserve, protect and defend the Constitution of the United States."

Section 2. [1] The President shall be Commander in Chief of the Army and Navy of the United States, and of the militia of the several States, when called into the actual Service of the United States; he may require the Opinion, in writing, of the principal Officer in each of the executive Departments, upon any Subject relating to the Duties of their respective Offices, and he shall have Power to grant Reprieves and pardons for Offenses against the United States, except in Cases of Impeachment.

[2] He shall have Power, by and with the Advice and Consent of the Senate, to make Treaties, provided two thirds of the Senators present concur; and he shall nominate, and by and with the Advice and Consent of the Senate, shall appoint Ambassadors, other public Ministers and Consuls, Judges of the Supreme Court, and all other Officers of the United States, whose Appointments are not herein otherwise provided for, and which shall be established by Law; but the Congress may by Law vest the Appointment of such inferior Officers, as they think proper, in the President alone, in the Courts of Law, or in the Heads of Departments.

[3] The President shall have power to fill up all Vacancies that may happen during the Recess of the Senate, by granting Commissions which shall expire at the End of their next Session.

Section 3. He shall from time to time give to the Congress Information of the State of the Union, and recommend to their Consideration such Measures as he shall judge necessary and expedient; he may, on extraordinary Occasions, convene both Houses, or either of them, and in Case of Disagreement between them, with Respect to the Time of Adjournment, he may adjourn them to such Time as he shall think proper; he shall receive Ambassadors and other public Ministers; he shall take Care that the Laws be faithfully executed, and shall Commission all the Officers of the United States.

Section 4. The President, Vice President and all civil Officers of the United States, shall be removed from Office on Impeachment for, and Conviction of, Treason, Bribery, or other high Crimes and Misdemeanors.

ARTICLE III

Section 1. The judicial Power of the United States, shall be vested in one Supreme Court, and in such inferior Courts as the Congress may from time to time ordain and establish. The Judges, both of the supreme and inferior Courts, shall hold their Offices during good Behavior, and shall, at stated Times, receive for their Services a Compensation, which shall not be diminished during their Continuance in Office.

Section 2. [1] The judicial Power shall extend to all Cases, in Law and Equity, arising under this Constitution, the Laws of the United States, and Treaties made, or which shall be made, under their Authority;—to all Cases affecting Ambassadors, other public Ministers and Consuls;—to all Cases of admiralty and maritime Jurisdiction;—to Controversies to which the Unites States shall be a Party;—to Controversies between two or more States;—between a State and Citizens of another State;—between Citizens of different States;—between Citizens of the same State claiming Lands under the Grants of different States, and between a State, or the Citizens thereof, and foreign States, Citizens or Subjects.

[2] In all Cases affecting Ambassadors, other public Ministers and Consuls, and those in which a State shall be a Party, the Supreme Court shall have original jurisdiction. In all the other Cases before mentioned, the Supreme Court shall have appellate Jurisdiction, both as to Law and Fact, with such Exceptions, and under such Regulations as the Congress shall make.

[3] The trial of all Crimes, except in Cases of Impeachment, shall be by Jury; and such Trial shall be held in the State where the said Crimes shall have been committed; but when not committed within any State, the Trial shall be at such Place or Places as the Congress may by Law have directed.

Section 3. [1] Treason against the United States, shall consist only in levying War against them, or, in adhering to their Enemies, giving them Aid and Comfort. No Person shall be convicted of Treason unless on the Testimony of two Witnesses to the same overt Act, or on Confession in open Court.

[2] The Congress shall have Power to declare the Punishment of Treason, but no Attainder of Treason shall work Corruption of Blood, or Forfeiture except during the Life of the Person attained.

ARTICLE IV

Section 1. Full Faith and Credit shall be given in each State to the public Acts, Records, and judicial Proceedings of every other State.

And the Congress may by general Laws prescribe the Manner in which such Acts, Records and Proceedings shall be proved, and the Effect thereof.

Section 2. [1] The Citizens of each State shall be entitled to all Privileges and Immunities of Citizens in the several States.

[2] A Person charged in any State with Treason, Felony, or other Crime, who shall flee from Justice, and be found in another State, shall on demand of the executive Authority of the State from which he fled, be delivered up, to be removed to the State having Jurisdiction of the Crime.

[3] No Person held to Service or Labour in one State, under the Laws thereof, escaping into another, shall, in Consequence of any Law or Regulation therein, be discharged from such Service or Labour, but shall be delivered up on Claim of the party to whom such Service or Labour, but shall be delivered up on Claim of the Party to whom such Service or Labour may be due.

Section 3, [1] New states may be admitted by the Congress into this Union; but no new State shall be formed or erected within the Jurisdiction of any other State; nor any State be formed by the Junction of two or more States, or Parts of States, without the Consent of the Legislatures of the States concerned as well as of the Congress.

[2] The Congress shall have Power to dispose of and make all needful Rules and Regulations respecting the Territory or other Property belonging to the United States; and nothing in this

Constitution shall be so construed as to Prejudice any Claims of the United States, or of any particular State.

Section 4. The United States shall guarantee to every State in this Union a Republican Form of Government, and shall protect each of them against Invasion; and on Application of the Legislature, or of the Executive (when the Legislature cannot be convened) against domestic Violence.

ARTICLE V

The Congress, whenever two thirds of both Houses shall deem it necessary, shall propose Amendments to this Constitution, or, on the Application of the Legislatures of two thirds of the several States, shall call a Convention for proposing Amendments, which, in either Case, shall be valid to all Intents and Purposes, as part of this Constitution, when ratified by the Legislatures of three fourths of the several States, or by Conventions in three fourths thereof, as the one or the other Mode of Ratification may be proposed by the Congress; Provided that no Amendment which may be made prior to the Year One thousand eight hundred and eight shall in any Manner affect the first and fourth Clauses in the Ninth Section of the first Article; and that no State, without its Consent, shall be deprived of its equal Suffrage in the Senate.

AMENDMENT XI [1798]

The judicial power of the United States shall not be construed to extend to any suit in law or equity. commenced or prosecuted against one of the United States by Citizens of another State, or by Citizens or Subjects of any Foreign State.

AMENDMENT XII [1804]

The Electors shall meet in their respective states and vote by ballot for President and Vice-President, one of whom, at least, shall not be an inhabitant of the same state with themselves; they shall name in their ballots the person voted for as President, and in distinct ballots the person voted for as Vice-President, and they shall make distinct lists of all persons voted for as President, and of all persons voted for as Vice-President, and of the number of votes for each, which lists they shall sign and certify, and transmit sealed to the seat of the government of the United States, directed to the President of the Senate; The President of the Senate shall, in the presence of the Senate and House of Representatives, open all the certificates and the votes shall then be counted;—The person having the greatest number of votes for President, shall be the President, if such numbers be a majority of the whole number of Electors appointed; and if no persons have such majority, then from the persons having the highest numbers not exceeding three on the list of those voted for as President, the House of Representatives shall choose immediately, by ballot, the President. But in choosing the President, the votes shall be taken by states, the representation from each state having one vote; a quorum for this purpose shall consist of a member or members from two-thirds of the states, and a majority of all the states shall be necessary to a choice. And if the House of Representatives shall not choose a President whenever the right of choice shall develop upon them before the fourth day of March next following, then the Vice-President, if such number be a majority of the whole number of Electors appointed, and if no person have a majority, then from the two highest numbers on the list, the Senate shall choose the Vice-President; a quorum for the purpose shall consist of two-thirds of the whole number of Senators, and a majority of the whole number shall be necessary to a choice. But no person constitutionally ineligible to the office of President shall be eligible to that of Vice-President of the United States.

AMENDMENT XIII [1865]

Section 1. Neither slavery nor involuntary servitude, expect as a punishment for crime whereof the party shall have been duly convicted, shall exist within the United States, or any place subject to their jurisdiction.

Section 2. Congress shall have power to enforce this article by appropriate legislation.

AMENDMENT XIV [1868]

Section 1. All persons born or naturalized in the United States, and subject to the jurisdiction thereof, are citizens of the United States and of the State wherein they reside. No State shall make or enforce any law which shall abridge the privileges or immunities of citizens of the United States; nor shall any State deprive any person of life, liberty, or property, without due process of law; nor deny to any person within its jurisdiction the equal protection of the laws.

Section 2. Representatives shall be apportioned among the several States according to their respective numbers, counting the whole number of persons in each State, excluding Indians not taxed. But when the right to vote at any election for the choice of electors for President and Vice President of the United States, Representatives in Congress, and Executive and Judicial officers of a State, or the members of the Legislature thereof, is denied to any of the male inhabitants of such State, being twenty-one years of age, and citizens of the United States, or in any way abridged, except for participation in rebellion, or other crime, the basis of representation therein shall be reduced in the proportion which the number of such male citizens shall bear to the whole number of male citizens twenty-one years of age in such State.

Section 3. No person shall be a Senator or Representative in Congress, or elector of President and Vice President, or hold any office, civil or military, under the United States, or under any State, who having previously taken an oath, as a member of Congress, or as an officer of the United States, or as a member o any State legislature, or as an executive or judicial officer of any State, to support the Constitution of the United States, shall have engaged in insurrection or rebellion against the same, or given aid or comfort to the enemies thereof. But Congress may by vote of two-thirds of each House, remove such disability.

Section 4. The validity of the public debt of the United States, authorized by law, including debts incurred for payment of pensions and bounties for services in suppressing insurrection or rebellion, shall not be questioned. But neither the United States nor any State shall assume or pay any debt or obligation incurred in aid of insurrection or rebellion against the United States, or any claim for the loss or emancipation of any slave; but all such debts, obligations and claims shall be held illegal and void.

Section 5. The Congress shall have power to enforce, by appropriate legislation, the provision of this article.

AMENDMENT XV [1870]

Section 1. The right of citizens of the United States to vote shall not be denied or abridged by the United States or by any State on account of race, color, or previous condition of servitude.

Section 2. The Congress shall have power to enforce this article by appropriate legislation.

AMENDMENT XVI [1913]

The Congress shall have power to lay and collect taxes on incomes, from whatever source derived, without apportionment among the several States, and without regard to any census or enumeration.

AMENDMENT XVII [1913]

Section 1. The Senate of the United States shall be composed of two Senators from each State, elected by the people thereof, for six years; and each Senator shall have one vote. The electors in each State shall have the qualifications requisite for electors of the most numerous branch of the State legislatures.

Section 2. When vacancies happen in the representation of any State in the Senate, the executive authority of such State shall issue writs of election to fill such vacancies: *Provided*, That the legislature of any State may empower the executive thereof to make temporary appointments until the people fill the vacancies by election as the legislature may direct.

Section 3. This amendment shall not be so construed as to affect the election or term of any Senator chosen before it becomes valid as part of the Constitution.

AMENDMENT XVIII [1919]

Section 1. After one year from the ratification of this article the manufacture, sale, or transportation of intoxicating liquors within, the importation thereof into, or the exportation thereof from the United States and all territory subject to the jurisdiction thereof for beverage purposes is hereby prohibited.

Section 2. The Congress and the several States shall have concurrent power to enforce this article by appropriate legislation.

Section 3. This article shall be inoperative unless it shall have been ratified as an amendment to the Constitution by the legislatures of the several States, as provided in the Constitution, within seven years from the date of the submission hereof to the States by the Congress.

AMENDMENT XIX [1920]

Section 1. The right of citizens of the United States to vote shall not be denied or abridged by the United States or by any State on account of sex.

Section 2. Congress shall have power to enforce this article by appropriate legislation.

AMENDMENT XX [1933]

Section 1. The terms of the President and Vice President shall end at noon on the 20th day of January, and the terms of Senators and Representatives at noon on the 3d day of January, of the years in which such terms would have ended if this article had not been ratified; and the terms of their successors shall then begin.

Section 2. The Congress shall assemble at least once in every year, and such meeting shall begin at noon on the 3d day of January, unless they shall by law appoint a different day.

Section 3. If, at the time fixed for the beginning of the term of the President, the President elect shall have died, the Vice President elect shall become President. If the President shall not have been chosen before the time fixed for the beginning of his term, or if the President elect shall have failed to qualify, the Vice President elect shall act as President until a President shall have qualified; and the Congress may by law provide for the case wherein neither a President elect nor a Vice President elect shall have qualified, declaring who shall then act as President, or the manner in which one who is to act shall be selected, and such person shall act accordingly until a President or Vice President shall have qualified.

Section 4. The Congress may by law provide for the case of the death of any of the persons from whom the House of Representatives may choose a President whenever the right of choice shall have developed upon them, and for the case of the death of any of the persons from whom the Senate may choose a Vice President whenever the right of choice shall have developed upon them.

Section 5. Section 1 and 2 shall take effect on the 15th day of October following the ratification of this article.

Section 6. This article shall be inoperative unless it shall have been ratified as an amendment to the Constitution by the legislatures of three-fourths of the several States within seven years from the date of its submission.

AMENDMENT XXI [1933]

Section 1. The eighteenth article of amendment to the Constitution of the United States is hereby repealed.

Section 2. The transportation or importation into any State, Territory, or possession of the United States for delivery or use therein of intoxicating liquors, in violation of the laws thereof, is hereby prohibited.

Section 3. This article shall be inoperative unless it shall have been ratified as an amendment to the Constitution by conventions in the several States, as provided in the Constitution, within seven years from the date of the submission hereof to the States by the Congress.

AMENDMENT XXII [1951]

Section 1. No person shall be elected to the office of the President more than twice, and no person who has held the office of President, or acted as President, for more than two years of a term to which some other person was elected President shall be elected to the office of President more than once. But this article shall not apply to any person holding the office of

President when this Article was proposed by the Congress, and shall not prevent any person who may be holding the office of President, or acting as President, during the term within which this Article becomes operative from holding the office of President or acting as President during the remainder of such term.

Section 2. This article shall be operative unless it shall have been ratified as an amendment to the Constitution by the legislatures of three-fourths of the several States within seven years from the date of its submission to the States by the Congress.

AMENDMENT XXIII [1961]

Section 1. The District constituting the seat of Government of the United States shall appoint in such manner as the Congress may direct:

A number of electors of President and Vice President equal to the whole number of Senators and Representatives in Congress to which the District would be entitled if it were a State, but in no event more than the least populous state; they shall be in addition to those appointed by the states, but they shall be considered, for the purposes of the election of President and Vice President, to be electors appointed by a state; and they shall meet in the District and perform such duties as provided by the twelfth article of amendment.

Section 2. The Congress shall have power to enforce this article by appropriate legislation.

AMENDMENT XXIV [1964]

Section 1. The right of citizens of the United States to vote in any primary or other election for President or Vice President, for electors for President or Vice President, or for Senator or Representative in Congress, shall not be denied or abridged by the United States or any State by reason of failure to pay any poll tax or other tax.

Section 2. The Congress shall have power to enforce this article by appropriate legislation.

AMENDMENT XXV [1967]

Section 1. In case of the removal of the President from office or of his death or resignation, the Vice President shall become President.

Section 2. Whenever there is a vacancy in the office of the Vice President, the President shall nominate a Vice President who shall take office upon confirmation by a majority vote of both Houses of Congress.

Section 3. Whenever the President transmits to the President pro tempore of the Senate and the Speaker of the House of Representatives his written declaration that he is unable to discharge the powers and duties of his office, and until he transmits to them a written declaration to the contrary, such powers and duties shall be discharged by the Vice President as Acting President.

Section 4. Whenever the Vice President and a majority of either the principal officers of the executive departments or of such other body as Congress may by law provide, transmit to the President pro tempore of the Senate and the Speaker of the House of Representatives their written declaration that the President is unable to discharge the powers and duties of his office, the Vice President shall immediately assume the powers and duties of the office as Acting President.

Thereafter, when the President transmits to the President pro tempore of the Senate and the Speaker of the House of Representatives his written declaration that no inability exists, he shall resume the powers and duties of his office unless the Vice President and a majority of either the principal officers of the executive department or of such other body as Congress may by law provide, transmit within four days to the President pro tempore of the Senate and the Speaker of the House of Representatives their written declaration that the President is unable to discharge the powers and duties of his office. Thereupon Congress shall decide the issue, assembling within forty-eight hours for that purpose if not in session. If the Congress, within twenty-one days after receipt of the latter written declaration, or, if Congress is not in session, within twenty-one days after Congress is required to assemble, determines by two-thirds of the vote of both Houses that the President is unable to discharge the powers and duties of his office, the Vice President shall continue to discharge the same as Acting President; otherwise, the President shall resume the powers and duties of his office.

AMENDMENT XXVI [1971]

Section 1. The right of citizens of the United States, who are eighteen years of age or older, to vote shall not be denied or abridged by the United States or by any State on account of age.

Section 2. The Congress shall have power to enforce this article by appropriate legislation.

AMENDMENT XXVII [1992]

Section 1. No law, varying the compensation for the services of the Senators and Representatives, shall take effect, until an election of representatives shall have intervened.

Miscellaneous Materials

Manuel Lujan, Jr., Secretary of the Interior, v. Defenders of Wildlife, et al.

United States Supreme Court, 1992

112 S.Ct. 2130

JUSTICE SCALIA delivered the opinion of the court with respect to Parts I, II, III-A, and IV, and an opinion with respect to Part III-B in which Chief Justice Rehnquist, Justice White, and Justice Thomas join.

I. The Endangered Species Act, 87 Stat. 884, as amended, 16 U.S.C. §1531 et seq., seeks to protect species of animals against threats to their continuing existence caused by man. See generally TVA v. Hill, 437 U.S. 153, 98 S.Ct. 2279, 57 L.Ed.2d 117 (1978). The ESA instructs the Secretary of the Interior to promulgate by regulation a list of those species which are either endangered or threatened under enumerated criteria, and to define the critical habitat of these species. 16 U.S.C. §§1533, 1536. Section 7(a)(2) of the Act then provides, in pertinent part: "Each Federal agency shall, in consultation with and with the assistance of the Secretary [of the Interior], insure that any action authorized, funded, or carried out by such agency ... is not likely to jeopardize the continued existence of any endangered species or threatened species or result in the destruction or adverse modification of habitat of such species which is determined by the Secretary, after consultation as appropriate with affected States, to be critical." 16 U.S.C. §1536(a)(2).

BACKGROUND

In 1978, the Fish and Wildlife Service (FWS) and the National Marine Fisheries Service (NMFS), on behalf of the Secretary of the Interior and the Secretary of Commerce respectively, promulgated a joint regulation stating that the obligations imposed by §7(a)(2) extend to actions taken in foreign nations. 43 Fed.Reg. 874 (1978). The next year, however, the Interior Department began to reexamine its position. Letter from Leo Krulitz, Solicitor, Department of the Interior, to Assistant Secretary, Fish and Wildlife and Parks, Aug. 8, 1979. A revised joint regulation, reinterpreting §7(a)(2) to require consultation only for actions taken in the United States or on the high seas, was proposed in 1983, 48 Fed.Reg. 29990 (1983), and promulgated in 1986, 51 Fed.Reg. 19926 (1986); 50 C.F.R. 402.01 (1991).

Shortly thereafter, respondents, organizations dedicated to wildlife conservation and other environmental causes, filed this action against the Secretary of the Interior, seeking a declaratory judgment that the new regulation is in error as to the geographic scope of §7(a)(2), and an injunction requiring the Secretary to promulgate a new regulation restoring the initial interpretation. The District Court granted the Secretary's motion to dismiss for lack of standing. Defenders of Wildlife v. Hodel, 658 F.Supp. 43, 47-48 (Minn.1987). The Court of Appeals for the Eighth Circuit reversed by a divided vote. Defenders of Wildlife v. Hodel, 851 F.2d 1035 (1988). On remand, the Secretary moved for summary judgment on the standing issue, and respondents moved for summary judgment on the merits. The District Court denied the Secretary's motion, on the ground that the Eighth Circuit had already determined the standing question in this case; it granted respondents' merits motion, and ordered the Secretary to publish a revised regulation. Defenders of Wildlife v. Hodel, 707 F.Supp. 1082 (Minn.1989). The Eighth Circuit affirmed. 911 F.2d 117 (1990). We granted certiorari, 500 U.S. ----, 111 S.Ct. 2008, 114 L.Ed.2d 97 (1991).

II . . . When the suit is one challenging the legality of government action or inaction, the nature and extent of facts that must be averred (at the summary judgment stage) or proved (at the trial stage) in order to establish standing depends considerably upon whether the plaintiff is himself an object of the action (or forgone action) at issue. If he is, there is ordinarily little question that the action or inaction has caused him injury, and that a judgment preventing or requiring the action will redress it. When, however, as in this case, a plaintiff's asserted injury arises from the government's allegedly unlawful regulation (or lack of regulation) of someone else, much more is needed. In that circumstance, causation and redressability ordinarily hinge on the response of the regulated (or regulable) third party to the government action or inaction--and perhaps on the response of others as well. The existence of one or more of the essential elements of standing "depends on the unfettered choices made by independent actors not before the courts and whose exercise of broad and legitimate discretion the courts cannot presume either to control or to predict," ASARCO Inc. v. Kadish, 490 U.S. 605, 615, 109 S.Ct. 2037, 2044, 104 L.Ed.2d 696 (1989) (opinion of Kennedy, J.); see also Simon, supra, 426 U.S., at 41-42, 96 S.Ct., at 1925, 1926; and it becomes the burden of the plaintiff to adduce facts showing that those choices have been or will be made in such manner as to produce causation and permit redressability of injury. E.g., Warth, supra, 422 U.S., at 505, 95 S.Ct., at 2208. Thus, when the plaintiff is not himself the object of the government action or inaction he challenges, standing is not precluded, but it is ordinarily "substantially more difficult" to establish. Allen, supra, 468 U.S., at 758, 104 S.Ct., at 3328; Simon, supra, 426 U.S., at 44-45, 96 S.Ct., at 1927; Warth, supra, 422 U.S., at 505, 95 S.Ct., at 2208.

III We think the Court of Appeals failed to apply the foregoing principles in denying the Secretary's motion for summary judgment. Respondents had not made the requisite demonstration of (at least) injury and redressability.

A Respondents' claim to injury is that the lack of consultation with respect to certain funded activities abroad "increas[es] the rate of extinction of endangered and threatened species." Complaint P 5, App. 13. Of course, the desire to use or observe an animal species, even for purely aesthetic purposes, is undeniably a cognizable interest for purpose of standing. See, e.g., Sierra Club v. Morton, 405 U.S., at 734, 92 S.Ct., at 1366. "But the 'injury in fact' test requires more than an injury to a cognizable interest. It requires that the party seeking review be himself among the injured." Id., at 734-735, 92 S.Ct., at 1366. To survive the Secretary's summary judgment motion, respondents had to submit affidavits or other evidence showing, through specific facts, not only that listed species were in fact being threatened by funded activities abroad, but also that one or more of respondents' members would thereby be "directly" affected apart from their " 'special interest' in th[e] subject." Id., at 735, 739, 92 S.Ct., at 1366, 1368. See generally Hunt v. Washington State Apple Advertising Comm'n, 432 U.S. 333, 343, 97 S.Ct. 2434, 2441, 53 L.Ed.2d 383 (1977).

With respect to this aspect of the case, the Court of Appeals focused on the affidavits of two Defenders' members--Joyce Kelly and Amy Skilbred. Ms. Kelly stated that she traveled to Egypt in 1986 and "observed the traditional habitat of the endangered Nile crocodile there and intend[s] to do so again, and hope[s] to observe the crocodile directly," and that she "will suffer harm in fact as a result of [the] American ... role ... in overseeing the rehabilitation of the Aswan High Dam on the Nile ... and [in] develop[ing] ... Egypt's ... Master Water Plan." App. 101. Ms. Skilbred averred that she traveled to Sri Lanka in 1981 and "observed th[e] habitat" of "endangered species such as the Asian elephant and the leopard" at what is now the site of the Mahaweli Project funded by the Agency for International Development (AID), although she "was unable to see any of the endangered species;" "this development project," she continued, "will seriously reduce endangered, threatened, and endemic species habitat including areas that I visited ... [, which] may severely shorten the future of these species;" that threat, she concluded, harmed her because she "intend[s] to return to Sri Lanka in the future and hope[s] to be more fortunate in spotting at least the endangered elephant and leopard." Id., at 145-146. When Ms. Skilbred was asked at a subsequent deposition if and when she had any plans to return to Sri Lanka, she reiterated that "I intend to go back to Sri Lanka," but confessed that she had no current plans: "I don't know [when]. There is a civil war going on right now. I don't know. Not next year, I will say. In the future." Id., at 318.

We shall assume for the sake of argument that these affidavits contain facts showing that certain agency-funded projects threaten listed species-- though that is questionable. They plainly contain no facts, however, showing how damage to the species will produce "imminent" injury to Mss. Kelly and Skilbred. That the women "had visited" the areas of the projects before the projects commenced proves nothing. As we have said in a related context, " '[p]ast exposure to illegal conduct does not in itself show a present case or controversy regarding injunctive relief ... if unaccompanied by any continuing, present adverse effects.' " Lyons, 461 U.S., at 102, 103 S.Ct., at 1665 (quoting O'Shea v. Littleton, 414 U.S. 488, 495-496, 94 S.Ct. 669, 676, 38 L.Ed.2d 674 (1974)). And the affiants' profession of an "inten[t]" to return to the places they had visited before--where they will presumably, this time, be deprived of the opportunity to observe animals of the endangered species--is simply not enough. Such "some day" intentions--without any description of concrete plans, or indeed even any specification of when the some day will be-- do not support a finding of the "actual or imminent" injury that our cases require.

Besides relying upon the Kelly and Skilbred affidavits, respondents propose a series of novel standing theories. The first, inelegantly styled "ecosystem nexus," proposes that any person who uses any part of a "contiguous ecosystem" adversely affected by a funded activity has standing even if the activity is located a great distance away. This approach, as the Court of Appeals correctly observed, is inconsistent with our opinion in National Wildlife Federation, which held that a plaintiff claiming injury from environmental damage must use the area affected by the challenged activity and not an area roughly "in the vicinity" of it. 497 U.S., at 887-889, 110 S.Ct., at --; see also Sierra Club, 405 U.S., at 735, 92 S.Ct., at 1366. It makes no difference that the general-purpose section of the ESA states that the Act was intended in part "to provide a means whereby the ecosystems upon which endangered species and threatened species depend may be conserved," 16 U.S.C. §1531(b). To say that the Act protects ecosystems is not to say that the Act creates (if it were possible) rights of action in persons who have not been injured in fact, that is, persons who use portions of an ecosystem not perceptibly affected by the unlawful action in question.

Respondents' other theories are called, alas, the "animal nexus" approach, whereby anyone who has an interest in studying or seeing the endangered animals anywhere on the globe has standing; and the "vocational nexus" approach, under which anyone with a professional interest in such animals can sue. Under these theories, anyone who goes to see Asian elephants in the Bronx Zoo, and anyone who is a keeper of Asian elephants in the Bronx Zoo, has standing to sue because the Director of AID did not consult with the Secretary regarding the AID-funded project in Sri Lanka. This is beyond all reason. Standing is not "an ingenious academic exercise in the conceivable," United States v. Students Challenging Regulatory Agency Procedures (SCRAP), 412 U.S. 669, 688, 93 S.Ct. 2405, 2416, 37 L.Ed.2d 254 (1973), but as we have said requires, at the summary judgment stage, a factual showing of perceptible harm. It is clear that the person who observes or works with a particular animal threatened by a federal decision is facing perceptible harm, since the very subject of his interest will no longer exist. It is even plausible-- though it goes to the outermost limit of plausibility--to think that a person who observes or works with animals of a particular species in the very area of the world where that species is threatened by a federal decision is facing such harm, since some animals that might have been the subject of his interest will no longer exist, see Japan Whaling Assn. v. American Cetacean Soc., 478 U.S. 221, 231, n. 4, 106 S.Ct. 2860, 2866, n. 4, 92 L.Ed.2d 166 (1986). It goes beyond the limit, however, and into pure speculation and fantasy, to say that anyone who observes or works with an endangered species, anywhere in the world, is appreciably harmed by a single project affecting some portion of that species with which he has no more specific connection.

B Besides failing to show injury, respondents failed to demonstrate redressability. Instead of attacking the separate decisions to fund particular projects allegedly causing them harm, the respondents chose to challenge a more generalized level of government action (rules regarding consultation), the invalidation of which would affect all overseas projects. This programmatic approach has obvious practical advantages, but also obvious difficulties insofar as proof of causation or redressability is concerned. As we have said in another context, "suits challenging, not specifically identifiable Government violations of law, but the particular programs agencies establish to carry out their legal obligations ... [are], even when premised on allegations of several instances of violations of law, ... rarely if ever appropriate for federal-court adjudication." Allen, 468 U.S., at 759-760, 104 S.Ct., at 3329.

The most obvious problem in the present case is redressability. Since the agencies funding the projects were not parties to the case, the District Court could accord relief only against the Secretary: He could be ordered to revise his regulation to require consultation for foreign projects. But this would not remedy respondents' alleged injury unless the funding agencies were bound by the Secretary's regulation, which is very much an open question. . .

IV The Court of Appeals found that respondents had standing for an additional reason: because they had suffered a "procedural injury." The so-called "citizen-suit" provision of the ESA provides, in pertinent part, that "any person may commence a civil suit on his own behalf (A) to enjoin any person, including the United States and any other governmental instrumentality or agency ... who is alleged to be in violation of any provision of this chapter." 16 U.S.C. §1540(g). The court held that, because §7(a)(2) requires interagency consultation, the citizen-suit provision creates a "procedural righ[t]" to consultation in all "persons"--so that anyone can file suit in federal court to challenge the Secretary's (or presumably any other official's) failure to follow the assertedly correct consultative procedure, notwithstanding their inability to allege any discrete injury flowing from that failure. 911 F.2d, at 121-122. To understand the remarkable nature of this holding one must be clear about what it does not rest upon: This is not a case where plaintiffs are seeking to enforce a procedural requirement the disregard of which could impair a separate concrete interest of theirs (e.g., the procedural requirement for a hearing prior to denial of their license application, or the procedural requirement for an environmental impact statement before a federal facility is constructed next door to them). Nor is it simply a case where concrete injury has been suffered by many persons, as in mass fraud or mass tort situations. Nor, finally, is it the unusual case in which Congress has created a concrete private interest in the outcome of a suit against a private party for the government's benefit, by providing a cash bounty for the victorious plaintiff. Rather, the court held that the injury-in-fact requirement had been satisfied by congressional conferral upon all persons of an abstract, self-contained, noninstrumental "right" to have the Executive observe the procedures required by law. We reject this view.

We have consistently held that a plaintiff raising only a generally available grievance about government--claiming only harm to his and every citizen's interest in proper application of the

Constitution and laws, and seeking relief that no more directly and tangibly benefits him than it does the public at large--does not state an Article III case or controversy. . .

In Ex parte Levitt, 302 U.S. 633, 58 S.Ct. 1, 82 L.Ed. 493 (1937), we dismissed a suit contending that Justice Black's appointment to this Court violated the Ineligibility Clause, Art. I, §6, cl. 2. "It is an established principle," we said, "that to entitle a private individual to invoke the judicial power to determine the validity of executive or legislative action he must show that he has sustained or is immediately in danger of sustaining a direct injury as the result of that action and it is not sufficient that he has merely a general interest common to all members of the public." Id., at 634, 58 S.Ct., at 1. See also Doremus v. Board of Ed. of Hawthorne, 342 U.S. 429, 433-434, 72 S.Ct. 394, 396-397, 96 L.Ed. 475 (1952) (dismissing taxpayer action on the basis of Frothingham).

. . . We reaffirm Levitt in holding that standing to sue may not be predicated upon an interest of th[is] kind...." Schlesinger, supra, at 217, 220, 94 S.Ct., at 2930, 2932. Since Schlesinger we have on two occasions held that an injury amounting only to the alleged violation of a right to have the Government act in accordance with law was not judicially cognizable because "assertion of a right to a particular kind of Government conduct, which the Government has violated by acting differently, cannot alone satisfy the requirements of Art. III without draining those requirements of meaning." Allen, 468 U.S., at 754, 104 S.Ct., at 3326; Valley Forge Christian College v. Americans United for Separation of Church and State, Inc., 454 U.S. 464, 483, 102 S.Ct. 752, 764, 70 L.Ed.2d 700 (1982). And only two Terms ago, we rejected the notion that Article III permits a citizen-suit to prevent a condemned criminal's execution on the basis of "the public interest protections of the Eighth Amendment;" once again, "[t]his allegation raise[d] only the generalized interest of all citizens in constitutional governance ... and [was] an inadequate basis on which to grant ... standing." Whitmore, 495 U.S., at 160, 110 S.Ct., at 1725.

To be sure, our generalized-grievance cases have typically involved Government violation of procedures assertedly ordained by the Constitution rather than the Congress. But there is absolutely no basis for making the Article III inquiry turn on the source of the asserted right. Whether the courts were to act on their own, or at the invitation of Congress, in ignoring the concrete injury requirement described in our cases, they would be discarding a principle fundamental to the separate and distinct constitutional role of the Third Branch--one of the essential elements that identifies those "Cases" and "Controversies" that are the business of the courts rather than of the political branches. "The province of the court," as Chief Justice Marshall said in Marbury v. Madison, 5 U.S. (1 Cranch) 137, 170, 2 L.Ed. 60 (1803) "is, solely, to decide on the rights of individuals." Vindicating the public interest (including the public interest in government observance of the Constitution and laws) is the function of Congress and the Chief Executive. The question presented here is whether the public interest in proper administration of the laws (specifically, in agencies' observance of a particular, statutorily prescribed procedure) can be converted into an individual right by a statute that denominates it as such, and that permits all citizens (or, for that matter, a subclass of citizens who suffer no distinctive concrete harm) to sue. If the concrete injury requirement has the separation- of-powers significance we have always said, the answer must be obvious: To permit Congress to convert the undifferentiated public interest in executive officers' compliance with the law into an "individual right" vindicable in the courts is to permit Congress to transfer from the President to the courts the Chief Executive's most important constitutional duty, to "take Care that the Laws be faithfully executed," Art. II, §3. It would enable the courts, with the permission of Congress, "to assume a position of authority over the governmental acts of another and co-equal department," Frothingham v. Mellon, 262 U.S., at 489, 43 S.Ct., at 601, and to become " 'virtually continuing monitors of the wisdom and soundness of Executive action.' " Allen, 468 U.S., at 760, 104 S.Ct., at 3329 (quoting Laird v. Tatum, 408 U.S. 1, 15, 92 S.Ct. 2318, 2326, 33 L.Ed.2d 154 (1972)). We have always rejected that vision of our role: "When Congress passes an Act empowering administrative agencies to carry on governmental activities, the power of those agencies is circumscribed by the authority granted. This permits the courts to participate in law enforcement entrusted to administrative bodies only to the extent necessary to protect justiciable individual rights against administrative action fairly beyond the granted powers.... This is very far from assuming that the courts are charged more than administrators or legislators with the protection of the rights of the people. Congress and the Executive supervise the acts of administrative agents.... But under Article III, Congress established courts to adjudicate cases and controversies as to claims of infringement of individual rights whether by unlawful action of private persons or by the exertion of unauthorized administrative power." Stark v. Wickard, 321 U.S. 288, 309-310, 64 S.Ct. 559, 571, 88 L.Ed. 733 (1944). "Individual rights," within the meaning of this passage, do not mean public rights that have been legislatively pronounced to belong to each individual who forms part of the public. See also Sierra Club, 405 U.S., at 740-741, n. 16, 92 S.Ct., at 1369, n. 16.

. . . it is clear that in suits against the government, at least, the concrete injury requirement must remain.

We hold that respondents lack standing to bring this action and that the Court of Appeals erred in denying the summary judgment motion filed by the United States. The opinion of the Court of Appeals is hereby reversed, and the cause remanded for proceedings consistent with this opinion.

It is so ordered.

JUSTICE KENNEDY, with whom JUSTICE SOUTER joins, concurring in part and concurring in the judgment.

I agree with the Court's conclusion in Part III-A that, on the record before us, respondents have failed to demonstrate that they themselves are "among the injured." Sierra Club v. Morton, 405 U.S. 727, 735, 92 S.Ct. 1361, 1366, 31 L.Ed.2d 636 (1972). . .

While it may seem trivial to require that Mss. Kelly and Skilbred acquire airline tickets to the project sites or announce a date certain upon which they will return, this is not a case where it is reasonable to assume that the affiants will be using the sites on a regular basis, see Sierra Club v. Morton, supra, 405 U.S., at 735, 92 S.Ct., at 1366, nor do the affiants claim to have visited the sites since the projects commenced. With respect to the Court's discussion of respondents' "ecosystem nexus," "animal nexus," and "vocational nexus" theories, I agree that on this record respondents' showing is insufficient to establish standing on any of these bases. I am not willing to foreclose the possibility, however, that in different circumstances a nexus theory similar to those proffered here might support a claim to standing. See Japan Whaling Assn. v. American Cetacean Soc., 478 U.S. 221, 231, n. 4, 106 S.Ct. 2860, 2866, n. 4, 92 L.Ed.2d 166 (1986) ("respondents ... undoubtedly have alleged a sufficient 'injury in fact' in that the whale watching and studying of their members will be adversely affected by continued whale harvesting").

In light of the conclusion that respondents have not demonstrated a concrete injury here sufficient to support standing under our precedents, I would not reach the issue of redressability that is discussed by the plurality in Part III-B.

I also join Part IV of the Court's opinion with the following observations. As government programs and policies become more complex and far-reaching, we must be sensitive to the articulation of new rights of action that do not have clear analogs in our common-law tradition. Modern litigation has progressed far from the paradigm of Marbury suing Madison to get his commission, Marbury v. Madison, 5 U.S. (1 Cranch) 137, 2 L.Ed. 60 (1803), or Ogden seeking an injunction to halt Gibbons' steamboat operations. Gibbons v. Ogden, 22 U.S. (9 Wheat.) 1, 6 L.Ed. 23 (1824). In my view, Congress has the power to define injuries and articulate chains of causation that will give rise to a case or controversy where none existed before, and I do not read the Court's opinion to suggest a contrary view. See Warth v. Seldin, 422 U.S. 490, 500, 95 S.Ct. 2197, 2205, 45 L.Ed.2d 343 (1975); In exercising this power, however, Congress must at the very least identify the injury it seeks to vindicate and relate the injury to the class of persons entitled to bring suit. The citizen-suit provision of the Endangered Species Act does not meet these minimal requirements, because while the statute purports to confer a right on "any person ... to enjoin ... the United States and any other governmental instrumentality or agency ... who is alleged to be in violation of any provision of this chapter," it does not of its own force establish that there is an injury in "any person" by virtue of any "violation." 16 U.S.C. §1540(g)(1)(A).

The Court's holding that there is an outer limit to the power of Congress to confer rights of action is a direct and necessary consequence of the case and controversy limitations found in Article III. I agree that it would exceed those limitations if, at the behest of Congress and in the absence of any showing of concrete injury, we were to entertain citizen-suits to vindicate the public's nonconcrete interest in the proper administration of the laws. . .

An independent judiciary is held to account through its open proceedings and its reasoned judgments. In this process it is essential for the public to know what persons or groups are invoking the judicial power, the reasons that they have brought suit, and whether their claims are vindicated or denied. The concrete injury requirement helps assure that there can be an answer to these questions; and, as the Court's opinion is careful to show, that is part of the constitutional design.

With these observations, I concur in Parts I, II, III-A, and IV of the Court's opinion and in the judgment of the Court.

JUSTICE STEVENS, concurring in the judgment.

Because I am not persuaded that Congress intended the consultation requirement in §7(a)(2) of the Endangered Species Act of 1973 (ESA), 16 U.S.C. §1536(a)(2), to apply to activities in foreign countries, I concur in the judgment of reversal. I do not, however, agree with the Court's conclusion that respondents lack standing because the threatened injury to their interest in protecting the environment and studying endangered species is not "imminent." Nor do I agree with the plurality's additional conclusion that respondents' injury is not "redressable" in this litigation.

I

In my opinion a person who has visited the critical habitat of an endangered species, has a professional interest in preserving the species and its habitat, and intends to revisit them in the future has standing to challenge agency action that threatens their destruction. Congress has found that a wide variety of endangered species of fish, wildlife, and plants are of "aesthetic, ecological, educational, historical, recreational, and scientific value to the Nation and its people." 16 U.S.C. §1531(a)(3). Given that finding, we have no license to demean the importance of the interest that particular individuals may have in observing any species or its habitat, whether those individuals are motivated by aesthetic enjoyment, an interest in professional research, or an economic interest in preservation of the species. Indeed, this Court has often held that injuries to such interests are sufficient to confer standing, and the Court reiterates that holding today.

The Court nevertheless concludes that respondents have not suffered "injury in fact" because they have not shown that the harm to the endangered species will produce "imminent" injury to them. I disagree. An injury to an individual's interest in studying or enjoying a species and its natural habitat occurs when someone (whether it be the government or a private party) takes action that harms that species and habitat. In my judgment, therefore, the "imminence" of such an injury should be measured by the timing and likelihood of the threatened environmental harm, rather than--as the Court seems to suggest--by the time that might elapse between the present and the time when the individuals would visit the area if no such injury should occur.

. . . In this case, however, the likelihood that respondents will be injured by the destruction of the endangered species is not speculative. If respondents are genuinely interested in the preservation of the endangered species and intend to study or observe these animals in the future, their injury will occur as soon as the animals are destroyed. Thus the only potential source of "speculation" in this case is whether respondents' intent to study or observe the animals is genuine. In my view, Joyce Kelly and Amy Skilbred have introduced sufficient evidence to negate petitioner's contention that their claims of injury are "speculative" or "conjectural." As Justice Blackmun explains, a reasonable finder of fact could conclude, from their past visits, their professional backgrounds, and their affidavits and deposition testimony, that Ms. Kelly and Ms. Skilbred will return to the project sites and, consequently, will be injured by the destruction of the endangered species and critical habitat. . .

II

Although I believe that respondents have standing, I nevertheless concur in the judgment of reversal because I am persuaded that the Government is correct in its submission that §7(a)(2) does not apply to activities in foreign countries. As with all questions of statutory construction, the question whether a statute applies extraterritorially is one of congressional intent. Foley Bros., Inc. v. Filardo, 336 U.S. 281, 284-285, 69 S.Ct. 575, 577, 93 L.Ed. 680 (1949). We normally assume that "Congress is primarily concerned with domestic conditions," id., at 285, 69 S.Ct., at 577, and therefore presume that " 'legislation of Congress, unless a contrary intent appears, is meant to apply only within the territorial jurisdiction of the United States.' " EEOC v. Arabian American Oil Co., 499 U.S. ----, 111 S.Ct. 1227, 113 L.Ed.2d 274 (1991) (quoting Foley Bros., 336 U.S., at 285, 69 S.Ct., at 577).

Section 7(a)(2) provides, in relevant part: "Each Federal agency shall, in consultation with and with the assistance of the Secretary [of the Interior or Commerce, as appropriate, insure that any action authorized, funded, or carried out by such agency (hereinafter in this section referred to as an 'agency action') is not likely to jeopardize the continued existence of any endangered species or threatened species or result in the destruction or adverse modification of habitat of such species which is determined by the Secretary, after consultation as appropriate with affected States, to be critical, unless such agency has been granted an exemption for such action by the Committee pursuant to subsection (h) of this section...." 16 U.S.C. §1536(a)(2).

Nothing in this text indicates that the section applies in foreign countries. Indeed, the only geographic reference in the section is in the "critical habitat" clause, which mentions "affected States." The Secretary of the Interior and the Secretary of Commerce have consistently taken the position that they need not designate critical habitat in foreign countries. See 42 Fed.Reg. 4869 (1977) (initial regulations of the Fish and Wildlife Service and the National Marine

Fisheries Service on behalf of the Secretary of Interior and the Secretary of Commerce). Consequently, neither Secretary interprets §7(a)(2) to require federal agencies to engage in consultations to insure that their actions in foreign countries will not adversely affect the critical habitat of endangered or threatened species.

That interpretation is sound, and, in fact, the Court of Appeals did not question it. There is, moreover, no indication that Congress intended to give a different geographic scope to the two clauses in §7(a)(2). To the contrary, Congress recognized that one of the "major causes" of extinction of endangered species is the "destruction of natural habitat." S.Rep. No. *2151 93-307, p. 2 (1973); see also, H.Rep. No. 93-412, p. 2 (1973), U.S.Code Cong. & Admin.News 1973, pp. 2989, 2990; TVA v. Hill, 437 U.S. 153, 179, 98 S.Ct. 2279, 2294, 57 L.Ed.2d 117 (1978). It would thus be illogical to conclude that Congress required federal agencies to avoid jeopardy to endangered species abroad, but not destruction of critical habitat abroad.

The lack of an express indication that the consultation requirement applies extraterritorially is particularly significant because other sections of the ESA expressly deal with the problem of protecting endangered species abroad. Section 8, for example, authorizes the President to provide assistance to "any foreign country (with its consent) ... in the development and management of programs in that country which [are] ... necessary or useful for the conservation of any endangered species or threatened species listed by the Secretary pursuant to section 1533 of this title." 16 U.S.C. §1537(a). It also directs the Secretary of Interior, "through the Secretary of State," to "encourage" foreign countries to conserve fish and wildlife and to enter into bilateral or multilateral agreements. §1537(b). Section 9 makes it unlawful to import endangered species into (or export them from) the United States or to otherwise traffic in endangered species "in interstate or foreign commerce." §1538(a)(1)(A), (E), (F). Congress thus obviously thought about endangered species abroad and devised specific sections of the ESA to protect them. In this context, the absence of any explicit statement that the consultation requirement is applicable to agency actions in foreign countries suggests that Congress did not intend that §7(a)(2) apply extraterritorially.

Finally, the general purpose of the ESA does not evince a congressional intent that the consultation requirement be applicable to federal agency actions abroad. The congressional findings explaining the need for the ESA emphasize that "various species of fish, wildlife, and plants in the United States have been rendered extinct as a consequence of economic growth and development untempered by adequate concern and conservation," and that these species "are of aesthetic, ecological, educational, historical, recreational, and scientific value to the Nation and its people." §1531(1), (3) (emphasis added). The lack of similar findings about the harm caused by development in other countries suggests that Congress was primarily concerned with balancing development and conservation goals in this country.

In short, a reading of the entire statute persuades me that Congress did not intend the consultation requirement in §7(a)(2) to apply to activities in foreign countries. Accordingly, notwithstanding my disagreement with the Court's disposition of the standing question, I concur in its judgment.

JUSTICE BLACKMUN, with whom JUSTICE O'CONNOR joins, dissenting.

I part company with the Court in this case in two respects. First, I believe that respondents have raised genuine issues of fact--sufficient to survive summary judgment--both as to injury and as to redressability. Second, I question the Court's breadth of language in rejecting standing for "procedural" injuries. I fear the Court seeks to impose fresh limitations on the constitutional authority of Congress to allow citizen-suits in the federal courts for injuries deemed "procedural" in nature. I dissent. . .

1. Were the Court to apply the proper standard for summary judgment, I believe it would conclude that the sworn affidavits and deposition testimony of Joyce Kelly and Amy Skilbred advance sufficient facts to create a genuine issue for trial concerning whether one or both would be imminently harmed by the Aswan and Mahaweli projects. In the first instance, as the Court itself concedes, the affidavits contained facts making it at least "questionable" (and therefore within the province of the factfinder) that certain agency-funded projects threaten listed species. The only remaining issue, then, is whether Kelly and Skilbred have shown that they personally would suffer imminent harm.

I think a reasonable finder of fact could conclude from the information in the affidavits and deposition testimony that either Kelly or Skilbred will soon return to the project sites, thereby satisfying the "actual or imminent" injury standard. The Court dismisses Kelly's and Skilbred's general statements that they intended to revisit the project sites as "simply not enough." But those statements did not stand alone. A reasonable finder of fact could conclude, based not only upon their statements of intent to return, but upon their past visits to the project sites, as well as their professional backgrounds, that it was likely that Kelly and Skilbred would make a return trip to the project areas. Contrary to the Court's contention that Kelly's and Skilbred's past visits "proves nothing," the fact of their past visits could demonstrate to a reasonable factfinder that Kelly and Skilbred have the requisite resources and personal interest in the preservation of the species endangered by the Aswan and Mahaweli projects to make good on their intention to return again. Cf. Los Angeles v. Lyons, 461 U.S. 95, 102, 103 S.Ct. 1660, 1665, 75 L.Ed.2d 675 (1983) ("Past wrongs were evidence bearing on whether there is a real and immediate threat of repeated injury") (internal quotations omitted). Similarly, Kelly's and Skilbred's professional backgrounds in wildlife preservation, see App. 100, 144, 309-310, also make it likely--at least far more likely than for the average citizen--that they would choose to visit these areas of the world where species are vanishing.

By requiring a "description of concrete plans" or "specification of when the some day [for a return visit] will be," the Court, in my view, demands what is likely an empty formality. No substantial barriers prevent Kelly or Skilbred from simply purchasing plane tickets to return to the Aswan and Mahaweli projects. This case differs from other cases in which the imminence of harm turned largely on the affirmative actions of third parties beyond a plaintiff's control. See Whitmore v. Arkansas, 495 U.S. 149, (1990) (harm to plaintiff death-row inmate from fellow inmate's execution depended on the court's one day reversing plaintiff's conviction or sentence and considering comparable sentences at resentencing); Los Angeles v. Lyons, 461 U.S., at 105, 103 S.Ct., at 1667 (harm dependent on police's arresting plaintiff again and subjecting him to chokehold); Rizzo v. Goode, 423 U.S. 362, 372, 96 S.Ct. 598, 605, 46 L.Ed.2d 561 (1976) (harm rested upon "what one of a small unnamed minority of policemen might do to them in the future because of that unknown policeman's perception of departmental disciplinary procedures"); O'Shea v. Littleton, 414 U.S. 488, 495-498, 94 S.Ct. 669, 675-677, 38 L.Ed.2d 674 (1974) (harm from discriminatory conduct of county magistrate and judge dependent on plaintiffs' being arrested, tried, convicted, and sentenced); Golden v. Zwickler, 394 U.S. 103, 109, 89 S.Ct. 956, 960, 22 L.Ed.2d 113 (1969) (harm to plaintiff dependent on a former Congressman's (then serving a 14-year term as a judge) running again for Congress). To be sure, a plaintiff's unilateral control over his or her exposure to harm does not necessarily render the harm non-speculative. Nevertheless, it suggests that a finder of fact would be far more likely to conclude the harm is actual or imminent, especially if given an opportunity to hear testimony and determine credibility.

I fear the Court's demand for detailed descriptions of future conduct will do little to weed out those who are genuinely harmed from those who are not. More likely, it will resurrect a code-pleading formalism in federal court summary judgment practice, as federal courts, newly doubting their jurisdiction, will demand more and more particularized showings of future harm. . .

2. The Court also concludes that injury is lacking, because respondents' allegations of "ecosystem nexus" failed to demonstrate sufficient proximity to the site of the environmental harm. To support that conclusion, the Court mischaracterizes our decision in Lujan v. National Wildlife Federation, 497 U.S. 871, 110 S.Ct. 3177, 111 L.Ed.2d 695 (1990), as establishing a general rule that "a plaintiff claiming injury from environmental damage must use the area affected by the challenged activity." In National Wildlife Federation, the Court required specific geographical proximity because of the particular type of harm alleged in that case: harm to the plaintiff's visual enjoyment of nature from mining activities. One cannot suffer from the sight of a ruined landscape without being close enough to see the sites actually being mined. Many environmental injuries, however, cause harm distant from the area immediately affected by the challenged action. Environmental destruction may affect animals traveling over vast geographical ranges, see, e.g., Japan Whaling Assn. v. American Cetacean Soc., 478 U.S. 221, 106 S.Ct. 2860, 92 L.Ed.2d 166 (1986) (harm to American whale watchers from Japanese whaling activities), or rivers running long geographical courses, see, e.g., Arkansas v. Oklahoma, 112 S.Ct. 1046, (1992) (harm to Oklahoma residents from wastewater treatment plant 39 miles from border). It cannot seriously be contended that a litigant's failure to use the precise or exact site where animals are slaughtered or where toxic waste is dumped into a river means he or she cannot show injury. . .

I have difficulty imagining this Court applying its rigid principles of geographic formalism anywhere outside the context of environmental claims. As I understand it, environmental plaintiffs are under no special constitutional standing disabilities. Like other plaintiffs, they need show only that the action they challenge has injured them, without necessarily showing they happened to be physically near the location of the alleged wrong. The Court's decision today should not be interpreted "to foreclose the possibility ... that in different circumstances a nexus theory similar to those proffered here might support a claim to standing." (Kennedy, J., concurring in part and concurring in the judgment).

B . . . I find myself unable to agree with the plurality's analysis of redressability, based as it is on its invitation of executive lawlessness, ignorance of principles of collateral estoppel, unfounded assumptions about causation, and erroneous conclusions about what the record does not say. In my view, respondents have satisfactorily shown a genuine issue of fact as to whether their injury would likely be redressed by a decision in their favor.

II The Court concludes that any "procedural injury" suffered by respondents is insufficient to confer standing. It rejects the view that the "injury-in-fact requirement ... [is] satisfied by congressional conferral upon all person of an abstract, self-contained, noninstrumental 'right' to have the Executive observe the procedures required by law." Whatever the Court might mean with that very broad language, it cannot be saying that "procedural injuries" as a class are necessarily insufficient for purposes of Article III standing.

Most governmental conduct can be classified as "procedural." Many injuries caused by governmental conduct, therefore, are categorizable at some level of generality as "procedural" injuries. Yet, these injuries are not categorically beyond the pale of redress by the federal courts. When the Government, for example, "procedurally" issues a pollution permit, those affected by the permittee's pollutants are not without standing to sue. Only later cases will tell just what the Court means by its intimation that "procedural" injuries are not constitutionally cognizable injuries. In the meantime, I have the greatest of sympathy for the courts across the country that will struggle to understand the Court's standardless exposition of this concept today.

The Court expresses concern that allowing judicial enforcement of "agencies' observance of a particular, statutorily prescribed procedure" would "transfer from the President to the courts the Chief Executive's most important constitutional duty, to 'take Care that the Laws be faithfully executed,' Art. II, sec. 3." In fact, the principal effect of foreclosing judicial enforcement of such procedues is to transfer power into the hands of the Executive at the expense--not of the courts--but of Congress, frm which that power originates and emanates.

Under the Court's anachronistically formal view of the separation of powers, Congress legislates pure, substantive mandates and has no business structuring the procedural manner in which the Executive implements these mandates. To be sure, in the ordinary course, Congress does legislate in black-and-white terms of affirmative commands or negative prohibitions on the conduct of officers of the Executive Branch. In complex regulatory areas, however, Congress often legislates, as it were, in procedural shades of gray. That is, it sets forth substantive policy goals and provides for their attainment by requiring Executive Branch officials to follow certain procedures, for example, in the form of reporting, consultation, and certification requirements. . .

The consultation requirement of §7 of the Endangered Species Act is a similar, action-forcing statute. Consultation is designed as an integral check on federal agency action, ensuring that such action does not go forward without full consideration of its effects on listed species. Once consultation is initiated, the Secretary is under a duty to provide to the action agency "a written statement setting forth the Secretary's opinion, and a summary of the information on which the opinion is based, detailing how the agency action affects the species or its critical habitat." 16 U.S.C. §1536(b)(3)(A). The Secretary is also obligated to suggest "reasonable and prudent alternatives" to prevent jeopardy to listed species. Ibid. The action agency must *2159 undertake as well its own "biological assessment for the purpose of identifying any endangered species or threatened species" likely to be affected by agency action. §1536(c)(1). After the initiation of consultation, the action agency "shall not make any irreversible or irretrievable commitment of resources" which would foreclose the "formulation or implementation of any reasonable and prudent alternative measures" to avoid jeopardizing listed species. §1536(d). These action-forcing procedures are "designed to protect some threatened concrete interest," of persons who observe and work with endangered or threatened species. That is why I am mystified by the Court's unsupported conclusion that "[t]his is not a case where plaintiffs are seeking to enforce a procedural requirement the disregard of which could impair a separate concrete interest of theirs."

Congress legislates in procedural shades of gray not to aggrandize its own power but to allow maximum Executive discretion in the attainment of Congress' legislative goals. Congress could simply impose a substantive prohibition on executive conduct; it could say that no agency action shall result in the loss of more than 5% of any listed species. Instead, Congress sets forth substantive guidelines and allows the Executive, within certain procedural constraints, to decide how best to effectuate the ultimate goal. See American Power & Light Co. v. SEC, 329 U.S. 90, 105, 67 S.Ct. 133, 142, 91 L.Ed. 103 (1946). The Court never has questioned Congress' authority to impose such procedural constraints on executive power. Just as Congress does not violate separation of powers by structuring the procedural manner in which the Executive shall carry out the laws, surely the federal courts do not violate separation of powers when, at the very instruction and command of Congress, they enforce these procedures.

To prevent Congress from conferring standing for "procedural injuries" is another way of saying that Congress may not delegate to the courts authority deemed "executive" in nature. (Congress may not "transfer from the President to the courts the Chief Executive's most important constitutional duty, to 'take Care that the Laws be faithfully executed,' Art. II, sec. 3"). Here Congress seeks not to delegate "executive" power but only to strengthen the procedures it has legislatively mandated. "We have long recognized that the nondelegation doctrine does not prevent Congress from seeking assistance, within proper limits, from its coordinate Branches." Touby v. United States,111 S.Ct. 1752, 1756 (1991). "Congress does not violate the Constitution merely because it legislates in broad terms, leaving a certain degree of discretion to executive or judicial actors " (emphasis added).

Ironically, this Court has previously justified a relaxed review of congressional delegation to the Executive on grounds that Congress, in turn, has subjected the exercise of that power to judicial review. INS v. Chadha, 462 U.S. 919, 953-954, n. 16, 103 S.Ct. 2764, 2785-2786, n. 16, 77 L.Ed.2d 317 (1983); American Power & Light Co. v. SEC, 329 U.S., at 105-106, 67 S.Ct. at 142-143. The Court's intimation today that procedural injuries are not constitutionally cognizable threatens this understanding upon which Congress has undoubtedly relied. In no sense is the Court's suggestion compelled by our "common understanding of what activities are appropriate to legislatures, to executives, and to courts." In my view, it reflects an unseemly solicitude for an expansion of power of the Executive Branch.

It is to be hoped that over time the Court will acknowledge that some classes of procedural duties are so enmeshed with the prevention of a substantive, concrete harm that an individual plaintiff may be able to demonstrate a sufficient likelihood of injury just through the breach of that procedural duty. For example, in the context of the NEPA requirement of environmental impact statements, this Court has acknowledged "it is now well settled that NEPA itself does not mandate particular results [and] simply prescribes the necessary process," but "these procedures are almost certain to affect the agency's substantive decision." Robertson v. Methow Valley Citizens Council, 490 U.S., 332, 350, 109 S.Ct. 1835, 1846, 104 L.Ed.2d 351 (1989) (emphasis added). See also Andrus v. Sierra Club, 442 U.S. 347, 350- 351, 99 S.Ct. 2335, 2337, 60 L.Ed.2d 943 (1979) ("If environmental concerns are not interwoven into the fabric of agency planning, the 'action-forcing' characteristics of [the environmental-impact statement requirement] would be lost"). This acknowledgement of an inextricable link between procedural and substantive harm does not reflect improper appellate factfinding. It reflects nothing more than the proper deference owed to the judgment of a coordinate branch--Congress--that certain procedures are directly tied to protection against a substantive harm.

In short, determining "injury" for Article III standing purposes is a fact-specific inquiry. "Typically ... the standing inquiry requires careful judicial examination of a complaint's allegations to ascertain whether the particular plaintiff is entitled to an adjudication of the particular claims asserted." Allen v. Wright, 468 U.S., at 752, 104 S.Ct., at 3325. There may be factual circumstances in which a congressionally imposed procedural requirement is so insubstantially connected to the prevention of a substantive harm that it cannot be said to work any conceivable injury to an individual litigant. But, as a general matter, the courts owe substantial deference to Congress' substantive purpose in imposing a certain procedural requirement. In all events, "[o]ur separation-of-powers analysis does not turn on the labeling of an activity as 'substantive' as opposed to 'procedural.' " Mistretta v. United States, 488 U.S. 361, 393, 109 S.Ct. 647, 665, 102 L.Ed.2d 714 (1989). There is no room for a per se rule or presumption excluding injuries labeled "procedural" in nature.

III In conclusion, I cannot join the Court on what amounts to a slash-and-burn expedition through the law of environmental standing. In my view, "[t]he very essence of civil liberty certainly consists in the right of every individual to claim the protection of the laws, whenever he receives an injury." Marbury v. Madison, 1 Cranch 137, 163, 2 L.Ed. 60 (1803). I dissent.

COMMENTARY AND QUESTIONS

1. After *Lujan*. After *Lujan*, what is the status of the international applicability of the Endangered Species Act? What appears to be the potential count on this point amongst the nine justices so far as can be divined from their opinions? Isn't Justice Stevens the only one who clearly says he doesn't think the ESA applies overseas?

2. How much harm is needed to find sufficient injury for standing? The Supreme Court as a whole agrees that if the two women had plane tickets in hand, they would have actionable injuries. Is the difference between having and not having plane tickets a serious distinction or a ridiculous technicality when determining standing?

3. "Nexus" approaches — a way to satisfy this standing hurdle? Which, if any, of the nexus approaches offers a workable doctrine from which to generate standing?

David H. Lucas v. South Carolina Coastal Council

United States Supreme Court, 1992

112 S.Ct. 2886

[In December 1986, petitioner Lucas bought two nonadjacent residential lots, #22 and #24, in a South Carolina barrier island development, intending to build single-family homes such as those on the immediately adjacent parcels. At that time, Lucas's lots were not subject to the State's coastal zone building permit requirements. In 1988, however, the state legislature enacted the Beachfront Management Act, which barred construction seaward of a coastal erosion line to be set by defendant Council after hydrological analysis of the barrier beach locations. The Council determined that Lucas's lots had been within the surf zone 50% of the time since 1949, and that they were well within the restricted 40-year erosion cycle area. Accordingly Lucas was prohibited from erecting any permanent habitable structures on his parcels.[1] He filed suit, arguing that the ban deprived him of all "economically viable use" of his property and therefore effected a "taking." The state trial court agreed, finding that the ban rendered Lucas's parcels "valueless," and entered an award exceeding $1.2 million. In reversing, 404 S.E.2d 895, citing the *Mugler*-type noxious use cases, the State Supreme Court held itself bound, in light of Lucas's failure to attack the Act's general validity, to accept the legislature's "uncontested ... findings" that new construction in the coastal zone threatened a valuable public resource, and that when a regulation is designed to prevent "harmful or noxious uses" of property akin to public nuisances, no compensation is owing under the Takings Clause regardless of the regulation's effect on the property's value.]

Scalia, J. ...Our decision in [Pennsylvania Coal v.] Mahon offered little insight into when, and under what circumstances, a given regulation would be seen as going "too far" for purposes of the Fifth Amendment. In 70-odd years of succeeding "regulatory takings" jurisprudence, we have generally eschewed any " 'set formula" ' for determining how far is too far, preferring to "engag[e] in ... essentially ad hoc, factual inquiries...." We have, however, described at least two discrete categories of regulatory action as compensable without case-specific inquiry into the public interest advanced in support of the restraint. The first encompasses regulations that compel the property owner to suffer a physical "invasion" of his property....

The second situation in which we have found categorical treatment appropriate is where regulation denies all economically beneficial or productive use of land. [citing:] Agins, 447 U.S., at 260; see also Nollan v. California Coastal Comm'n, 483 U.S. 825, 834 (1987); Keystone Bituminous Coal Assn. v. DeBenedictis, 480 U.S. 470, 495 (1987); Hodel v. Virginia Surface Mining & Reclamation Assn., Inc., 452 U.S. 264, 295-296 (1981).[2] As we have said on numerous

---

[1] The Act did allow the construction of certain nonhabitable improvements, e.g., "wooden walkways no larger in width than six feet," and "small wooden decks no larger than one hundred forty-four square feet."

[2] [Original fn 6] We will not attempt to respond to all of JUSTICE BLACKMUN's mistaken citation of case precedent. Characteristic of its nature is his assertion that the cases we discuss here stand merely for the proposition "that proof that a regulation does not deny an owner economic use of his property is sufficient to defeat a facial taking challenge" and not for the point that "denial of such use is sufficient to establish a taking claim regardless of any other consideration." Post, at 15, n. 11. The cases say, repeatedly and unmistakably, that " '[t]he test to be applied in considering [a] facial [takings] challenge is fairly straightforward. A statute regulating the uses that can be made of property effects a taking if it "denies an owner economically viable use of his land."' " Keystone, 480 U.S., at 495 (quoting Hodel, 452

occasions, the Fifth Amendment is violated when land-use regulation "does not substantially advance legitimate state interests *or denies an owner economically viable use of his land.*" Agins, supra, at 260 (emphasis added). [3]

We have never set forth the justification for this rule. Perhaps it is simply, as Justice Brennan suggested, that total deprivation of beneficial use is, from the landowner's point of view, the equivalent of a physical appropriation. See San Diego Gas & Electric Co. v. San Diego, 450 U.S., at 652 (Brennan, J., dissenting). "[F]or what is the land but the profits thereof [?]" 1 E. Coke, Institutes ch. 1, §1 (1st Am. ed. 1812). Surely, at least, in the extraordinary circumstance when no productive or economically beneficial use of land is permitted, it is less realistic to indulge our usual assumption that the legislature is simply "adjusting the benefits and burdens of economic life," *Penn Central,* 438 U.S., at 124, in a manner that secures an "average reciprocity of advantage" to everyone concerned. *Pennsylvania Coal,,* 260 U.S., at 415. And the functional basis for permitting the government, by regulation, to affect property values without compensation– that "Government hardly could go on if to some extent values incident to property could not be diminished without paying for every such change in the general law," id., at 413 – does not apply to the relatively rare situations where the government has deprived a landowner of all economically beneficial uses.

On the other side of the balance, affirmatively supporting a compensation requirement, is the fact that regulations that leave the owner of land without economically beneficial or productive options for its use – typically, as here, by requiring land to be left substantially in its natural state – carry with them a heightened risk that private property is being pressed into some form of public service under the guise of mitigating serious public harm.... We think, in short, that there are good reasons for our frequently expressed belief that when the owner of real property has been called upon to sacrifice all economically beneficial uses in the name of

---

U.S., at 295-296 (quoting Agins, 447 U.S., at 260)) (emphasis added). JUSTICE BLACKMUN describes that rule (which we do not invent but merely apply today) as "alter[ing] the long-settled rules of review" by foisting on the State "the burden of showing [its] regulation is not a taking." Post, at 11, 12. This is of course wrong. Lucas had to do more than simply file a lawsuit to establish his constitutional entitlement; he had to show that the Beachfront Management Act denied him economically beneficial use of his land. Our analysis presumes the unconstitutionality of state land-use regulation only in the sense that any rule-with- exceptions presumes the invalidity of a law that violates it.... JUSTICE BLACKMUN's realquarrel is with the substantive standard of liability we apply in this case, a long-established standard we see no need to repudiate.

[3] [Original fn 7] Regrettably, the rhetorical force of our "deprivation of all economically feasible use" rule is greater than its precision, since the rule does not make clear the "property interest" against which the loss of value is to be measured. When, for example, a regulation requires a developer to leave 90% of a rural tract in its natural state, it is unclear whether we would analyze the situation as one in which the owner has been deprived of all economically beneficial use of the burdened portion of the tract, or as one in which the owner has suffered a mere diminution in value of the tract as a whole.... Unsurprisingly, this uncertainty regarding the composition of the denominator in our "deprivation" fraction has produced inconsistent pronouncements by the Court. Compare Pennsylvania Coal ...Keystone Bituminous.... The answer to this difficult question may lie in how the owner's reasonable expectations have been shaped by the State's law of property-i. e., whether and to what degree the State's law has accorded legal recognition and protection to the particular interest in land with respect to which the takings claimant alleges a diminution in (or elimination of) value. In any event, we avoid this difficulty in the present case, since the "interest in land" that Lucas has pleaded (a fee simple interest) is an estate with a rich tradition of protection at common law, and since the South Carolina Court of Common Pleas found that the' Beachfront Management Act left each of Lucas's beachfront lots without economic value.

the common good, that is, to leave his property economically idle, he has suffered a taking.[4]

B ...It is correct that many of our prior opinions have suggested that "harmful or noxious uses" of property may be proscribed by government regulation without the requirement of compensation. For a number of reasons, however, we think the South Carolina Supreme Court was too quick to conclude that that principle decides the present case. The "harmful or noxious uses" principle was the Court's early attempt to describe in theoretical terms why government may, consistent with the Takings Clause, affect property values by regulation without incurring an obligation to compensate – a reality we nowadays acknowledge explicitly with respect to the full scope of the State's police power.... "Harmful or noxious use" analysis was, in other words, simply the progenitor of our more contemporary statements that "land-use regulation does not effect a taking if it 'substantially advance[s] legitimate state interests'...." Nollan, supra, at 834 (quoting Agins v. Tiburon, 447 U.S., at 260); see also Penn Central Transportation Co., supra, at 127; Euclid v. Ambler Realty Co., 272 U.S. 365, 387-388 (1926).

The transition from our early focus on control of "noxious" uses to our contemporary understanding of the broad realm within which government may regulate without compensation was an easy one, since the distinction between "harm-preventing" and "benefit-conferring" regulation is often in the eye of the beholder. It is quite possible, for example, to describe in either fashion the ecological, economic, and aesthetic concerns that inspired the South Carolina legislature in the present case. One could say that imposing a servitude on Lucas's land is necessary in order to prevent his use of it from "harming" South Carolina's ecological resources; or, instead, in order to achieve the "benefits" of an ecological preserve.[5] ...

---

[4] [Original fn 8] JUSTICE STEVENS criticizes the "deprivation of all economicallybeneficial use" rule as "wholly arbitrary", in that "[the] landowner whose property is diminished in value 95% recovers nothing," while the landowner who suffers a complete elimination of value "recovers the land's full value." Post, at 4. This analysis errs in its assumption that the landowner whose deprivation is one step short of complete is not entitled to compensation. Such an owner might not be able to claim the benefit of our categorical formulation, but, as we have acknowledged time and again, "[t]he economic impact of the regulation on the claimant and ... the extent to which the regulation has interfered with distinct investment- backed expectations" are keenly relevant to takings analysis generally. Penn Central Transportation Co. v. New York City, 438 U.S. 104, 124 (1978). It is true that in at least some cases the landowner with 95% loss will get nothing, while the landowner with total loss will recover in full. But that occasional result is no more strange than the gross disparity between the landowner whose premises are taken for a highway (who recovers in full) and the landowner whose property is reduced to 5% of its former value by the highway (who recovers nothing). Takings law is full of these "all-or-nothing" situations....

[5] [Original fn 10, 11] The legislature's express findings include the following: "The General Assembly finds that: "(1) The beach/dune system along the coast of South Carolina is extremely important to the people of this State and serves the following functions: "(a) protects life and property by serving as a storm barrier which dissipates wave energy and contributes to shoreline stability in an economical and effective manner; "(b) provides the basis for a tourism industry that generates approximately two-thirds of South Carolina's annual tourism industry revenue which constitutes a significant portion of the state's economy. The tourists who come to the South Carolina coast to enjoy the ocean and dry sand beach contribute significantly to state and local tax revenues; "(c) provides habitat for numerous species of plants and animals, several of which are threatened or endangered. Waters adjacent to the beach/dune system also provide habitat for many other marine species; "(d) provides a natural health environment for the citizens of South Carolina to spend leisure time which serves their physical and mental well- being. "(2) Beach/dune system vegetation is unique and extremely important to the vitality and preservation of the system. "(3) Many miles of South Carolina's beaches have been identified as critically eroding. " (4) ... [D]evelopment unwisely has been sited too close to the [beach/dune] system. This type of development

A given restraint will be seen as mitigating "harm" to the adjacent parcels or securing a "benefit" for them, depending upon the observer's evaluation of the relative importance of the use that the restraint favors. See Sax, Takings and the Police Power, 74 Yale L. J. 36, 49 (1964).... Whether Lucas's construction of single-family residences on his parcels should be described as bringing "harm" to South Carolina's adjacent ecological resources thus depends principally upon whether the describer believes that the State's use interest in nurturing those resources is so important that any competing adjacent use must yield.... [6]

Noxious-use logic cannot serve as a touchstone to distinguish regulatory "takings"-which require compensation-from regulatory deprivations that do not require compensation. A fortiori the legislature's recitation of a noxious-use justification cannot be the basis for departing from our categorical rule that total regulatory takings must be compensated. If it were, departure would virtually always be allowed. The South Carolina Supreme Court's approach would essentially nullify Mahon's affirmation of limits to the noncompensable exercise of the police

---

has jeopardized the stability of the beach/dune system, accelerated erosion, and endangered adjacent property. It is in both the public and private interests to protect the system from this unwise development. "(5) The use of armoring in the form of hard erosion control devices such as seawalls, bulkheads, and rip-rap to protect erosion-threatened structures adjacent to the beach has not proven effective. These armoring devices have given a false sense of security to beachfront property owners. In reality, these hard structures, in many instances, have increased the vulnerability of beachfront property to damage from wind and waves while contributing to the deterioration and loss of the dry sand beach which is so important to the tourism industry. "(6) Erosion is a natural process which becomes a significant problem for man only when structures are erected in close proximity to the beach/dune system. It is in both the public and private interests to afford the beach/dune system space to accrete and erode in its natural cycle. This space can be provided only by discouraging new construction in close proximity to the beach/dune system and encouraging those who have erected structures too close to the system to retreat from it. ..... "(8) It is in the state's best interest to protect and to promote increased public access to South Carolina's beaches for out-of-state tourists and South Carolina residents alike." S. C. Code s 48-39-250 (Supp. 1991).

[11] In the present case, in fact, some of the "[South Carolina] legislature's 'findings" ' to which the South Carolina Supreme Court purported to defer in characterizing the purpose of the Act as "harmpreventing," 304 S. C. 376, 385, 404 S. E. 2d 895, 900 (1991), seem to us phrased in "benefit-conferring" language instead. For example, they describe the importance of a construction ban in enhancing "South Carolina's annual tourism industry revenue," S. C. Code s 48- 39250(1)(b) (Supp. 1991), in "provid[ing] habitat for numerous species of plants and animals, several of which are threatened or endangered," s 48- 39-250(1)(c), and in "provid[ing] a natural healthy environment for the citizens of South Carolina to spend leisure time which serves their physical and mental well-being." s 48-39-250(1)(d). It would be pointless to make the outcome of this case hang upon this terminology, since the same interests could readily be described in "harm-preventing" fashion. JUSTICE BLACKMUN, however, apparently insists that we must make the outcome hinge (exclusively) upon the South Carolina Legislature's other, "harm- preventing" characterizations, focusing on the declaration that "prohibitions on building in front of the setback line are necessary to protect people and property from storms, high tides, and beach erosion." Post, at 6. He says "[n]othing in the record undermines [this] assessment," ibid., apparently seeing no significance in the fact that the statute permits owners of existing structures to remain (and even to rebuild if their structures are not "destroyed beyond repair," S. C. Code Ann. s 48- 39-290(B)), and in the fact that the 1990 amendment authorizes the Council to issue permits for new construction in violation of the uniform prohibition.

[6] [Original fn 12] In JUSTICE BLACKMUN's view, even with respect to regulations that deprive an owner of all developmental or economically beneficial land uses, the test for required compensation is whether the legislature has recited a harm-preventing justification for its action. See post, at 5, 13-17. Since such a justification can be formulated in practically every case, this amounts to a test of whether the legislature has a stupid staff....

power. Our cases provide no support for this: None of them that employed the logic of "harmful use" prevention to sustain a regulation involved an allegation that the regulation wholly eliminated the value of the claimant's land. See Keystone Bituminous, 480 U.S. at 513-514 (REHNQUIST, C.J., dissenting).

Where the State seeks to sustain regulation that deprives land of all economically beneficial use, we think it may resist compensation only if the logically antecedent inquiry into the nature of the owner's estate shows that the proscribed use interests were not part of his title to begin with. This accords, we think, with our "takings" juris prudence, which has traditionally been guided by the understandings of our citizens regarding the content of, and the State's power over, the "bundle of rights" that they acquire when they obtain title to property. It seems to us that the property owner necessarily expects the uses of his property to be restricted, from time to time, by various measures newly enacted by the State in legitimate exercise of its police powers; "[a]s long recognized, some values are enjoyed under an implied limitation and must yield to the police power." Pennsylvania Coal, 260 U.S.,at 413. And in the case of personal property, by reason of the State's traditionally high degree of control over commercial dealings, he ought to be aware of the possibility that new regulation might even render his property economically worthless (at least if the property's only economically productive use is sale or manufacture for sale), see Andrus v. Allard, 444 U.S. 51, 66-67 (1979)(prohibition on sale of eagle feathers). In the case of land, however, we think the notion pressed by the Council that title is somehow held subject to the "implied limitation" that the State may subsequently eliminate all economically valuable use is inconsistent with the historical compact recorded in the Takings Clause that has become part of our constitutional culture. [7] [

Where "permanent physical occupation" of land is concerned, we have refused to allow the government to decree it anew (without compensation), no matter how weighty the asserted "public interests" involved.... We believe similar treatment must be accorded confiscatory regulations, i. e., regulations that prohibit all economically beneficial use of land: Any limitation so severe cannot be newly legislated or decreed (without compensation), but must inhere in the title itself, in the restrictions that background principles of the State's law of property and nuisance already place upon land ownership. A law or decree with such an effect must, in other words, do no more than duplicate the result that could have been achieved in the courts-by adjacent landowners (or other uniquely affected persons) under the State's law of private nuisance, or by the State under its complementary power to abate nuisances that affect

---

[7] [Original fn 15] After accusing us of "launch[ing] a missile to kill a mouse," post, at 1, JUSTICE BLACKMUN expends a good deal of throw-weight of his own upon a noncombatant, arguing that our description of the "understanding" of land ownership that informs the Takings Clause is not supported by early American experience. That is largely true, but entirely irrelevant. The practices of the States prior to incorporation of the Takings and Just Compensation Clauses, see Chicago, B. & Q. R. Co. v. Chicago, 166 U.S. 226 (1897)-which, as JUSTICE BLACKMUN acknowledges, occasionally included outright physical appropriation of land without compensation, see post, at 22-were out of accord with any plausible interpretation of those provisions. JUSTICE BLACKMUN is correct that early constitutional theorists did not believe the Takings Clause embraced regulations of property at all, see post, at 23, and n. 23, but even he does not suggest (explicitly, at least) that we renounce the Court's contrary conclusion in Mahon. Since the text of the Clause can be read to encompass regulatory as well as physical deprivations (in contrast to the text originally proposed by Madison, see Speech Proposing Bill of Rights (June 8, 1789), in 12 J. Madison, The Papers of James Madison 201 (C. Hobson, R. Rutland, W. Rachal, & J. Sisson ed. 1979) ("No person shall be ... obliged to relinquish his property, where it may be necessary for public use, without a just compensation"), we decline to do so as well.

the public generally, or otherwise.[8]

On this analysis, the owner of a lake bed, for example, would not be entitled to compensation when he is denied the requisite permit to engage in a landfilling operation that would have the effect of flooding others' land. Nor the corporate owner of a nuclear generating plant, when it is directed to remove all improvements from its land upon discovery that the plant sits astride an earthquake fault. Such regulatory action may well have the effect of eliminating the land's only economically productive use, but it does not proscribe a productive use that was previously permissible under relevant property and nuisance principles. The use of these properties for what are now expressly prohibited purposes was always unlawful, and (subject to other constitutional limitations) it was open to the State at any point to make the implication of those background principles of nuisance and property law explicit. See Michelman, Property, Utility, and Fairness, Comments on the Ethical Foundations of "Just Compensation" Law, 80 Harv. L. Rev. 1165, 1239- 1241 (1967). In light of our traditional resort to "existing rules or understandings that stem from an independent source such as state law" to define the range of interests that qualify for protection as "property" under the Fifth (and Fourteenth) amendments [citations omitted], this recognition that the Takings Clause does not require compensation when an owner is barred from putting land to a use that is proscribed by those "existing rules or understandings" is surely unexceptional. When, however, a regulation that declares "off-limits" all economically productive or beneficial uses of land goes beyond what the relevant background principles would dictate, compensation must be paid to sustain it.[9]

The "total taking" inquiry we require today will ordinarily entail (as the application of state nuisance law ordinarily entails) analysis of, among other things, the degree of harm to public lands and resources, or adjacent private property, posed by the claimant's proposed activities, see, e.g., Restatement (Second) of Torts §§826, 827, the social value of the claimant's activities and their suitability to the locality in question, see, e.g., id., §§828(a) and (b), 831, and the relative ease with which the alleged harm can be avoided through measures taken by the claimant and the government (or adjacent private landowners) alike, see, e.g., id., §§827(e), 828(c), 830. The fact that a particular use has long been engaged in by similarly situated owners ordinarily imports a lack of any common-law prohibition (though changed circumstances or new knowledge may make what was previously permissible no longer so, see Restatement (Second) of Torts, supra, §827, comment g. So also does the fact that other landowners, similarly situated, are permitted to continue the use denied to the claimant.

It seems unlikely that common-law principles would have prevented the erection of any habitable or productive improvements on petitioner's land; they rarely support prohibition of the "essential use" of land, Curtin v. Benson, 222 U.S. 78, 86 (1911). The question, however, is one of state law to be dealt with on remand. We emphasize that to win its case South Carolina must do more than proffer the legislature's declaration that the uses Lucas desires are

---

8 [Original fn 16] The principal "otherwise" that we have in mind is litigation absolving the State (or private parties) of liability for the destruction of "real and personal property, in cases of actual necessity, to prevent the spreading of a fire" or to forestall other grave threats to the lives and property of others. Bowditch v. Boston, 101 U.S. 16, 18-19 (1880); see United States v. Pacific Railroad, 120 U.S. 227, 238-239 (1887).

9 [Original fn 17] Of course, the State may elect to rescind its regulation and thereby avoid having to pay compensation for a permanent deprivation. See First English Evangelical Lutheran Church, 482 U.S., at 321. But "where the [regulation has] already worked a taking of all use of property, no subsequent action by the government can relieve it of the duty to provide compensation for the period during which the taking was effective." Ibid.

inconsistent with the public interest, or the conclusory assertion that they violate a common-law maxim such as sic utere tuo ut alienum non laedas. As we have said, a "State, by ipse dixit, may not transform private property into public property without compensation...." Webb's Fabulous Pharmacies, Inc. v. Beckwith, 449 U.S. 155, 164 (1980). Instead, as it would be required to do if it sought to restrain Lucas in a common-law action for public nuisance, South Carolina must identify background principles of nuisance and property law that prohibit the uses he now intends in the circumstances in which the property is presently found. Only on this showing can the State fairly claim that, in proscribing all such beneficial uses, the Beachfront Management Act is taking nothing.[10] The judgment is reversed and the cause remanded....

JUSTICE KENNEDY, concurring in the judgment.

...The South Carolina Court of Common Pleas found that petitioner's real property has been rendered valueless by the State's regulation.... This is a curious finding, and I share the reservations of some of my colleagues about a finding that a beach front lot loses all value because of a development restriction....

The finding of no value must be considered under the Takings Clause by reference to the owner's reasonable, investment-backed expectations. Kaiser Aetna v. United States, 444 U.S. 164, 175 (1979); Penn Central Transportation Co. v. New York City, 438 U.S. 104, 124 (1978); see also W. B. Worthen Co. v. Kavanaugh, 295 U.S. 56 (1935)....

In my view, reasonable expectations must be understood in light of the whole of our legal tradition. The common law of nuisance is too narrow a confine for the exercise of regulatory power in a complex and interdependent society. Goldblatt v. Hempstead, 369 U.S. 590, 593 (1962). The State should not be prevented from enacting new regulatory initiatives in response to changing conditions, and courts must consider all reasonable expectations whatever their source. The Takings Clause does not require a static body of state property law; it protects private expectations to ensure private investment. I agree with the Court that nuisance prevention accords with the most common expectations of property owners who face regulation, but I do not believe this can be the sole source of state authority to impose severe restrictions. Coastal property may present such unique concerns for a fragile land system that the State can go further in regulating its development and use than the common law of nuisance might otherwise permit.

The Supreme Court of South Carolina erred, in my view, by reciting the general purposes for which the state regulations were enacted without a determination that they were in accord with the owner's reasonable expectations and therefore sufficient to support a severe restriction on specific parcels of property.... With these observations, I concur in the judgment of the Court.

JUSTICE BLACKMUN, dissenting.

Today the Court launches a missile to kill a mouse.

---

10 [Original fn 18] JUSTICE BLACKMUN decries our reliance on background nuisance principles at least in part because he believes those principles to be as manipulable as we find the "harm prevention"/"benefit conferral" dichotomy, see post, at 20-21. There is no doubt some leeway in a court's interpretation of what existing state law permits-but not remotely as much, we think, as in a legislative crafting of the reasons for its confiscatory regulation. We stress that an affirmative decree eliminating all economically beneficial uses may be defended only if an objectively reasonable application of relevant precedents would exclude those beneficial uses in the circumstances in which the land is presently found.

The State of South Carolina prohibited petitioner Lucas from building a permanent structure on his property from 1988 to 1990. Relying on an unreviewed (and implausible) state trial court finding that this restriction left Lucas' property valueless, this Court granted review to determine whether compensation must be paid in cases where the State prohibits all economic use of real estate. According to the Court, such an occasion never has arisen in any of our prior cases, and the Court imagines that it will arise "relatively rarely" or only in "extraordinary circumstances." Almost certainly it did not happen in this case.

Nonetheless, the Court presses on to decide the issue, and as it does, it ignores its jurisdictional limits, remakes its traditional rules of review, and creates simultaneously a new categorical rule and an exception (neither of which is rooted in our prior case law, common law, or common sense). I protest not only the Court's decision, but each step taken to reach it. More fundamentally, I question the Court's wisdom in issuing sweeping new rules to decide such a narrow case. Surely, as JUSTICE KENNEDY demonstrates, the Court could have reached the result it wanted without inflicting this damage upon our Taking Clause jurisprudence.

My fear is that the Court's new policies will spread beyond the narrow confines of the present case. For that reason, I, like the Court, will give far greater attention to this case than its narrow scope suggests-not because I can intercept the Court's missile, or save the targeted mouse, but because I hope perhaps to limit the collateral damage....

I B

Petitioner Lucas is a contractor, manager, and part owner of the Wild Dune development on the Isle of Palms. He has lived there since 1978. In December 1986, he purchased two of the last four pieces of vacant property in the development.[11] The area is notoriously unstable. In roughly half of the last 40 years, all or part of petitioner's property was part of the beach or flooded twice daily by the ebb and flow of the tide. See Transcript, 84-102. Between 1957 and 1963, petitioner's property was under water. Between 1963 and 1973 the shoreline was 100 to 150 feet onto petitioner's property. In 1973 the first line of stable vegetation was about halfway through the property. Between 1981 and 1983, the Isle of Palms issued 12 emergency orders for sandbagging to protect property in the Wild Dune development....

The Beachfront Management Act includes a finding by the South Carolina General Assembly that the beach/dune system serves the purpose of "protect[ing] life and property by serving as a storm barrier which dissipates wave energy and contributes to shoreline stability in an economical and effective manner." §48-39-250(1)(a). The General Assembly also found that "development unwisely has been sited too close to the [beach/dune] system. This type of development has jeopardized the stability of the beach/dune system, accelerated erosion, and endangered adjacent property." §48-39-250(4); see also §48-39- 250(6) (discussing the need to "afford the beach/dune system space to accrete and erode").

If the state legislature is correct that the prohibition on building in front of the setback line prevents serious harm, then, under this Court's prior cases, the Act is constitutional.... The Court consistently has upheld regulations imposed to arrest a significant threat to the common welfare, whatever their economic effect on the owner....

Nothing in the record undermines the General Assembly's assessment that prohibitions on

---

[11] The properties were sold frequently at rapidly escalating prices before Lucas purchased them. Lot 22 was first sold in 1979 for $96,660, sold in 1984 for $187,500, then in 1985 for $260,000, and, finally, to Lucas in 1986 for $475,000. He estimated its worth in 1991 at $650,000. Lot 24 had a similar past. The record does not indicate who purchased the properties prior to Lucas, or why none of the purchasers held on to the lots and built on them.

building in front of the setback line are necessary to protect people and property from storms, high tides, and beach erosion. Because that legislative determination cannot be disregarded in the absence of such evidence, see, e.g., Euclid, 272 U.S., at 388; O'Gorman & Young v. Hartford Fire Ins. Co, 282 U.S. 251, 257-258 (1931) (Brandeis, J.), and because its determination of harm to life and property from building is sufficient to prohibit that use under this Court's cases, the South Carolina Supreme Court correctly found no taking....

The trial court...found the property "valueless." The court accepted no evidence from the State on the property's value without a home, and petitioner's appraiser testified that he never had considered what the value would be absent a residence. The appraiser's value was based on the fact that the "highest and best use of these lots ... [is] luxury single family detached dwellings." The trial court appeared to believe that the property could be considered "valueless" if it was not available for its most profitable use....

Clearly, [this] Court was eager to decide this case. But eagerness, in the absence of proper jurisdiction, must-and in this case should have been-met with restraint.

III The Court's willingness to dispense with precedent in its haste to reach a result is not limited to its initial jurisdictional decision. The Court also alters the long-settled rules of review.

The South Carolina Supreme Court's decision to defer to legislative judgments in the absence of a challenge from petitioner comports with one of this Court's oldest maxims: "the existence of facts supporting the legislative judgment is to be presumed." United States v. Carolene Products Co., 304 U.S. 144, 152 (1938). Indeed, we have said the legislature's judgment is "well-nigh conclusive." Berman v. Parker, 348 U.S. 26, 32 (1954). ...

IV The Court does not reject the South Carolina Supreme Court's decision simply on the basis of its disbelief and distrust of the legislature's findings. It also takes the opportunity to create a new scheme for regulations that eliminate all economic value. From now on, there is a categorical rule finding these regulations to be a taking unless the use they prohibit is a background common-law nuisance or property principle.

A. I first question the Court's rationale in creating a category that obviates a "case-specific inquiry into the public interest advanced," if all economic value has been lost. If one fact about the Court's taking jurisprudence can be stated without contradiction, it is that "the particular circumstances of each case" determine whether a specific restriction will be rendered invalid by the government's failure to pay compensation....

This Court repeatedly has recognized the ability of government, in certain circumstances, to regulate property without compensation no matter how adverse the financial effect on the owner may be.... In Keystone Bituminous Coal, the Court summarized over 100 years of precedent: "the Court has repeatedly upheld regulations that destroy or adversely affect real property interests."[12] The Court recognizes that "our prior opinions have suggested that

---

12 [Dissent fn 10, 11] [In the First English Evangelica casel,] on remand, the California court found no taking in part because the zoning regulation "involves this highest of public interests – the prevention of death and injury." First Lutheran Church v. Los Angeles, 210 Cal. App. 3d 1353, 1370, 258 Cal. Rptr. 893, (1989), cert. denied, 493 U.S. 1056 (1990). [11] The Court's suggestion that Agins v. Tiburon, 447 U.S. 255 (1980), a unanimous opinion, created a new per se rule, only now discovered, is unpersuasive. In Agins, the Court stated that "no precise rule determines when property has been taken" but instead that "the question necessarily requires a weighing of public and private interest." Id., at 260-262. The other cases cited by the Court, ante, at 9, repeat the Agins sentence, but in no way suggest that the public interest is irrelevant if total value has been taken. The Court has indicated that proof that a regulation does not

'harmful or noxious uses' of property may be proscribed by government regulation without the requirement of compensation," ante, at 17, but seeks to reconcile them with its categorical rule by claiming that the Court never has upheld a regulation when the owner alleged the loss of all economic value. Even if the Court's factual premise were correct, its understanding of the Court's cases is distorted. In none of the cases did the Court suggest that the right of a State to prohibit certain activities without paying compensation turned on the availability of some residual valuable use. Instead, the cases depended on whether the government interest was sufficient to prohibit the activity, given the significant private cost.

These cases rest on the principle that the State has full power to prohibit an owner's use of property if it is harmful to the public. "[S]ince no individual has a right to use his property so as to create a nuisance or otherwise harm others, the State has not 'taken' anything when it asserts its power to enjoin the nuisance-like activity." Keystone Bituminous Coal, 480 U.S., at 491, n. 20. It would make no sense under this theory to suggest that an owner has a constitutionally protected right to harm others, if only he makes the proper showing of economic loss....[13] Ultimately even the Court cannot embrace the full implications of its per se rule: it eventually agrees that there cannot be a categorical rule for a taking based on economic value that wholly disregards the public need asserted. Instead, the Court decides that it will permit a State to regulate all economic value only if the State prohibits uses that would not be permitted under "background principles of nuisance and property law."[14]

Until today, the Court explicitly had rejected the contention that the government's power to act without paying compensation turns on whether the prohibited activity is a common-law nuisance.[15] The brewery closed in Mugler itself was not a common-law nuisance, and the Court

---

deny an owner economic use of his property is sufficient to defeat a facial taking challenge. See Hodel v. Virginia Surface Mining & Reclamation Assn., Inc., 452 U.S. 264, 295-297 (1981). But the conclusion that a regulation is not on its face a taking because it allows the landowner some economic use of property is a far cry from the proposition that denial of such use is sufficient to establish a taking claim regardless of any other consideration. The Court never has accepted the latter proposition. The Court relies today on dicta in Agins, Hodel, Nollan v. California Coastal Comm'n, 483 U.S. 825 (1987), and Keystone Bituminous Coal v. DeBenedictis, 480 U.S. 470 (1987), for its new categorical rule. Ante, at 10.

13 "Indeed, it would be extraordinary to construe the Constitution to require a government to compensate private landowners because it denied them 'the right' to use property which cannot be used without risking injury and death." First Lutheran Church, 210 Cal. App. 3d, at 1366

14 Although it refers to state nuisance and property law, the Court apparently does not mean just any state nuisance and property law. Public nuisance was first a common-law creation, see Newark, The Boundaries of Nuisance, 65 L. Q. Rev. 480, 482 (1949) (attributing development of nuisance to 1535), but by the 1800s in both the United States and England, legislatures had the power to define what is a public nuisance, and particular uses often have been selectively targeted. See Prosser, Private Action for Public Nuisance, 52 Va. L. Rev. 997, 999-1000 (1966); J.F. Stephen, A General View of the Criminal Law of England 105-107 (2d ed. 1890). The Court's references to "common-law" background principles, however, indicate that legislative determinations do not constitute "state nuisance and property law" for the Court.

15 Also, until today the fact that the regulation prohibited uses that were lawful at the time the owner purchased did not determine the constitutional question. The brewery, the brickyard, the cedar trees, and the gravel pit were all perfectly legitimate uses prior to the passage of the regulation. See Mugler v. Kansas, 123 U.S. 623, 654 (1887); Hadacheck v. Los Angeles, 239 U.S. 394 (1915); Miller, 276 U.S., at 272; Goldblatt v. Hempstead, 369 U.S. 590 (1962). This Court explicitly acknowledged in Hadacheck that "[a] vested interest cannot be asserted against [the police power] because of conditions once obtaining. To so hold would preclude development and fix a city forever in its primitive conditions." 239 U.S., at 410.

specifically stated that it was the role of the legislature to determine what measures would be appropriate for the protection of public health and safety....

The Court rejects the notion that the State always can prohibit uses it deems a harm to the public without granting compensation because "the distinction between 'harm-preventing' and 'benefit-conferring' regulation is often in the eye of the beholder." ... The Court, however, fails to explain how its proposed common law alternative escapes the same trap.

The threshold inquiry for imposition of the Court's new rule, "deprivation of all economically valuable use," itself cannot be determined objectively. As the Court admits, whether the owner has been deprived of all economic value of his property will depend on how "property" is defined....

The Court's decision in Keystone Bituminous Coal illustrates this principle perfectly. In Keystone, the Court determined that the "support estate" was "merely a part of the entire bundle of rights possessed by the owner." 480 U.S., at 501. Thus, the Court concluded that the support estate's destruction merely eliminated one segment of the total property. Ibid. The dissent, however, characterized the support estate as a distinct property interest that was wholly destroyed. Id., at 519. The Court could agree on no "value-free basis" to resolve this dispute.

Even more perplexing, however, is the Court's reliance on common-law principles of nuisance in its quest for a value-free taking jurisprudence. In determining what is a nuisance at common law, state courts make exactly the decision that the Court finds so troubling when made by the South Carolina General Assembly today: they determine whether the use is harmful. Common-law public and private nuisance law is simply a determination whether a particular use causes harm. See Prosser, Private Action for Public Nuisance, 52 Va. L. Rev. 997, 997 (1966) ("Nuisance is a French word which means nothing more than harm"). There is nothing magical in the reasoning of judges long dead. They determined a harm in the same way as state judges and legislatures do today. If judges in the 18th and 19th centuries can distinguish a harm from a benefit, why not judges in the 20th century, and if judges can, why not legislators? There simply is no reason to believe that new interpretations of the hoary common law nuisance doctrine will be particularly "objective" or "value-free." Once one abandons the level of generality of sic utere tuo ut alienum non laedas, ante, at 26, one searches in vain, I think, for anything resembling a principle in the common law of nuisance.

C ... The principle that the State should compensate individuals for property taken for public use was not widely established in America at the time of the Revolution. "The colonists ... inherited ... a concept of property which permitted extensive regulation of the use of that property for the public benefit- regulation that could even go so far as to deny all productive use of the property to the owner if, as Coke himself stated, the regulation 'extends to the public benefit ... for this is for the public, and every one hath benefit by it." ' F. Bosselman, D. Callies & J. Banta, The Taking Issue 80-81 (1973)....

Although, prior to the adoption of the Bill of Rights, America was replete with land use regulations,... the Fifth Amendment's Taking Clause originally did not extend to regulations of property,.whatever the effect.[16] Most state courts agreed with this narrow interpretation of a

[16] James Madison, author of the Taking Clause, apparently intended it to apply only to direct, physical takings of property by the Federal Government. See Treanor, The Origins and Original Significance of the Just Compensation Clause of the Fifth Amendment, 94 Yale L.J., 694, 711 (1985). Professor Sax argues that although "contemporaneous commentary upon the meaning of the compensation clause is in very short supply," 74 Yale L.J., at 58, the "few authorities that are available" indicate that the clause was

taking. "Until the end of the nineteenth century ... jurists held that the constitution protected possession only, and not value." Siegel, Understanding the Nineteenth Century Contract Clause: The Role of the Property-Privilege Distinction and "Takings" Clause Jurisprudence, 60 S. Cal. L. Rev. 1, 76 (1986); Bosselman 106....

In short, I find no clear and accepted "historical compact" or "understanding of our citizens" justifying the Court's new taking doctrine. Instead, the Court seems to treat history as a grab-bag of principles, to be adopted where they support the Court's theory, and ignored where they do not. ... What makes the Court's analysis unworkable is its attempt to package the law of two incompatible eras and peddle it as historical fact.

The Court makes sweeping and, in my view, misguided and unsupported changes in our taking doctrine. While it limits these changes to the most narrow subset of government regulation- those that eliminate all economic value from land- these changes go far beyond what is necessary to secure petitioner Lucas' private benefit. One hopes they do not go beyond the narrow confines the Court assigns them to today. I dissent.

JUSTICE STEVENS, dissenting.

...II. In its analysis of the merits, the Court starts from the premise that this Court has adopted a "categorical rule that total regulatory takings must be compensated," and then sets itself to the task of identifying the exceptional cases in which a State may be relieved of this categorical obligation. The test the Court announces is that the regulation must do no more than duplicate the result that could have been achieved under a State's nuisance law. Ante, at 24. Under this test the categorical rule will apply unless the regulation merely makes explicit what was otherwise an implicit limitation on the owner's property rights.

In my opinion, the Court is doubly in error. The categorical rule the Court establishes is an unsound and unwise addition to the law and the Court's formulation of the exception to that rule is too rigid and too narrow.

THE CATEGORICAL RULE

As the Court recognizes, Pennsylvania Coal Co. v. Mahon, 260 U.S. 393 (1922), provides no support for its-or, indeed, any-categorical rule. To the contrary, Justice Holmes recognized that such absolute rules ill fit the inquiry into "regulatory takings." Thus, in the paragraph that contains his famous observation that a regulation may go "too far" and thereby constitute a taking, the Justice wrote: "As we already have said, this is a question of degree-and therefore cannot be disposed of by general propositions." Id. at 416. What he had "already ... said" made perfectly clear that Justice Holmes regarded economic injury to be merely one factor to be weighed: "One fact for consideration in determining such limits is the extent of the diminution [of value.] So the question depends upon the particular facts." Id. at 413.

Nor does the Court's new categorical rule find support in decisions following Mahon. Although in dicta we have sometimes recited that a law "effects a taking if [it] ... denies an owner economically viable use of his land," Agins v. Tiburon, 447 U.S. 255, 260 (1980), our rulings have rejected such an absolute position. We have frequentlyand recently-held that, in some circumstances, a law that renders property valueless may nonetheless not constitute a taking. See, e.g., First English Evangelical Lutheran Church of Glendale v. County of Los Angeles, 482 U.S. 304, 313 (1987); Goldblatt v. Hempstead, 369 U.S. 590, 596 (1962); United States v. Caltex, 344 U.S. 149, 155 (1952); Miller v. Schoene, 276 U.S. 272 (1928); Hadachek v. Sebastian, 239

"designed to prevent arbitrary government action," not to protect economic value. Id., at 58-60.

U.S. 394, 405 (1915); Mugler v. Kansas, 123 U.S. 623, 657 (1887); cf. Ruckelshaus v. Monsanto Co., 467 U.S. 986, 1011 (1984); Connolly v. Pension Benefit Guaranty Corporation, 475 U.S. 211, 225 (1986). In short, as we stated in Keystone Bituminous Coal Assn. v. DeBenedictis, 480 U.S. 470, 490 (1987), " 'Although a comparison of values before and after' a regulatory action 'is relevant, ... it is by no means conclusive." '

In addition to lacking support in past decisions, the Court's new rule is wholly arbitrary. A landowner whose property is diminished in value 95% recovers nothing, while an owner whose property is diminished 100% recovers the land's full value. The case at hand illustrates this arbitrariness well. The Beachfront Management Act not only prohibited the building of new dwellings in certain areas, it also prohibited the rebuilding of houses that were "destroyed beyond repair by natural causes or by fire." 1988 S. C. Acts 634, §3; see also Esposito v. South Carolina Coastal Council, 939 F. 2d 165, 167 (CA4 1991). Thus, if the homes adjacent to Lucas' lot were destroyed by a hurricane one day after the Act took effect, the owners would not be able to rebuild, nor would they be assured recovery. Under the Court's categorical approach, Lucas (who has lost the opportunity to build) recovers, while his neighbors (who have lost both the opportunity to build and their homes) do not recover. The arbitrariness of such a rule is palpable....

Moreover, because of the elastic nature of property rights, the Court's new rule will also prove unsound in practice. In response to the rule, courts may define "property" broadly and only rarely find regulations to effect total takings. This is the approach the Court itself adopts in its revisionist reading of venerable precedents. We are told that-notwithstanding the Court's findings to the contrary in each case-the brewery in Mugler, the brickyard in Hadacheck, and the gravel pit in Goldblatt all could be put to "other uses" and that, therefore, those cases did not involve total regulatory takings.

On the other hand, developers and investors may market specialized estates to take advantage of the Court's new rule. The smaller the estate, the more likely that a regulatory change will effect a total taking. Thus, an investor may, for example, purchase the right to build a multi-family home on a specific lot, with the result that a zoning regulation that allows only single-family homes would render the investor's property interest "valueless." In short, the categorical rule will likely have one of two effects: Either courts will alter the definition of the "denominator" in the takings "fraction," rendering the Court's categorical rule meaningless, or investors will manipulate the relevant property interests, giving the Court's rule sweeping effect. To my mind, neither of these results is desirable or appropriate, and both are distortions of our takings jurisprudence.

Finally, the Court's justification for its new categorical rule is remarkably thin. The Court mentions in passing three arguments in support of its rule; none is convincing. First, the Court suggests that "total deprivation of feasible use is, from the landowner's point of view, the equivalent of a physical appropriation." Ante, at 12. This argument proves too much. From the "landowner's point of view," a regulation that diminishes a lot's value by 50% is as well "the equivalent" of the condemnation of half of the lot. Yet, it is well established that a 50% diminution in value does not by itself constitute a taking. See Euclid v. Ambler Realty Co., 272 U.S. 365, 384 (1926) (75% diminution in value). Thus, the landowner's perception of the regulation cannot justify the Court's new rule....

In short, the Court's new rule is unsupported by prior decisions, arbitrary and unsound in practice, and theoretically unjustified. In my opinion, a categorical rule as important as the one established by the Court today should be supported by more history or more reason than has yet been provided.

THE NUISANCE EXCEPTION

Like many bright-line rules, the categorical rule established in this case is only "categorical" for a NLSe or two in the U.S. Reports. No sooner does the Court state that "total regulatory takings must be compensated," ante, at 21, than it quickly establishes an exception to that rule.

The exception provides that a regulation that renders property valueless is not a taking if it prohibits uses of property that were not "previously permissible under relevant property and nuisance principles." Ante, at 24. The Court thus rejects the basic holding in Mugler v. Kansas, 123 U.S. 623 (1887). There we held that a state-wide statute that prohibited the owner of a brewery from making alcoholic beverages did not effect a taking, even though the use of the property had been perfectly lawful and caused no public harm before the statute was enacted....

The Court's holding today effectively freezes the State's common law, denying the legislature much of its traditional power to revise the law governing the rights and uses of property. Until today, I had thought that we had long abandoned this approach to constitutional law. More than a century ago we recognized that "the great office of statutes is to remedy defects in the common law as they are developed, and to adapt it to the changes of time and circumstances." Munn v. Illinois, 94 U.S. 113, 134 (1877). As Justice Marshall observed about a position similar to that adopted by the Court today: "If accepted, that claim would represent a return to the era of Lochner v. New York, 198 U.S. 45 (1905), when common-law rights were also found immune from revision by State or Federal Government. Such an approach would freeze the common law as it has been constructed by the courts, perhaps at its 19th- century state of development. It would allow no room for change in response to changes in circumstance. The Due Process Clause does not require such a result." PruneYard Shopping Center v. Robins, 447 U.S. 74, 93 (1980) (concurring opinion).

Arresting the development of the common law is not only a departure from our prior decisions; it is also profoundly unwise. The human condition is one of constant learning and evolution-both moral and practical. Legislatures implement that new learning; in doing so they must often revise the definition of property and the rights of property owners. Thus, when the Nation came to understand that slavery was morally wrong and mandated the emancipation of all slaves, it, in effect, redefined "property." On a lesser scale, our ongoing self-education produces similar changes in the rights of property owners: New appreciation of the significance of endangered species, see, e.g., Andrus v. Allard, 444 U.S. 51 (1979); the importance of wetlands, see, e.g., 16 U.S. C. §3801 et seq.; and the vulnerability of coastal lands, see, e.g., 16 U.S. C. §1451 et seq., shapes our evolving understandings of property rights.

Of course, some legislative redefinitions of property will effect a taking and must be compensated – but it certainly cannot be the case that every movement away from common law does so. There is no reason, and less sense, in such an absolute rule. We live in a world in which changes in the economy and the environment occur with increasing frequency and importance. If it was wise a century ago to allow Government " 'the largest legislative discretion" ' to deal with " 'the special exigencies of the moment," ' Mugler, 123 U.S., at 669, it is imperative to do so today. The rule that should govern a decision in a case of this kind should focus on the future, not the past. [17]The Court's categorical approach rule will, I fear, greatly hamper the efforts of

[17] Even measured in terms of efficiency, the Court's rule is unsound. The Court today effectively establishes a form of insurance against certain changes in land-use regulations. Like other forms of insurance, the Court's rule creates a "moral hazard" and inefficiencies: In the face of uncertainty about changes in the law, developers will overinvest, safe in the knowledge that if the law changes adversely, they will be entitled to compensation. See generally Farber, Economic Analysis and Just Compensation, 12 Int'l Rev. of Law & Econ. 125 (1992).

local officials and planners who must deal with increasingly complex problems in land-use and environmental regulation. As this case-in which the claims of an individual property owner exceed $1 million-well demonstrates, these officials face both substantial uncertainty because of the ad hoc nature of takings law and unacceptable penalties if they guess incorrectly about that law....

III. It is well established that a takings case "entails inquiry into [several factors:] the character of the governmental action, its economic impact, and its interference with reasonable investment-backed expectations." PruneYard, 447 U.S., at 83. The Court's analysis today focuses on the last two of these three factors: the categorical rule addresses a regulation's "economic impact," while the nuisance exception recognizes that ownership brings with it only certain "expectations." Neglected by the Court today is the first, and in some ways, the most important factor in takings analysis: the character of the regulatory action....

In analyzing takings claims, courts have long recognized the difference between a regulation that targets one or two parcels of land and a regulation that enforces a state-wide policy....

The impact of the ban on developmental uses must also be viewed in light of the purposes of the Act. The legislature stated the purposes of the Act as "protect[ing], preserv[ing], restor[ing] and enhanc[ing] the beach/dune system" of the State not only for recreational and ecological purposes, but also to "protec[t] life and property." S. C. Code §48-39-260(1)(a) (Supp. 1990). The State, with much science on its side, believes that the "beach/dune system [acts] as a buffer from high tides, storm surge, [and] hurricanes." This is a traditional and important exercise of the State's police power, as demonstrated by Hurricane Hugo, which in 1989, caused 29 deaths and more than $6 billion in property damage in South Carolina alone.

In view of all of these factors, even assuming that petitioner's property was rendered valueless, the risk inherent in investments of the sort made by petitioner, the generality of the Act, and the compelling purpose motivating the South Carolina Legislature persuade me that the Act did not effect a taking of petitioner's property.

Accordingly, I respectfully dissent.-

Statement of JUSTICE SOUTER.

I would dismiss the writ of certiorari in this case as having been granted improvidently. After briefing and argument it is abundantly clear that an unreviewable assumption on which this case comes to us is both questionable as a conclusion of Fifth Amendment law and sufficient to frustrate the Court's ability to render certain the legal premises on which its holding rests.

The petition for review was granted on the assumption that the state by regulation had deprived the owner of his entire economic interest in the subject property. Such was the state trial court's conclusion, which the state supreme court did not review. It is apparent now that in light of our prior cases,... the trial court's conclusion is highly questionable....

Because the questionable conclusion of total deprivation cannot be reviewed, the Court is precluded from attempting to clarify the concept of total (and, in the Court's view, categorically compensable) taking on which it rests, a concept which the Court describes, see ante, at 11 n. 6, as so uncertain under existing law as to have fostered inconsistent pronouncements by the Court itself. Because that concept is left uncertain, so is the significance of the exceptions to the compensation requirement that the Court proceeds to recognize. This alone is enough to show that there is little utility in attempting to deal with this case on the merits....

The Court will be understood to suggest...that there are in fact circumstances in which state-law nuisance abatement may amount to a denial of all beneficial land use as that concept is to be employed in our takings jurisprudence under the Fifth and Fourteenth Amendments. The nature of nuisance law, however, indicates that application of a regulation defensible on grounds of nuisance prevention or abatement will quite probably not amount to a complete deprivation in fact. The nuisance enquiry focuses on conduct, not on the character of the property on which that conduct is performed.... Under these circumstances, I believe it proper for me to vote to dismiss the writ....

COMMENTARY AND QUESTIONS

1. On reading *Lucas*. The Lucas case is a vast, rich accumulation of takings jurisprudence that by itself will undoubtedly be the basis of semester-long law school seminars. The full, unedited text of the various *Lucas* opinions totals 75 pages.

Behind the pitched arguments about what substantive takings tests should apply to property value wipeouts – and subsidiary questions like whether this action was truly "ripe" for review, whether the land was truly valueless, and how much a federal court should defer to the findings of state legislatures and supreme courts – lie a concatenation of judicial politics. Has this majority overthrown the *Keystone Bituminous* majority? Is *Lucas* an assertion of the prior decade's Meese-Sununu judicial agenda? Why was certiorari granted in this case and not to *First English* after the California court had upheld that wipeout on remand? Does the majority decide this case as an extraordinary exception, where there is a total wipeout, or is it setting a test to encourage wider invalidations of regulatory restrictions? Would the votes have been quite different if it had not be such an extreme case? Does the harsh rhetoric of some of the exchanges evidence a breakdown in the Rehnquist Court's erstwhile attempts to maintain collegial respect?

Like many legal cases, this one could support several screenplays.

2. The Takings Test after *Lucas*. What if anything has changed after *Lucas*? If it is quite clear that there was no categorical "bright line" test for regulatory takings before *Lucas* (is it?), is there one now? A major caveat was built into the test by Justice Scalia at the paragraph ending with original footnote 16 –

> Any limitation [that creates a wipeout] cannot be newly legislated or decreed without compensation, but must inhere in the title itself, in the restrictions that background principles of the State's law of property and nuisance already place upon land ownership...[as] could have been achieved in the courts...under the State's law of private nuisance, or [a state's] complementary power to abate nuisances that affect the public generally, or otherwise.

But what does this mean? Is the extant common law the limit? What's this "otherwise," beyond the extreme examples given inthe footnote?

Here is a way to test what *Lucas* means: Would Justice Scalia, based on his *Lucas* reasoning, have held that Los Angeles County had to pay the First English corporation full market value for the flood hazard restrictions in *First English*, if it wanted to prevent the plaintiff from lodging 200 handicapped children in cabins in a floodway that had been completely destroyed by flashfloods several years before? Or what about regulations restricting construction on earthquake faults? (See Scalia in *Lucas* after fn 16, and coursebook at 466-467.) It would appear that the majority would not require compensation in such ludicrous cases, but why? The common law does not recognize flood jeopardy or earthquake location as a tort, so the Court must be adopting a flexible modern view of what constitutes "nuisance-like" restraints.

This re-imports judicial harm-weighing judgments into takings jurisprudence, and goes far beyond traditional common law. The only possible shift is of the burden of proof, but even this is not clear. If defining the property rights in the context of public harms is the basis of Scalia's test, then the state's public harm argument is not an exception to the new rule but an element of the takings challenge formula. Or if the state must prove the substantial existence of (a risk of) harm, how is that to be weighed in order to know whether it shifts the burden back to plaintiff? This is not a bright line test.

3. What's a wipeout? Among the questions that Lucas stirs up but doesn't resolve is the question – when is property value wiped out? In fact, although the Court chose to accept the trial judge's finding that the land was "valueless," it is almost impossible to believe that Lucas's seafront lots, and any other parcel in the land for that matter, had absolutely no market value remaining.

In future cases, when will courts be able to find that there has been a total wipeout so as to apply *Lucas*, or will that never be possible? In original footnote 7, Justice Scalia says—

> When...a regulation requires a developer to leave 90% of a rural tract in its natural state, it is unclear whether we would analyze the situation as one in which the owner has been deprived of all economically beneficial use of the burdened portion of the tract, or as one in which the owner has suffered a mere diminution in value of the tract as a whole.

Thus the definition of the term "valueless" is more expansive than "having no value," and Scalia may have opened the door for subjective extensions of his categorical rule by the federal judiciary to property restriction cases far less pronounced than *Lucas*.

And does footnote 7 now re-open the baseline games? If I have a 150-acre parcel of land, two acres of which are restricted against any development because they are wetlands, haven't I suffered a 100% loss of those two acres? See Tull v. Virginia, US SupCt, No. 92-112.

4. The story behind the story. Do you detect an attempt by Justice Blackmun to raise skepticism about Mr. Lucas's bona fides? Lucas was portrayed in the media as just like any other private citizen who wanted to build a home for himself and his family and another for resale and got steamrolled by government. Lucas plunked down almost a million bucks for the two lots. This apparently was the highest price ever paid for lots in the Beachwood subdivision of the Wild Dunes development. ¥et Lucas had been intimately associated with that development since 1979, having served as a contractor, a realtor, and as an assistant in planning to the Wild Dunes board. (see trial transcript at 24, 33-34.) Is it likely that such insiders normally wait until the last, so as to be able to pay top dollar for a lot? And then for 19 months, from December 1986 until passage of the new act in June 1988 Lucas did nothing with the land, except, presumptively, paying approximately $10,000 a month in payments of interest charges and principal. (In media interviews, Lucas complained about his payments for taxes and insurance, but did not mention that he was paying carrying charges on his property.) Was the case a put-up job, trying to create a good test case for the privateering "wise-use" movement? Does it matter?

5. Environmental policy: back off from challenging the sea.

> Everyone who hears these words of mine and does not put them into practice is like a foolish man who builds his house on sand. The rains come down, the streams rise, and the winds

blow, and it falls with a great crash. Matthew 7:26-27

The folly of the modern real estate market's drive to develop prime residential housing on the barrier beaches of the U.S. has led to a series of disasters but no diminution of the building boom. The rate of building on our coastal beaches is five times greater than on inland locations. The threat of hurricane wipeouts is blunted by federally-subsidized flood hazard insurance that provides a base for mortgage financing that otherwise would not exist. (The insurance requires that localities be zoned with storm and erosion setback regulations, but the model regulations provide for variances where enforcement would impose economic burdens.) The obvious wise policy in confronting the inevitable onslaughts of coastal storms is not to stake out private property development lines at the shifting fragile edge of the seacoast, but to manage a measured retreat from the confrontation with nature. See Hearings on H.R. 5981 to establish a Barrier Islands Protection System, Before the Subcommittee on National Parks and Insular Affairs, 96th Cong. 2d Sess., March 1980.

And in eco-economic terms, what would the commercial market value of Mr. Lucas's million-dollar property be if it were not for the massive public subsidies that the real estate industry lobbied for and now takes for granted? Subtract from market value the amounts attributable to subsidized flood insurance; highway, causeway, and bridge construction and reconstruction; linear barrier beach extension of sewer and utilities; beach re-nourishment and beach protection; rescue operations; disaster aid; reconstruction financing; and the like, and the willingness of buyers to pay for risky barrier beach location would drop to very little. See Siffin, Bureaucracy, Entrepreneurship, and Natural Resources: Witless Policy and the Barrier Islands, 1 Cato Journal (1981). But the constitutional calculus apparently cannot offset public elements in private property value, and must use full market value as the constitutional starting point.

Kathleen Les et al. v. William K. Reilly
United States Court of Appeals for the Ninth Circuit, 1992
No. 91-70234, __F.2d__, 1992 WestLaw 153883

Schroeder, Circuit Judge. Petitioners seek review of a final order of the Environmental Protection Agency permitting the use of four pesticides as food additives although they have been found to induce cancer. Petitioners challenge the final order on the ground that it violates the provisions of the Delaney clause, 21 U.S.C. §348(c)(3), which prohibits the use of any food additive that is found to induce cancer.

Prior to 1988, EPA regulations promulgated in the absence of evidence of carcinogenicity permitted use of the four pesticides at issue here as food additives. In 1988, however, the EPA found these pesticides to be carcinogens. Notwithstanding the Delaney clause, the EPA refused to revoke the earlier regulations, reasoning that, although the chemicals posed a measurable risk of causing cancer, that risk was "de minimis."

We set aside the EPA's order because we agree with the petitioners that the language of the Delaney clause, its history and purpose all reflect that Congress intended the EPA to prohibit all additives that are carcinogens, regardless of the degree of risk involved.

BACKGROUND

The Federal Food, Drug, and Cosmetic Act (FFDCA), 21 U.S.C. §§301-394 (West 1972 & Supp. 1992), is designed to ensure the safety of the food we eat by prohibiting the sale of food that is "adulterated." 21 U.S.C. §331(a). Adulterated food is in turn defined as food containing any unsafe food "additive." 21 U.S.C. §342(a)(2)(C). A food "additive" is defined broadly as "any substance the intended use of which results or may reasonably be expected to result ... in its becoming a component ... of any food." 21 U.S.C. §321(s). A food additive is considered unsafe unless there is a specific exemption for the substance or a regulation prescribing the conditions under which it may be used safely. 21 U.S.C. §348(a).

Before 1988, the four pesticide chemicals with which we are here concerned- benomyl, mancozeb, phosmet and trifluralin-were all the subject of regulations issued by the EPA permitting their use. In October 1988, however, the EPA published a list of substances, including the pesticides at issue here, that had been found to induce cancer. Regulation of Pesticides in Food: Addressing the Delaney Paradox Policy Statement, 53 Fed. Reg. 41,104, 41,119 (Oct. 19, 1988). As known carcinogens, the four pesticides ran afoul of a special provision of the FFDCA known as the Delaney clause, which prescribes that additives found to induce cancer can never be deemed "safe" for purposes of the FFDCA. The Delaney clause is found in FFDCA section 409, 21 U.S.C. §348. That section limits the conditions under which the Secretary may issue regulations allowing a substance to be used as a food additive: No such regulation shall issue if a fair evaluation of the data before the Secretary-(A) fails to establish that the proposed use of the food additive, under the conditions of use to be specified in the regulation, will be safe: Provided, That no additive shall be deemed to be safe if it is found to induce cancer when ingested by man or animal, or if it is found, after tests which are appropriate for the evaluation of the safety of food additives, to induce cancer in man or animal.... 21 U.S.C. §348(c)(3).

The FFDCA also contains special provisions which regulate the occurrence of pesticide residues on raw agricultural commodities. Section 402 of the FFDCA, 21 U.S.C. §342(a)(2)(B), provides that a raw food containing a pesticide residue is deemed adulterated unless the residue is authorized under §408 of the FFDCA, 21 U.S.C. §346a, which allows tolerance regulations setting maximum permissible levels and also provides for exemption from tolerances under certain circumstances. When a tolerance or an exemption has been established for use of a pesticide on a raw agricultural commodity, then the FFDCA allows for the "flow-through" of such pesticide residue to processed foods, even when the pesticide may be a carcinogen. This flow- through is allowed, however, only to the extent that the concentration of the pesticide in the processed food does not exceed the concentration allowed in the raw food. . . . It is undisputed that the EPA regulations at issue in this case allow for the concentration of cancer-causing pesticides during processing to levels in excess of those permitted in the raw foods.

The proceedings in this case had their genesis in October 1988 when the EPA published a list of substances, including these pesticides, that were found to induce cancer. 53 Fed. Reg. 41,104, App. B. Simultaneously, the EPA announced a new interpretation of the Delaney clause: the EPA proposed to permit concentrations of cancer-causing pesticide residues greater than that tolerated for raw foods so long as the particular substances posed only a "de minimis" risk of actually causing cancer. 53 Fed. Reg. at 41,110. Finding that benomyl, mancozeb, phosmet and trifluralin (among others) posed only such a de minimis risk, the Agency announced that it would not immediately revoke its previous regulations authorizing use of these substances as food additives.

Petitioners filed an administrative petition in May 1989 requesting the EPA to revoke those food additive regulations. Following public comment, the EPA issued a Notice of Response refusing to revoke the regulations. After the petitioners filed objections to that response, the EPA published its final order denying the petition to revoke the food additive regulations. This petition for review . . . followed.

The issue before us is whether the EPA has violated §409 of the FFDCA, the Delaney clause, by permitting the use of carcinogenic food additives which it finds to present only a de minimis or negligible risk of causing cancer. The Agency acknowledges that its interpretation of the law is a new and changed one. From the initial enactment of the Delaney clause in 1958 to the time of the rulings here in issue, the statute had been strictly and literally enforced. 56 Fed. Reg. at 7751-52. The EPA also acknowledges that the language of the statute itself appears, at first glance, to be clear on its face. Id. at 7751 ("[S]ection 409 mandates a zero risk standard for carcinogenic pesticides in processed foods in those instances where the pesticide concentrates during processing or is applied during or after processing.").

The language is clear and mandatory. The Delaney clause provides that no additive shall be deemed safe if it induces cancer. 21 U.S.C. §348(c)(3). The EPA states in its final order that appropriate tests have established that the pesticides at issue here induce cancer in humans or animals. 56 Fed. Reg. at 7774-75. The statute provides that once the finding of carcinogenicity is made, the EPA has no discretion. As a leading work on food and drug regulation notes: [T]he Delaney Clause leaves the FDA room for scientific judgment in deciding whether its conditions are met by a food additive. But the clause affords no flexibility once FDA scientists determine that these conditions are satisfied. A food additive that has been found in an appropriate test to induce cancer in laboratory animals may not be approved for use in food for any purpose, at any level, regardless of any "benefits" that it might provide. Richard A. Merrill and Peter B. Hutt, Food and Drug Law 78 (1980).

This issue was litigated before the D.C. Circuit in connection with the virtually identical "color additive" prohibition of 21 U.S.C. §376(b)(5)(B). The D.C. Circuit concluded that "[t]he natural-almost inescapable-reading of this language is that if the Secretary finds the additive to induce' cancer in animals, he must deny listing." Public Citizen v. Young, 831 F.2d 1108, 1112 (D.C. Cir. 1987), cert. denied, 485 U.S. 1006 (1988). The court concluded that the EPA's de minimis interpretation of the Delaney clause in 21 U.S.C. §376 was "contrary to law." 831 F.2d at 1123. The Public Citizen decision reserved comment on whether the result would be the same under the food additive provisions as it was under the food color provisions, 831 F.2d at 1120, but its reasoning with respect to the language of the statute is equally applicable to both.

The Agency asks us to look behind the language of the Delaney clause to the overall statutory scheme governing pesticides, which permits the use of carcinogenic pesticides on raw food without regard to the Delaney clause. Yet section 402 of the FFDCA, 21 U.S.C. §342(a)(2)(C), expressly harmonizes that scheme with the Delaney clause by providing that residues on processed foods may not exceed the tolerance level established for the raw food. The statute unambiguously provides that pesticides which concentrate in processed food are to be treated as food additives, and these are governed by the Delaney food additive provision contained in §409. If pesticides which concentrate in processed foods induce cancer in humans or animals, they render the food adulterated and must be prohibited.

The legislative history, too, reflects that Congress intended the very rigidity that the language it chose commands. The food additive Delaney clause was enacted in response to increasing public concern about cancer. It was initially part of a bill, introduced in the House of Representatives in 1958 by Congressman Delaney, to amend the FFDCA. H.R. 7798, 85th Cong., 1st Sess. (1957), reprinted in XIV A Legislative History of the Federal Food, Drug, and Cosmetic Act and its Amendments 91 (1979) (hereinafter, "Legislative History "). The bill, intended to ensure that no carcinogens, no matter how small the amount, would be introduced into food, was at least in part a response to a decision by the FDA to allow a known carcinogen, the pesticide Aramite, as an approved food additive. Food Additives: Hearings Before a Subcommittee of the House Committee on Interstate and Foreign Commerce, 85th Cong., 1st and 2d Sess. 171 (1958), reprinted in XIV Legislative History 163, 336. Of the FDA's approval for sale of foods containing small quantities of Aramite, Congressman Delaney stated: The part that chemical additives play in the cancer picture may not yet be completely understood, but enough is known to put us on our guard. The safety of the public health demands that chemical additives should be specifically pretested for carcinogenicity, and this should be spelled out in the law. The precedent established by the Aramite decision has opened the door, even if only a little, to the use of carcinogens in our foods. That door should be slammed shut and locked. That is the purpose of my anticarcinogen provision. Id. at 498, reprinted in XIV Legislative History at 660. The scientific witnesses who testified before Congress stressed that because current scientific techniques could not determine a safe level for carcinogens, all carcinogens should be prohibited. See 56 Fed. Reg. at 7769. While Congressman Delaney's bill was not ultimately passed, the crucial anticancer language from the bill was incorporated into the Food Additives Amendment of 1958 which enacted section 409 of the FFDCA into law. H.R. 13254, 85th Cong., 2d Sess. (1958), reprinted in XIV Legislative History 880, 887. Thus, the legislative history supports the conclusion that Congress intended to ban all carcinogenic food additives, regardless of amount or significance of risk, as the only safe alternative.

Throughout its 30-year history, the Delaney clause has been interpreted as an absolute bar to all carcinogenic food additives. See 53 Fed. Reg. at 41,104 (announcing a shift in the EPA's position, away from reading section 409's Delaney clause "literally"). . .

The EPA contends that the legislative history shows that Congress never intended to regulate pesticides, as opposed to other additives, with extraordinary rigidity under the food additives provision. The Agency is indeed correct that the legislative history of the food additive provision does not focus on pesticides, and that pesticides are regulated more comprehensively under the Federal Insecticide, Fungicide, and Rodenticide Act (FIFRA), 7 U.S.C. §136-136y (West 1980 & Supp. 1992). Nevertheless, the EPA's contention that Congress never intended the food additive provision to encompass pesticide residues is belied by the events prompting passage of the provision into law: FDA approval of Aramite was the principal impetus for the food additive Delaney clause and Aramite was itself a regulated pesticide. Thus, Congress intended to regulate pesticides as food additives under §409 of the FFDCA, at least to the extent that pesticide residues concentrate in processed foods and exceed the tolerances for raw foods.

Finally, the EPA argues that a de minimis exception to the Delaney clause is necessary in order to bring about a more sensible application of the regulatory scheme. It relies particularly on a recent study suggesting that the criterion of concentration level in processed foods may bear little or no relation to actual risk of cancer, and that some pesticides might be barred by rigid enforcement of the Delaney clause while others, with greater cancer-causing risk, may be permitted through the flow-through provisions because they do not concentrate in processed foods. See National Academy of Sciences, Regulating Pesticides in Food: The Delaney Paradox (1987). The EPA in effect asks us to approve what it deems to be a more enlightened system than that which Congress established. The EPA is not alone in criticizing the scheme established by the Delaney clause. See, e.g., Richard A. Merrill, FDA's Implementation of the Delaney Clause: Repudiation of Congressional Choice or Reasoned Adaptation to Scientific Progress, 5 Yale J. on Reg. 1, 87 (1988) (concluding that the Delaney clause is both unambiguous and unwise: "at once an explicit and imprudent expression of legislative will"). Revising the existing statutory scheme, however, is neither our function nor the function of the EPA. There are currently bills pending before the House and the Senate which would amend the food additive provision to allow the Secretary to establish tolerance levels for carcinogens, including pesticide residues in processed foods, which impose a negligible risk. H.R. 2342, 102d Cong., 1st Sess. (1991); S. 1074, 102d Cong., 1st Sess. (1991). If there is to be a change, it is for Congress to direct.

The EPA's refusal to revoke regulations permitting the use of benomyl, mancozeb, phosmet and trifluralin as food additives on the ground the cancer risk they pose is de minimis is contrary to the provisions of the Delaney clause prohibiting food additives that induce cancer. The EPA's final order is set aside.

COMMENTARY AND QUESTIONS

1. Zero risk or reasonable risk? The court's reasoning goes even further than the court itself appears to perceive. If the Delaney Clause must be interpreted literally, then EPA not only must prohibit the sale of agricultural products "to the extent that pesticide residues concentrate in processed foods and exceed the tolerances for raw foods, "but EPA also, as the Merrill and Hutt quotation makes clear, cannot set any tolerance levels for pesticides that have been found to cause cancer in laboratory animals. Thus, we have the anomalous result that EPA can registrar for use, under FIFRA, a pesticide that has been found to be weakly carcinogenic in test animals but that has important social and economic benefits and cannot feasible be replaced by substitute pest control methods: however, EPA must, at the same time, interdict the sale of raw agricultural products or processed foods containing any trace of this pesticide. Congress must obviously clear this pesticide policy logjam. should Congress adopt a zero risk approach, a reasonable risk approach, or some combination of both? For example, should Congress mandate a zero risk approach for strong carcinogens (e.g., for those causing a higher than one in a million risk of cancer) and a reasonable risk approach for weaker carcinogens?

2. What's an agency to do? Is an agency ever justified in not reading a clear statutory mandate literally? The Delaney Clause, enacted in 1958, is a crude regulatory device that makes a number of questionable toxicological assumptions, including (1) that high-dose, relatively small group animals tests can accurately predict low-dose, large group human responses, and (2) that substances causing cancer in animals also invariably cause cancer in human beings. (See Chapter 2). The atmosphere in Congress during hearings on the Delaney Clause was one of pervasive "cancer phobia" But isn't an unambiguous legislative directive to be followed to the letter, regardless of its scientific or policy merits?

The following Overview of The Federal Clean Water Act mentioned on page 210 in Part II of the Teacher's Manual was inadvertently omitted. This Overview should appear in Part III of your main Teacher's Manual at page 313.

W. Goldfarb, An Overview of The Federal Clean Water Act

The Clean Water Act is difficult to understand and teach because of its confusing combination of a technology-based foundation and a water quality-based superstructure. The historical reason for this statutory architecture was that the Senate, in order to enact a statute featuring its innovative technology-based approach, was compelled to compromise with the House and accept the water quality-based approach — which the Senate considered to be outmoded and unenforceable — as a subordinate means of control where technology-based standards did not result in acceptable water quality. Between 1972 and 1987, EPA and the States did their best to ignore water quality-based controls without publicly admitting to this strategy. Thus, there is a wide divergence between law-on-the-books and law-in-action in this area. In the Clean Water Act Amendments of 1987, Congress reaffirmed the water quality-based approach, but there is reason to believe that the "back burner gamesmanship" is continuing.

TECHNOLOGY-BASED CONTROLS

The first and most important level of CWA controls — technology-based effluent limitations (TBELs) — is relatively straightforward once it is understood that TBELs vary by type of discharger and type of pollutant.

There are a limited number of options open to industrial units with unpreventable wastewater streams: (1) discharge into pits, ponds, or lagoons (covered by RCRA); (2) discharge into shallow groundwater formations (not regulated by federal law but frequently subject to state regulations where the groundwater is or could be a potable water supply); (3) discharge into deep underground wells (covered by the Underground Injection Control (UIC) provisions of the federal Safe Drinking Water Act); (4) discharge into sanitary sewers, or combined sanitary and storm sewers, leading to POTWs (i.e., become indirect dischargers); (5) discharge into municipal separate storm sewers (such discharges will soon be regulated under EPA stormwater regulations) or (6) discharge directly to waterbodies. Only options (4), (5) and (6) fall within the CWA's ambit.

Indirect dischargers must meet "prohibited discharge standards" so as not to disrupt the operations of POTWs, and "national pretreatment standards," similar to TBELs for direct dischargers with the exception of the hitherto un-implemented "removal allowances" based on the abilities of POTWs to treat toxic pollutants. Pretreatment standards are generally enforced by local sewerage authorities with approved pretreatment programs. If an authority does not enforce against an indirect discharger of toxics, and if the POTW's discharge permit contains effluent limitations for those passthrough toxics, the POTW may be in violation of its own permit.

Direct dischargers' TBELs depend on the types of pollutants being discharged. the nature and evolution of TBELs is presented in the main volume (835-848), but Table 1 (which may be distributed in class) should simplify matters even further.

In practice, however, the applications of TBELs to particular industrial dischargers are frequently not mechanical derivations from categorical effluent limitations guidelines contained in EPA regulations because many industrial dischargers are either not yet covered by federal regulations or else are unique, multifaceted facilities that produce various products utilizing water for diverse process (including batch and continuous processes), heating, cooling, and plant sanitation purposes. In composite facilities, waste streams of all sorts may be kept separate or mixed; some waste streams may be discharged into POTWs, others to waterbodies, and still others disposed of by underground injection. The opportunities for saving money through pollution prevention, recycling and reuse, and waste exchange with neighboring facilities are vast with regard to composite facilities. Attorneys should recommend that waste audits be performed in order to explore these possibilities. If discharge permits are necessary for composite plants, the "effluent numbers" are generally developed by "Best Professional Judgment" (BPJ) of state or federal permit writers. The "Fundamentally Different Factors" (FDF) variance is not often resorted to in such situations because permit writers recognize at the outset that federal categorical effluent limitations do not neatly apply to composite facilities. BPJ is based on utilizing categorical effluent limitations as analogies, applying complex mixed-wastestream formulas for combined toxic and non-toxic streams, whole effluent testing (bioassays), past performance, and other factors. Because of the gestalt nature of BPJ, informal negotiations frequently occur among permit writers, dischargers, and in some states environmental groups, during the development of draft discharge permits. These negotiations are critical because BPJ determinations are appealed more often than permit numbers based directly on effluent limitations guidelines.

WATER QUALITY-BASED CONTROLS

According to the CWA and EPA regulations, where applications of TBELs to point sources and Best Management Practices (BMPs) to nonpoint sources (which EPA has no legal authority to impose) will not meet applicable water quality standards based on antidegradation or fishable-swimmable quality (i.e., on "water quality-limited stretches"), water quality-based effluent limitations (WQBELs) must be imposed requiring point sources to apply controls "beyond BAT."

Our understanding of the complex natural systems that manifest themselves as water quality and the human health effects of polluted water is comparatively primitive. thus, setting numerical water quality standards (WQS), establishing Total Maximum Daily Loads (TMDLs) of pollutants to meet WQS on particular stretches, assigning Waste Load Allocations (WLAs) — based on water-quality models — to point source dischargers located on those stretches, and developing WQBEL permit numbers that account for mixing zones, fish corridors, different and volatile temperature and flow regimes, and the eccentricities of individual dischargers is scientifically questionable and resource-intensive. [18]

In addition to these methodological problems, water quality-based controls are politically problematic. they disrupt the national uniformity achieved by technology-based limitations

---

[18]. For an informative discussion of the difficulties inherent in the process of setting WQBELs, see Houck, Regulation of Toxic Pollutants Under the Clean Water Act, 21 ELR 10528, 10542-10547 (September 21, 1991).

and revive the race of laxity (forum-shopping) that subverted the 1965 Water Quality Act. Highly industrialized states with numerous water quality-limited stretches are inherently penalized by the water quality-based approach, especially because antidegradation policies in less industrialized states are generally ineffective (see main volume, 853-864). Second, industrialized states are reluctant to remove ("downgrade") fishable-swimmable uses on heavily polluted waterways — which EPA regulations allow — because of the negative political fallout that such a move would provoke. Third, it is patently unfair to impose WQBELs, which are developed without reference to lead times or economic and technological achievability, on point sources when nonpoint sources — which account for up to 70% of water pollution in some states — go unregulated under the CWA. And fourth, with the decrease in federal program funding for state water pollution control programs, states have been increasingly financing their permit programs through permit fees imposed on dischargers. However, because water quality-based permitting is so complex and resource-intensive, it would be politically infeasible to charge fees that would adequately fund such programs.

Between 1972 and 1987, EPA and the states concentrated on technology-based controls, paying only lip service to water quality-based controls. States set, and EPA routinely approved, narrative water quality criteria (e.g., "free from toxicity") even when EPA had published recommended numeric criteria for toxics; requirements to establish TMDLs and WLAs were disregarded; and water quality-based permits, where they existed at all, were developed using rough mass balances and in the context of informal (and probably illegal) negotiations with dischargers regarding economic and technological feasibility.

States, under the indulgent gaze of EPA, adopted innovative (and sometimes dubious) strategems for circumventing water quality-based controls. Some set water quality standards that varied by water temperature, flow, or time of year. Others developed finely-tuned, site-specifiic water quality standards. Others, such as Connecticut and North Carolina, promulgated easily enforceable rules that prohibited discharges of toxics above potable water intake points. More and more states began to rely on whole effluent testing (bioassays) and whole effluent toxicity (WET) permit conditions for dischargers of mixed waste streams containing toxic pollutants. Ohio keyed its water quality standards to the ecological conditions of receiving waterbodies rather than insteam water quality. Sixteen states granted over 400 legally questionable variances, based on econmic impact, from water quality standards.[19]

By 1987, most states had adopted few, if any, water quality criteria for the 126 priority toxic pollutants, nor did many states possess effective water quality-based controls on toxic discharges. In the Clean Water Act Amendments of 1987, Congress expressed its impatience with the slow pace of toxic substances control by enacting section 303(c)(2)(B), which required states to adopt numeric criteria for all priority pollutants for which EPA had itself published numeric criteria, and section 304(1), which required states to establish a process to identify toxic hot spots and the point sources impacting them, and then to impose Individual Control Strategies (ICSs) on relevant point sources so as to attain water quality criteria. (See pages 848-853 of the main volume.)[20]

---

[19]. See USGAO, Stronger Efforts Needed by EPA to Control Toxic Water Pollution, 32-33 (July 1991) for a critique of state variances.

[20]. A worthwhile history and summary of the CWA's regulatory program for toxics can be found in EPA, Proposal to Establish Water Quality Criteria For Toxic Pollutants In States That Lack Such Standards (56 FR 58420; Nov. 19, 1991).

Congress' affirmation of the water quality-based approach in the 1987 CWA amendments generated another round of gamesmanship. By February 1990, when all states should have adopted fully acceptable numeric criterial for priority pollutants which were the subjects of EPA-published numeric criteria, only four states and two territories had actually done so. On November 19, 1991, EPA proposed federal water quality criteria for toxics for 22 states that did not have acceptable criteria.[21] Because section 303(c)(2)(B) did not establish a federal floor for state water quality standards for toxics, most states that have adopted criteria for toxics have set standards that are weaker than EPA's recommendations.[22]

Section 304(1) — the toxic hotspot identification and cleanup provision — has thus far also been ineffective in appreciably reducing toxic loadings in waterways. The EPA toxic hotspot listing regulations were remanded by the Ninth Circuit Court of Appeals (see main volume, 849-850). Furthermore, according to the USGAO:[23]

(1) EPA and states were unable to identify all impaired waters because most states have assessed the quality of less than half of their surface waters;

(2) EPA required that ICSs be developed only for those waters impaired by point sources discharging any of the 126 priority pollutants;

(3) Nonpoint sources, unregulated by section 304(1), are major sources of toxics; and

(4) Major dischargers, in order to avoid the stigma of being listed as toxic polluters, have either persuaded states to make their water quality criteria less stringent or hooked up to POTWs in order to obtain more lenient treatment (see main volume, 844).

Meanwhile, as the water quality-based control process flounders yet again, the real action "beyond BAT" is in the area of discharge permits based on biological WET (whole effluent testing) limits (see main volume, 852-853).[24]

---

21. Id.

22. Houck, footnote 1 supra, 10543-10544.

23. Footnote 2, supra, 16-20.

24. Houck, footnote 1, supra, 10555-10558.

• The Rio Conference — 1992

"Progress in many fields, too little progress in most fields, and no progress at all in some fields....We will be held accountable...We are heading toward a crisis of uncontrollable dimensions unless we change course."

— Norwegian Prime Minister Gro Harlem Bruntland

The United Nations Conference on Environment and Development took place in Rio de Janeiro, Brazil from June 3rd to June 14th, 1992. It took years of preparation, attracted worldwide attention, and generated controversy, hope, and a tremendous amount of paperwork. It also gave rise to five significant documents, briefly outlined below:

THE RIO DECLARATION

A statement of 27 principles underlying the "Earth Summit," which was approved by all of the nations attending UNCED. It reaffirms the 1972 Stockholm Declaration on Human Environment, and proclaims the goal of UNCED to be the establishment of "a new and equitable global partnership." Principle 1 declares that "Human beings are at the centre of concerns for sustainable development. They are entitled to a healthy and productive life in harmony with nature." The Declaration goes on to affirm "the right to development", and states that "eradicating poverty" is an "indispensable requirement for sustainable development". It goes on to encourage elimination of "unsustainable patterns of production and consumption", "right-to-know" provisions, and the development of environmental laws. It stresses the importance of internalizing the environmental costs of production, and concludes with a call for the "further development of international law in the field of sustainable development".

CONVENTION ON BIODIVERSITY

This convention aims to lower the rate of global plant and animal extinction by establishing national conservation management systems. It also seeks to establish international standards for the biotechnology industry, including rules governing the commercial use of genetic resources. Under the terms of the convention, nations with natural resources valued by the biotechnology industry have an interest in both the direct sale of the natural resource, and in any patent or royalty arising from biotechnology derived from that resource. The accord between Merck Pharmaceutical and the government of Costa Rica is often used as an example. Signatories also agree to establish ecosytem inventories, and to develop national strategies and programs to implement the principles of the Biodiversity Convention. It was signed by 153 nations. The only delegation refusing to sign was that of the United States, citing concerns over "financing and protection of intellectual property rights". Thirty nations must ratify this convention for it to become a part of international law.

CONVENTION ON CLIMATE CHANGE

Anthropogenic emission of greenhouse gases is the focus of this framework convention, specifically; how to stabilize global emissions of carbon dioxide, methane and chlorofluorocarbons while achieving "sustainable social and economic growth". Article 3 sets forth the principles that should guide this endeavor, urging the parties to "protect the climate system for the benefit of present and future generations", and to "take precautionary measures to anticipate, prevent or minimize...climate change". Article 4 outlines the commitments of the signatories, including the sponsorship and exchange of research findings, and the development of national programs designed to mitigate climate change. References to specific timetables and precise emission levels were deleted in order to gain the endorsement of the U.S. delegation. All attending nations signed this convention. It must be ratified by fifty nations to become international law.

FOREST PRINCIPLES

This statement sets worldwide standards for good forestry practices, stressing the importance of "sustainable use" in developing management regimes. It also addresses the financial and ecological relationships between timber-importing and timber-exporting countries. It urges that total global forest cover be increased, but puts no special emphasis on old growth forests. Though it was finished during UNCED, the final wording is considerably weaker than the original version, a result of pronounced disagreements in point of view between "developed" and "developing" nations. The developed nations persisted in characterizing tropical forests as the world's "carbon sinks" or "carbon sponges", while the developing nations who control these forests saw them as sovereign national resources, to be dealt with as they saw fit. From this "Southern" perspective, the "Northern" countries were trying to buy the "right to pollute"; first generating the vast majority of the world's anthropogenic greenhouse gases, and then telling the South not to cut its forests so as to help soak up the excess carbon dioxide the Northern lifestyle required. This convention could lead to a binding treaty, but at this writing, no arrangements have been made to begin this process.

AGENDA 21

This is an 800-page, 120-chapter guide to the implementation of the Conventions on Climate Change and Biodiversity, and of the "sustainable development" principles contained within the Rio Declaration. It is designed to serve as the foundation for international environmental law and cooperation into the next century. It addresses everything from marine pollution to desertification to population dynamics to patterns of consumption. There are chapters on management of resources, the roles of "subgroups" (women, children, indigenous peoples, NGO's, etc.) within the environmental context, the development of a body of environmental laws within existing legal systems, and the actual "Means of Implementation" required to achieve these goals. Agenda 21 creates a permanent United Nations Commission on Sustainable Development, which will oversee compliance with the provisions of the Conventions on Climate Change and Biodiversity by their signatories. It also establishes a Global Environmental Facility to work with the World Bank on coordinating aid transfer from richer to poorer countries, calls for increased levels of aid from richer countries, and suggests that a Convention on Desertification be held to address this growing environmental challenge.

Partially derived from Nicholas Yost's article, "Rio and the Road Beyond", in the Environmental Law Quarterly, Summer 1992, Volume 11, Number 4, published by the American Bar Association

For copies of these documents, as well as other information on the UNCED Conference, sustainable development and international environmental law,
the following organizations should prove helpful:

United Nations Publications
Sales Section, 2 United Nations Plaza
Room DC2-853
Dept. 416
New York, NY 10017
(Tel) (212) 963-8302 or (800) 253-9646

American Bar Association
1800 M Street, NW, S-200
Washington, D.C. 20036

• THE RIO DECLARATION (aka EARTH CHARTER)

Following is a text of The Rio Declaration on Environment and Development, adopted by world leaders June 14, 1992, at the final session of the U.N. Conference on Environment and Development:

THE UNITED NATIONS CONFERENCE ON ENVIRONMENT AND DEVELOPMENT,

Having met at Rio de Janeiro from 3 to 14 June 1992,

Reaffirming the Declaration of the United Nations Conference on the Human Environment, adopted at Stockholm on 16 June 1972, and seeking to build upon it,

With the goal of establishing a new and equitable global partnership through the creation of new levels of cooperation among States, key sectors of societies and people,

Working towards international agreements which respect the interests of all and protect the integrity of the global environmental and developmental system,

Recognizing the integral and interdependent nature of the Earth, our home,

Proclaims that:

PRINCIPLE 1

Human beings are at the center of concerns for sustainable development. They are entitled to a healthy and productive life in harmony with nature.

PRINCIPLE 2

States have, in accordance with the Charter of the United Nations and the principles of international law, the sovereign right to exploit their own resources pursuant to their own environmental and developmental policies, and the responsibility to ensure that activities within their jurisdiction or control do not cause damage to the environment of other States or of areas beyond the limits of national jurisdiction.

PRINCIPLE 3

The right to development must be fulfilled so as to equitably meet developmental and environmental needs of present and future generations.

PRINCIPLE 4

In order to achieve sustainable development, environmental protection shall constitute an integral part of the development process and cannot be considered in isolation from it.

PRINCIPLE 5

All States and all people shall cooperate in the essential task of eradicating poverty as an indispensable requirement for sustainable development, in order to decrease the disparities in standards of living and better meet the needs of the majority of the people of the world.

PRINCIPLE 6

The special situation and needs of developing countries, particularly the least developed and those most environmentally vulnerable, shall be given special priority. International actions in the field of environment and development should also address the interests and needs of all countries.

PRINCIPLE 7

States shall cooperate in a spirit of global partnership to conserve, protect and restore the health and integrity of the Earth's ecosystem. In view of the different contributions to global environmental degradation, States have common but differentiated responsibilities.The developed countries acknowledge the responsibility that they bear in the international pursuit of sustainable development in view of the pressures their societies place on the global environment and the technologies and financial resources they command.

PRINCIPLE 8

To achieve sustainable development and a higher quality of life for all people, States should reduce and eliminate unsustainable patterns of production and consumption and promote appropriate demographic policies.

PRINCIPLE 9

States should cooperate to strengthen endogenous capacity-building for sustainable development by improving scientific understanding through exchanges of scientific and technological knowledge, and by enhancing the development, adaptation, diffusion and transfer of technologies, including new and innovative

technologies.

PRINCIPLE 10

Environmental issues are best handled with the participation of all concerned citizens, at the relevant level. At the national level, each individual shall have appropriate access to information concerning the environment that is held by public authorities, including information on hazardous materials and activities in their communities, and the opportunity to participate in decision-making processes. States shall facilitate and encourage public awareness and participation by making information widely available. Effective access to judicial and administrative proceedings, including redress and remedy, shall be provided.

PRINCIPLE 11

States shall enact effective environmental legislation. Environmental standards, management objective and priorities should reflect the environmental and developmental context to which they apply. Standards applied by some countries may be inappropriate and of unwarranted economic and social cost to other countries, in particular developing countries.

PRINCIPLE 12

States should cooperate to promote a supportive and open international economic system that would lead to economic growth and sustainable development in all countries, to better address the problems of environmental degradation. Trade policy measures for environmental purposes should not constitute a means of arbitrary or unjustifiable discrimination or a disguised restriction on international trade. Unilateral actions to deal with environmental challenges outside the jurisdiction of the importing country should be avoided. Environmental measures addressing transboundary or global environmental problems should, as far as possible, be based on an international consensus.

PRINCIPLE 13

States shall develop national law regarding liability and compensation for the victims of pollution and other environmental damage. States shall also cooperate in an expeditious and more determined manner to develop further international law regarding liabililty and compensation for adverse effects of environmental damage caused by activities within their jurisdiction or control to areas beyond their jurisdiction.

PRINCIPLE 14

States should effectively cooperate to discourage or prevent the relocation and transfer to other States of any activities and substances that cause severe environmental degradation or are found to be harmful to human health.

PRINCIPLE 15

In order to protect the environment, the precautionary approach shall be widely applied by States according to their capabilities. Where there are threats of serious or irreversible damage, lack of full scientific certainty shall not be used as a reason for postponing cost-effective measures to prevent environmental degradation.

PRINCIPLE 16

National authorities should endeavor to promote the internalization of environmental costs and the use of economic instruments, taking into account the approach that the polluter should, in principle, bear the cost of pollution, with due regard to the public interest and without distorting international trade and investment.

PRINCIPLE 17

Environmental impact assessment, as a national instrument, shall be undertaken for proposed activities that are likely to have a significant adverse impact on the environment and are subject to a decision of a competent national authority.

PRINCIPLE 18

States shall immediately notify other States of any natural disasters or other emergencies that are likely to produce sudden harmful effects on the environment of those States. Every effort shall be made by the international community to help States so afflicted.

PRINCIPLE 19

States shall provide prior and timely notification and relevant information to potentially affected States on activities that may have a significant adverse transboundary environmental effect and shall consult with those States at an early stage and in good faith.

PRINCIPLE 20

Women have a vital role in environmental management and development. Their full participation is therefore essential to achieve sustainable development.

PRINCIPLE 21

The creativity, ideals and courage of the youth of the world should be mobilized to forge a global partnership in order to achieve sustainable development and ensure a better future for all.

PRINCIPLE 22

Indigenous people and their communities, and other local communities, have a vital role in environmental management and development because of their knowledge and traditional practices. States should recognize and duly support their identity, culture and interests and enable their effective participation in the achievement of sustainable development.

PRINCIPLE 23

The environment and natural resources of people under oppression, domination and occupation shall be protected.

PRINCIPLE 24

Warfare is inherently destructive of sustainable development. States shall therefore respect international law providing protection for the environment in times of armed conflict and cooperate in its further development, as necessary.

PRINCIPLE 25

Peace, development and environmental protection are interdependent and indivisible.

PRINCIPLE 26

States shall resolve all their environmental disputes peacefully and by appropriate means in accordance with the Charter of the United Nations.

PRINCIPLE 27

States and people shall cooperate in good faith and in a spirit of partnership in the fulfillment of the principles embodied in this Declaration and in the further development of international law in the field of sustainable development.

AGENDA 21
OUTLINE

SECTION III: STRENGTHENING THE ROLE OF MAJOR GROUPS

SECTION IV: MEANS OF IMPLEMENTATION

• A Collection of Past Examination Questions

FOR EXAMS GIVEN AT LAW SCHOOLS,, SEE PAGE 320 OF THE MAIN TEACHERS MANUAL

1992

Multiple Choice Exam Questions:
written by student teachers for the undergraduate offerings of NLS at Boston College

1. In a cost-benefit analysis, environmentalists seek to encourage industry toward all of the following <u>except</u>:
    a. cost-internalization
    b. cost-externalization
    c. realization of environmental effects on humans
    d. recognizing the costs of development is our natural resources.

2. An injunction to shut down operations will most likely be entered.
    a. against an iron ore processing plant emitting air and water pollution that cause property damage but cause no human harm.
    b. against a chemical waste disposal site despite an absence of any damages.
    c. against a Dairy Queen that uses whole milk instead of low fat.
    d. A court will never issue an injunction which shuts down a company's operation.

3. The citizens of Yakima Valley have been plagued by the constant dispersal of smog in their beautiful valley by Dow Chemical Co. To remedy this situation, Yakima chooses to sue Dow instead of going to state or federal regulators because:
    a. government agencies are inadequately staffed.
    b. government agencies are unwilling to go against a major source of revenue.
    c. the citizens feel they have insufficient influence on the agencies decisional process.
    d. statutory remedies do not focus on the individual harmed.
    e. all of the above.

4. All the following are true for the tort of intentional trespass <u>except:</u>
    a. trespass protects possessor's interest in exclusive possession of property.
    b. nominal damages are not available.
    b. punitive damages are available.
    d. intent is required.
    e. a trespass invasion may exist based on the new wave particle theory.

5. Annabelle owns a 100 acre tract of land in Montana which contains some of the most unique forms of vegetation and plant life in the U.S. Crafty Corp. purchases the land next to Annabelle's property for the purpose of building a shopping mall. In the process of bulldozing their land, Crafty cuts down nearly 20 acres of Annabelle's property, whose boundaries were properly marked. Annabelle sues and seeks a restorative injunction for the loss of the unique plant life and vegetation. In its argument against the restorative injunction, Crafty will most likely argue that:
   a. it is too expensive.
   b. the value of the land has increased by the commercial development.
   c. they could not see the boundary markers when they were bulldozing.
   d. both a. and b.
   e. none of the above.

6. You are being sued, along with three other defendants, for pollution of a reservoir. It has been determined that joint and several liability applies. Just before the jury verdict of $8,000,000 comes out, your fellow defendants, along with all of their money take a convenient holiday of indefinite duration to South America. You will be:
   a. soon joining them.
   b. liable for all $8,000,000.
   c. liable for your joint share, $2,000,000.
   d. not liable, unless the other three defendants and their money are available to contribute their fair share.
   e. liable only for the portion of damages that the plaintiffs can prove were caused directly by you.

7. Patriot, Inc., a Massachusetts based corporation, manufactures part of the new Bullseye missile for the U.S. army. While loading the plutonium core into the Bullseye casing, there is an accident and radiation leaks form the containment area. Some months after the U.S. government reveals the nature of the accident, several citizens living closest to the missile plant sue Patriot, Inc. for damages including "increased risk of future illness". Plaintiffs would be entitled to this type of compensation only where:
   a. they had expert witnesses testify that there is a slight chance plaintiffs may develop cancer from the exposure to radiation.
   b. the plaintiffs have manifestly developed symptoms of cancer.
   c. the plaintiffs testify that they are experiencing changes in their bodies but show no symptoms of cancer.
   d. they have experts testify that plutonium radiation if good for tanning.

8. P brings a suit under nuisance for pollution of his land by D. In defense, D asserts that P's common law suit is foreclosed by a state statute covering the same kind of pollution. Which is the correct statement of the rule the court will apply?
   a. Where statutes and the common law conflict, it is within the judge's discretion to decide which will be applied.
   b. statutes that occupy the same area as common law must be narrowly construed; the presumption is that common law remains.
   c. where common law and statutes conflict, common law always prevail, because it is court-made law.
   d. none of the above.

9. Hanz and Franz, two vice presidents of Terminator, Inc., were informed by the foreman at their Miami plant that there were high levels of asbestos in the older area of the plant. To comply with the new federal regulations on asbestos, Hanz and Franz ordered the foremen to remove the asbestos after hours and dispose of it in a nearby lake. Two children swimming in the lake subsequently died of asbestos poisoning. Hanz and Franz can be held criminally liable for these deaths because:
   - a. they were acting under the auspices of the corporation.
   - b. they complied with the federal regulations on asbestos.
   - c. they directly ordered the disposal of the asbestos into the lake.
   - d. they had control over the Miami plant finances and processing activities.

10. Corporation Xeon purchases 100 acres of forest land in Montana from the Pattersons to build a retirement village with condos and stores. On the 100 acres is Mithusala, the oldest tress in the United States. What would be your best option as the attorney for the "Concerned Citizens for a Caring Environment" in halting the ruination of the forest and chopping down of Mithusala?
    - a. Sue Corporation Xeon in court for a preliminary injunction.
    - b. Sue Corporation Xeon under the theory of public trust.
    - c. Go to the historic preservation society and have Mithusala declared a national land Mark.
    - d. Go to the Bureau of Land Management and hold a public hearing on the issue.

11. The State of Alaska wishes to install part of its pipeline to California across 40 acres of woodland owned by Christine Starr. Ms. Starr has never developed the land but has set aside this land as a wildlife preserve. Alaska condemns Ms. Starr's land for the pipeline route. Ms. Starr's strongest challenge to Alaska's exercise of its condemnation power is:
    - a. the route Alaska has chosen is arbitrary because there is a more direct route through a neighboring junk yard.
    - b. the pipeline provides no useful benefit to any community.
    - c. Alaska did not have the authority to condemn Ms. Starr's land for the pipeline route.
    - d. Alaska must consider the preservation of the wildlife in its exercise of the condemnation power.

12. The U.S. Department of Energy has decided to place a low-level nuclear waste depository in Walpole, Massachusetts, pursuant to power delegated to it by the Atomic Energy Act. The town fathers of Walpole have just passed an ordinance decreeing that, "There shall be no nuclear waste depositories of any type within the confines of the Town of Walpole; not now; not ever." The nuclear depository in Walpole will
    - a. not be built because the Energy Department was acting ultra vires .
    - b. will be built because the Federal Government pre-empts state and local actions in the field of nuclear energy.
    - c. will be built because the town, despite good intentions, cannot impose land use restrictions or regulations even within its own jurisdiction.
    - d. will not be build unless it is the "only rationally-remaining alternative."

13. If a court determines that an agency's decision was arbitrary and capricious,
    a. the court disagrees with the agency's conclusions based on the court's own review of the facts.
    b. the court has hound the agency's factual record insufficient for purposes of review.
    c. the court has applied the lowest standard of review to the agency's decision.
    d. the court has applied the strictest standard of review to the agency's decision.

14. In Florida, the Kissimmee River, which had been channeled into a straight, rapid-flowing, canal-like watercourse, is now scheduled to be returned to its original, slow-moving, curvy path. Although it will cost a substantial amount of money, the riverine ecosystem is expected to significantly improve. An Environmental Impact Statement
    a. must be prepared be fore any money at al is spent on the project.
    b. is not necessary because the project is expected to improve the environment rather than harm it.
    c. must be prepared at some point before major construction begins.
    d. should be prepared early enough so that environmental pros and cons can be considered along with other factors in deciding whether to proceed with the project.

15. *Allen v. U.S.*, involved a plaintiff who had been exposed to radiation during government weapons testing. In analyzing the plaintiff's case, the court held that it would be sufficient if the plaintiff showed that the weapon's fallout was a "substantial factor" in his subsequent illness. This is an example of:
    a. loosening the requirement of a "cause-in-fact" relationship between the conduct and the harm.
    b. making the plaintiff's case more difficult to prove in court.
    c. dispensing with the "proximate" cause requirement.
    d. none of the above.

16. The State of North Dakota wants to build a super highway through major forested areas of the state. Using its condemnation power, North Dakota acquires all of the land for this project. 75% of the project is funded by the Federal Highway Management Bureau (FHMB). The NRDC sues the state of North Dakota because it has not filed an environmental impact statement. The court is most likely to rule that
    a. NEPA applies specifically to state action and therefore, North Dakota must file an EIS.
    b. it is too late to require North Dakota to file an EIS because they have already acquired the land.
    c. this is a ploy by the federal government to circumvent the EIS requirement by funneling federal projects to states.
    d. the mandate of FHMB is in direct conflict with NEPA and therefore, North Dakota does not have to file an EIS.
    e. there is insufficient federal action to require an EIS.

17. Which of the following is true?
    a. EPA may not consider economic or technological feasibility for setting emission standards for hazardous pollutants.
    b. EPA may consider technological feasibility because the 1990 Amendments to the Clean Air Act codified Judge Burk's opinion in the vinyl chloride case.
    c. EPA may consider technological feasibility because a "harm-based" approach to hazardous pollutants is not workable because of the uncertainty involved in regulating these substances.
    d. both b. and c.
    e. none of the above

18. "Inverse condemnation" is
    a. a decision by a government agency to purchase the land of citizens at market value.
    b. unlawful.
    c. only proper for purposes of public health.
    d. a legal theory employed by owners of regulated land to claim that the regulation has caused such a diminution in property value that a regulatory taking has occurred.

19. The EPA under the Clean Water Act determines that the technology based standard for the iron ore mining industry is BPT–best practicable control technology. In order for Rock Hard Corp. to comply with this standard it
    a. must use the top of the line equipment in its plant.
    b. can consider costs as an outweighing factor and ignore the CWA standard.
    c. can adopt the technology within the iron ore industry best suited to its needs if it falls within the range of the BPT standard.
    d. must build a research and design unit to constantly develop more efficient technology.

20. The state of New York wants to establish a recreation facility on your land. They initiate condemnation proceedings against your property. What would be your best argument?
    a. Private land cannot be transferred by a state to private parties.
    b. The building of recreation facilities is not a proper public purpose.
    c. New York already owns over 500,000 acres of land which it could alternatively use.
    d. Financial compensation is not enough because of the sentimental attachment to the land.

21. Acme, Inc. releases acid into the groundwater surrounding its processing plant. The Johnsons live 2 miles from the Acme plant and have a well in their backyard which they use for drinking water. The Johnson's youngest son, Tommy, develops intestinal problems requiring hospital visits and examinations. The Johnsons sue Acme. The standard the court will apply to impute liability to Acme, Inc.'s behavior will be
    a. Acme's action was a substantial factor in bringing about the harm.
    b. Acme's action caused the Johnsons' harm beyond any doubt.

c. Acme's action could have caused the Johnsons' harm.
d. all of the above.
e. none of the above.

22. The two main problems with RCRA are:

1.______________________________

2.______________________________

23. All of the following are true regarding CERCLA except:
a. Courts have created a CERCLA "common law".
b. Liability under CERCLA is narrowly construed.
c. CERCLA uses strict liability.
d. CERCLA goes to actual as well as threatened releases.
e. A guilty defendant is liable for government response cost sunder CERCLA.

24. The Endangered Species Act only affects species that are indigenous to the United States.
a. true
b. false

25. Fire Side Co., a New York company, has receive numerous complaints from its Canadian neighbors that the emissions from its smoke stacks has intensified the acid rain problem in its cities. A group of Canadian citizens seeks to halt this activity and destruction of their cities. Their option is
a. to bring this case before the International Court of Justice on the theory of trespass or intentional nuisance.
b. Petition the U.N. Security Council to pass a resolution condemning Fire Side's actions.
c. to rely on a treaty signed and ratified by both the U.S. and Canada on the control of transboundary pollution.
d. rely on the treaty of absolute territorial integrity in petitioning the U.S. State Department to respect Canadian rights to a clean environment.

26. Cost externalization is exemplified by:
a. The salt paradigm discussed in class.
b. A factory discharging wastes into a river.
c. Evading statutory permitting requirements and the installation of pollution control equipment by hooking in to a municipality's sewage treatment center.
d. Dumping barrels of toxic waste in an isolated field in New Hampshire.
e. All of the above.

27. Assume that the New Hampshire dump site turned residential neighborhood we discussed in class has been listed #436 on the NPL. When developing a remedial design plan to clean up the site, the EPA may:
    - a. consider the cost and effectiveness of various approaches as one factor in the decision-making process.
    - b. use only those clean-up requirements which have previously been prescribed for the particular toxins found in the site.
    - c. ignore cost since the goal of CERCLA is cleaning up sites and Superfund money is available now that the site has been listed on the NPL.
    - d. pull requirements for the clean-up form non-environmental, unpublished materials produced by a chemical company's R&D lab.

28. The bank who loaned the developer money for the residential housing project:
    - a. has no liability risk.
    - b. may be liable, but only if the bank knew the land was a toxic dump site.
    - c. will be liable to the homeowners since they have lost everything.
    - d. may be held responsible as a PRP for the clean-up if the bank participated in the management of the development project.

29. The EPA may not consider economic or technological feasibility in setting primary and secondary NAAQSs under § 109 because:
    - a. The CAA specifically forbids the consideration of these factors in standard setting under § 109.
    - b. It was Congress' intent that these factors would not be considered in standard setting under § 109.
    - c. The common law of the CAA forbids the consideration of these factors.
    - d. both a. and c.
    - e. both b. and c.

30. As president of the town's history club, you have discovered that a house on Commonwealth Avenue was the site of George Washington's conception. A bill is pending in the legislature to purchase the house. In practical terms, your best shot at preventing the current plan to demolish the house is:
    - a. Enact a NEPA-type statute to prevent demolition unless a historical value assessment is filed with your office.
    - b. Sue for an injection halting demolition based on public trust argument.
    - c. File your own eminent domain proceedings.
    - d. Form a human chain around the building to ward off the bulldozers.

31. For the preceding question:
    - a. a) is the best choice because it is proactive as a statutory stop-and-think response to the problem.
    - b. b) is not clearly a winner, but there is legal doctrine on point.
    - c. c) is the best choice because it guarantees transfer of legal title of the building to the town.
    - d. d) is the best choice because the publicity it will generate will surely save the building.

32. A local statute prevents emissions of Has X in access of 2 has units per hour. This emissions goal can only be met by installing an X-emit Has X pipe on all air handlers. This statutory approach is an example of what statutory type?
    a. roadblock
    b. stop and think
    c. harm-based
    d. technology-based
    e. both c. and d.

33. Mr. Zany, your next door neighbor, after obtaining a permit from the zoning board, built a chicken coop in his backyard while you were in Miami Beach sunning yourself over spring bread and is planning to move in a flock of noisy chickens.
Your best game plan is:
    a. Sue Zany.
    b. Sue the zoning board.
    c. Petition to amend the zoning process to ensure no more chicken coops are built in the neighborhood
    d. Call a town meeting to organize opposition to Zany

34. The remedy you should seek is:
    a. money damages
    b. an injunction
    c. revocation of the permit
    d. amendment of the permitting process
    e. a community petition demanding that Zany remove the chicken coop.

35. Public nuisance ———— be an effective cause of action in this scenario since ———.
    a. would; property values will suffer
    b. would; the harm is common to everyone in the neighborhood
    c. might; you have a special injury
    d. would not; money damages are not available in a public nuisance action.

36. Curves Unlimited markets a breast implant device which was the subject of an intercompany memo reporting negative results of a products safety test. Your client's Curves Unlimited breast implant has ruptured. She suffers from a nervous disorder detailed as a health risk in the company's memo. Assuming the memo was discovered and is admissible as evidence at trial and that the company is found liable for your client's injury, punitive would be a proper element of the damage award:
    a. since punitives are intended to provide "extra" compensation when companies decide to "cost in" harms to people (ala Ford and the Pinto).
    b. since punitives are intended to deter and punish egregious behavior.
    c. if the company attempted to pay your client off.
    d. if compensatory damages are limited by statute in your jurisdiction.

37. MA REC, Inc. has joined with the state in a project to establish a state forest recreational area. The state has initiated condemnation proceedings against several parcels of land. The property owners effected have come to you for representation. The best argument available to you is:
    a. Eminent domain cannot be used to transfer private property to a private party.
    b. Building a recreation area is not a proper public purpose.
    c. The state already owns 500,000 acres of forest on which it could site the proposed recreational area.
    d. Financial compensation based on market value is insufficient for your clients given that these parcels have great sentimental value as homesteads.

38. Your neighbor's sewage drain backed up last week during a heavy spring rain. The torrent of water which rushed across you flower bed uprooted and destroyed the Mucho Expensivo tulips you planted last month. A likely cause of action is:
    a. intentional private nuisance
    b. negligent private nuisance
    c. strict liability
    d. public nuisance
    e. all of the above; at least one of them will stick.

39. You should be able to obtain:
    a. compensatory damages
    b. compensatory and punitive damages
    c. compensatory damages and an injunction requiring your neighbor to fix the drain
    d. compensatory damages and an injunction barring your neighbor from using the drain
    e. compensatory damages plus initiation of an eminent domain action to transfer title of the drain to the town to ensure that the drain is repaired properly.

40. Julia Childnose was distraught when her hit show "Cooking with Julia" was canceled by the CBA network. To console Julia, her husband built a beautiful retirement home, complete with a huge gourmet kitchen for Julia. Julia admitted to her husband that her favorite part of cooking was sitting back and letting her ultra-sensitive noise wallow in the delicious aromas which she created in the kitchen.
One day when Julia was sitting at the kitchen table, her olfactory nerve in ecstasy over a beautiful quiche, she let out a shrill cream. Her husband came running in to see what happened. Julia screamed hysterically, "My nose has been violated by that horrible stench coming in through the kitchen window. My nose will never be the same." Mr. Childnose was in awe since he smelled nothing. As time went by, Julia complained frequently about the stench, though Mr. Childnose and their frequent dinner guests did not notice the complained of smell.

Julia eventually traced the stench to her neighbor's kitchen where she fainted from the odor's intensity. It turns out that Julia's next door neighbor's started a home-based company, Domesti-Desserts, to make gourmet desserts for farm and pet animals. Julia wants to shut down Domesti-Desserts and collect money damages. In private nuisance action, what is the likely outcome?

a. Julia will probably lose because the neighbors will successfully raise a "coming to the nuisance" defense.
b. Julia will probably lose because this is not substantial unreasonable interference with property use since probably no reasonable person would objet to the odor.
c. Julia will probably lose because the elements of a prima facie case of private nuisance have not been satisfied.
<u>d</u>. Both b. and c.
e. None of the above.

41. Domesti-Dessert was so successful, the neighbors opened a factory. The horse meat used in production emits "saddle hoof chloride," a hazardous pollutant. The EPA recently established an emissions level for saddle hoof chloride based on best available technology. The Environmental Defense Fund (EDF) is furious that the EPA considered technological feasibility when setting the standard and claims that the standard is far too lax for such a dangerous pollutant. They challenge this action and insist on a zero emissions level. The year is 1991. What will the court find?

a. The EPA may not consider economic or technological feasibility in setting emissions standards for hazardous pollutants because Congress intended the CAA to be of a technology forcing character.
b. The EPA may consider technological feasibility because the 1990 Amendments to the CAA codified Judge Bork's opinion in the vinyl chloride litigation.
c. The EPA may consider technological feasibility but only where it is reasonable assumed that there is a sufficient safety butter given the uncertainty involved in regulating these substances.
<u>d</u>. both b. and c.
e. None of the above.

42. Cher Nobyl owns and operates the Three-Acre Hazardous Waste Dump in Hate Canal, New York. Cher fills her 3 acres to capacity in a very short time, then begins stacking barrels of waste along the perimeters of the property. Soon all of the neighborhood kids are glowing like light bulbs and becoming sick. Silky Wood's daughter is one of the sick children. Silky, on behalf of her child, decides to file a public nuisance action. Which statement(s) is true?

<u>a</u>. Silky Wood may not have standing to bring a public nuisance action.
b. Silky wood can clearly recover damages for her child's specific harms, as well as for harms suffered by the public in general.
c. Only the state can bring a public nuisance action.
d. Both a. and c.
e. Both a. and b.

43. Peter, Petra, Paul, Patricia, and Petula are all residents of a large town which is surrounded by various chemical producing industries. The source of water for all is the same–a deep well in the middle of town. Peter gets stomach cancer, Petra develops emphysema, Paul gets skin cancer, Patricia gets bladder cancer, and Petula gets leukemia, all within the same general time period. Tim Tort, a personal injury lawyer thinks they may have grounds for a class action (a la *Woburn.*). Once the suit is brought, the trial court judge will probably:

a. Consider causation to e a minor issue.
b. Provide separate proof of their different claims.
c. Hold that Joint and Several Liability does not apply to the defendant chemical industries.
d. Recommend that one of the Plaintiffs should bring a Flagship suit.
e. None of the above.

44. The State of New York transfers to Schenectady Snack Stands, Inc. (SSS), a private corporation operated by Sid Schlock, large plots of land within the various New York State parks. SSS plans to build on each plot a recreation complex for which they are famous. Each complex will contain a four story concession stand/gift shop; a mini-amusement park; Ripley's Believe It Or Not museum; a Tanning parlor; and an erotic bakery. What has just occurred?

a. Polyfurcation of state park lands.
b. Derogation of park lands.
c. Euthrophication of park lands.
d. Diversion of park lands.
e. Alienation of park lands.

45. One of the most important attributes of the ESA and other road block statutes is that:

a. They are flexible in their application.
b. They may be slipped through Congress under camouflage very effectively.
c. Litigation, such as that involving the sail darter, helps the cause of environmentalism.
d. The "God Squad" sits to supervise all roadblock statutes, thus these statutes are very effectively enforced.
e. They have teeth.

46. The "tragedy of the commons" is a model of decision-making that predicts the eventual exhaustion of resources. Which of the following assumptions is not contained in the model?

a. that each decision-maker seeks to maximize his own profits
b. that the commons is accessible only to those who have a private property interest in it
c. that the resources on the commons are finite
d. that decisions made will tend to internalize benefits and externalize cost
e. none of the above

47. There are three basic theories of tort liability available under tort causes of action: that the defendant acted intentionally, that the defendant was negligent, and that the defendant should be held strictly liable. Of the three, which does <u>not</u> call for an inquiry into the defendant's state of mind?

 a. defendant acted negligently
 <u>b</u>. defendant should be held strictly liable
 c. defendant acted intentionally
 d. a. and c.
 e. b. and c.

48. In *Florissant v. Park Land Company*, a public interest group successfully used the public trust doctrine to prevent a development company form bulldozing unique fossil beds. This case demonstrates that:

 <u>a</u>. the public trust doctrine can impose public trust constraints on private property owners as well as the government
 b. the public trust doctrine can only be used to protect values other than water rights
 c. the public trust doctrine cannot be extended to protect treasured man-made artifacts, like painting
 d. b. and c.

49. United States law has been adopted by the United Nations to be the legal system of the recently united world. Mars has long been colonized by the industrial nations of Earth because it has immense resources to be exploited. A number of industrialized nations have already set up both publicly and privately owned factories taking full advantage of the plentiful iron oxides of the red deserts of Mars. These factories manufacture spaceship hills and components and release a great deal of highly toxic and non-toxic compounds into the newly coalescing atmosphere. Human population is growing steadily as a small groups spread over the Martian surface setting up communities supported by mechanized mining sites and agriculture) water for agriculture and other uses must be pumped form deep underground–which is the only place is exists in quantity so far).

There is also a UN terraforming project will underway that will eventually build and Earth-like atmosphere for Mars. The UN intends to make Mars a resource for all humankind. Currently, the atmosphere is partially breathable (light weight oxygen face masks are needed to supplement the as yet oxygen-poor atmosphere). As more countries join in the industrial bonanza, and add their factory emissions to the atmosphere the terraforming project shows down because the factory emissions interfere with the terraforming process. Both toxic and non-toxic emissions have also hampered agriculture and interfered with some of the more sensitive mining machinery used by many private mining operations on the planets surface. Recently, one of the main terraforming plants began having nuclear reactor trouble. The UN, knew of the problem but kept quiet. A week later, there was an accident and a resulting melt-down which poisoned a 100 square kilometer area and ruined robot mining ad agricultural operations in the area. The colonists are not enthused by the thought of toxics in their air and have noted increases in the frequency of respiratory ailments.

A number of potential causes of action are available to those seeking to protect against the hazards of toxic and non-toxic factory and terraforming plant emissions. Remember that these are the only facts we have. Which cause of action is the least effective as it applies to the fact pattern above?

a. Public Nuisance
b. Public Trust
c. Private Nuisance
d. Pre-emption

50. The process by which government agencies receive the powers that they apply in their various regulatory settings is:

a. Separation of Powers Doctrine
b. Delegation Doctrine
c. Preemption Doctrine
d. Agency Doctrine

51. The Endangered Species Act is an example of a "roadblock" statute because:

a. it's technology-forcing to preserve endangered species.
b. it provides a financial incentive to preserve endangered species.
c. it indirectly prohibits the trade of Appendix III species, unless the exporter receives a permit from the importing country.
d. it prohibits an agency action if that action triggers the statute.

52. The primary mechanism by which states implement the Clean Air Act is the:

a. National Ambient Air Quality Standard
b. State Implementation Plan
c. Best Available Control Technology
d. Lowest Achievable Emission Reduction

53. The National Pollution Discharge Elimination System is:

a. a permit system which addresses water pollution from point sources.
b. a method of reducing the amount of hazardous waste generated by industry.
c. a way for municipalities to set standards which address air pollution.
d. none of the above.

54. CERCLA requires courts to apply what common law theory or tort liability:

a. Joint & Several Liability
b. Comparative Fault
c. Strict Liability
d. None of the above.

55. Punitive damage awards are inappropriate where;

a. they would unfairly punish a corporation's shareholders
b. there has been a change in corporate personnel since the time of the wrongdoing
c. the punitive damages are not proportional to the harm caused by the wrongdoing
d. none of the above

56. The Resource Conservation & Recovery Act (RCRA) regulates the use and disposal of hazardous waste by:
    a. Requiring generators of hazardous waste to pay for clean-up of abandoned hazardous waste sites.
    b. Requiring an environmental impact statement before every shipment of hazardous waste.
    c. Requiring "cradle to grave" regulation of hazardous waste for generators of hazardous waste, transporters of hazardous waste, and owners/operators of hazardous waste disposal sites.
    d. Requiring a state implementation plan for all hazardous waste.

Questions 57-59 are based on this fact pattern:

Toxic Inc. is a large San Antonio, Texas company (employing approximately 5000 people) specializing in X-ray film. Part of Toxic Inc.'s operations involve removing silver from x-ray film. The workers are largely illegal aliens, few of whom speak English. In order to separate the silver from the film, the workers hunch over bubbling foaming cauldrons of sodium cyanide. They were issued no gear and were not instructed about safety issues. While stirring the vats, sodium cyanide slopped over the sides, soaking the workers' clothing and skin. The air was choked with the fumes of hydrogen cyanide gas. Studies revealed that several workers at Toxic Inc. died as a result of cyanide poisoning and several others were seriously ill.

57. Assume that Toxic Inc. complied with all Occupational Safety ad Health Act (OSHA) regulations. OSHA compliance bars Texas from criminally prosecuting the management of Toxic Inc., because OSHA as a federal statute pre-empts a state statute.
    a. True
    b. False

58. If the state decided to criminally prosecute the Chief Executive Officer of Toxic Inc., which of the following defenses might help the Chief Executive Officer to avoid prosecution:
    a. "I didn't know the employees were ill."
    b. "I reasonably relieved that employees were instructed about safety issues."
    c. "I reasonably believed that the employees were not illegal aliens."
    d. "I didn't know cyanide has was lethal."

59. If one of the seriously ill employees decided to sue Toxic Inc. under a common law tort theory, which would be most applicable:
    a. Public Nuisance
    b. Private Nuisance
    c. Trespass
    d. Negligence

60. The Central Intelligence Agency has decided that it wants f fitness center in a wetlands area near the Potomac River. The best reason why the CIA should draft an Environmental Impact Statement (EIS) is:
    a. as an intelligence agency, it should know better

b. construction of a fitness center will destroy 2 acres of wetlands and may eliminate a butterfly species
c. the fitness center will occupy a building presently owned by the CIA
d. the fitness center was donated by a private individual

61. Suppose in *Adams v. Murphy*, the Supreme Court held that Massachusetts could not supplement the federal Natural Gas Act, which thoroughly regulates natural has transportation, by requiring a public utility transporting natural has to also seek approval from the Massachusetts Public Service Commission. The Supreme Court's decision was based on which type of preemption analysis?
a. Express intent to pre-empt
b. Conflict of laws
c. Similar purpose and objective
d. Comprehensive regulation

62. As justice Rehnquist explained in *Vermont Yankee* (the case which discussed the relationship between reviewing courts, the Administrative Procedure Act, Congress, and the agency's rulemaking procedures):
a. The Administrative Procedure Act established the maximum procedural requirements which Congress was willing to have the courts impose upon agencies in conducting rulemaking procedure.
b. Courts may increase procedural requirements in rulemaking proceedings if the agency determination is "quasi-judicial" which involves a very small number of persons exceptionally affected.
c. Courts may increase procedural requirements in rulemaking proceedings if the agency decision is a totally unjustified departure from well-settled agency procedures of long standing.
d. All of the above.
e. None of the above.

63. When deciding if a government regulation has resulted win an uncompensated taking of private property, a court probably will <u>not</u> consider:
a. the public benefit from the government regulation
b. the burden on the property owner resulting form the government regulation
c. the diminution in the value of the property
d. the property owner's financial condition

64. Generally, a federal court will apply which standard of review to an informal agency decision:

a. substantial evidence test
b. arbitrary and capricious test
c. de novo review
d. none of the above

65. Federal agencies which are required to complete an Environmental Impact Statement (EIS) under the National Environmental Policy Act (NEPA) <u>must</u> consider:
a. alternatives to the proposed action

b. the price of the proposed action
c. the burden of the proposed action on individual property owners
d. conflicts with state laws

66. The Clean Water Act (CWA) provides for effluent limitations which are based upon:
a. primarily, control technology and secondly, water quality
b. primarily, water quality of rivers and streams and secondly, control technology
c. primarily, drinking water quality
d. none of the above

67. Which of the following statutes does not provide substantive protections, only procedural ones?
a. RCRA (Resource Conservation & Recovery Act)
b. CERCLA (Comprehensive Environmental Response Compensation and Liability Act)
c. ESA (Endangered Species Act)
d. NEPA (National Environmental Policy Act)

68. Based on common law (i.e. there is no statutory provision) which is the following places would most likely be found by a reviewing court as a public trust?
a. Fenway Park
b. O'Neill Library
c. John Hancock Building
d. Boston Common

69. Suppose, again, the Central intelligence Agency wished to build a fitness center in your backyard. In order to build the fitness center, they invoke the eminent domain doctrine to obtain the necessary land, including your Olympic-sized swimming pool and Jacuzzi. You challenge the decision in a federal district court, which of the following inquiries would a reviewing court make:
I. Does the CIA have the authority to at?
II. Does the CIA's decision address a public purpose?
III. Is the taking of your property rationally related to the CIA's goal of building a fitness center?
IV. Does the CIA compensation adequately reflect the fair market value of the property?

a. I and IV only
b. IV only
c. I, II, III
d. II, III, and IV
e. All the above

70. The "tragedy of the commons" is a model of decision-making that predicts the eventual exhaustion of resources. Which of the following assumptions is <u>not</u> contained in the model?
a. that each decision-maker seeks to maximize his own profit
b. that the commons is accessible only to those who have a property interest in it

c. that the resources on the commons are finite
d. that decisions made will tend to internalize benefits and externalize costs.

71. The story of Allied Chemical's production of Kepone presents an example of the tragedy of the commons in a complicated, real-life form. In 1973, Allied entered into a "rolling" agreement with LSP, whereby LSP would produce Kepone in exchange for economic and technical assistance. From an environmental standpoint, this was:
a. good, because it spreads out the harmful effects of the pollution among more than one source
b. good, because Kepone production was limited by the small size of LSP
c. bad, because small polluters usually are lax in their treatment of wastes
d. bad, because it allowed Allied to avoid imposition of costs through the legal system through the use of LSP as a "shield"

72. *Boomer v. Atlantic Cement Company* presents an example of one common law tort, in which the plaintiff must prove that the defendant acted in a way that caused the plaintiff harm to his use and enjoyment of property, such that the plaintiff should receive a remedy. This is a prima facie case of:
a. private nuisance
b. public nuisance
c. trespass
d. negligence

73. Which of the following is not an element of the prima facie case of international private nuisance:
a. defendant caused the interference with plaintiff's property rights
b. defendant knew with substantial certainty that harm would result
c. the defendant intended to harm the plaintiff
d. the plaintiff suffered a substantial and unreasonable interference with its property rights

74. Negligent private nuisance cases are easier to rove and more difficult to defend then intentional private nuisance cases.
a. true
b. false

75. A private plaintiff can use a public nuisance cause-of-action when:
a. special injury can be shown
b. the government could have prevented the harm to this plaintiff
c. no other private parties are injured
d. there is no alternative

76. Possible defenses to a charge of negligent private nuisance include all of the following except:
a. the plaintiff assumed the risk
b. the plaintiff contributed to the negligence
c. the defendant followed industry practice and custom

d. the defendant came to the nuisance

77. The operations of local factory (D) result in the emission of aluminum particles that settle on the ground up to 2 miles downwind. Paula (P) sues based on harm to her livestock. A court is likely to hold that
   a. this is not a nuisance, because there was no physical invasion
   b. this is not a trespass, because a person must "break the close" of one's property for there to be a trespass
   c. both s. and b.
   d. none of the above

78. You live downwind from a major industrial park and have recently suffered health problems form the air pollution. However, there are five factories in this park that could be contributing to your injuries. What legal doctrine is most likely to help you overcome this problem?
   a. permissive joinder of claims
   b. a class action suit
   c. right of contribution
   d. joint and several liability

79. *Allen v. U.S.* involved a plaintiff who had been exposed to radiation during government weapons testing. In analyzing the plaintiff's case, the court held that it would be sufficient if the plaintiff showed that the weapon's fallout was a "substantial factor" in his subsequent illness. This is an example of:
   a. loosening the requirement of "cause-in-fact" relationship between the conduct and the harm
   b. making the plaintiff's case more difficult to prove in court
   c. dispensing with the "proximate cause" requirement
   d. none of the above

80. In a toxic tort action, P sues D, his emphysema of 20 years, for emphysema which he alleges resulted from ongoing exposure to sulfur dioxide. At trial, it is shown that P is a 2-pack-a-day smoker, that the rate of emphysema among his co-workers is roughly equal to the national average among men his age; and that P has been in retirement for 8 years. Faced with these facts, a court is likely to:
   a. find for D, because the equal rates of emphysema indicate that the sulfur dioxide can't be the cause
   b. find for D, because P's case falls short of showing that D's conduct was a "substantial factor" in causing the emphysema
   c. find for P, because policy reasons dictate that we compensate plaintiffs who are subjected to only-term harm
   d. none of the above

81. Toxic Tort Claims against the government might not be defeated by a defense of sovereign immunity if the plaintiff(s) can show:
   a. the government acted unreasonable
   b. the government was not engaging in activities similar to those of private enterprises
   c. actual harm

d. causation

82. Which of the following remedies is most unlikely to be available to a private plaintiff:
   a. an injunction
   b. recovery for the unknown risk of future illness
   c. recovery for economic losses
   d. recovery for pain and suffering

83. Courts might prefer to make an award of permanent damages when a plaintiff has successfully shown that the defendant interfered with the plaintiff's use and enjoyment of its land, because permanent damages are:
   a. easier to assess
   b. more expedient
   c. more fair
   d. more comprehensive

84. Punitive damages should be awarded when a defendant:
   a. acts intentionally
   b. acts with malice
   c. follows industry standards and customs
   d. acts negligently

85. Environmental losses are difficult to assess. Ideally they may be recoverable through an award of:
   a. the shadow price of the resource
   b. punitive damages
   c. loss of economic uses
   d. restoration of the resource

86. Which of the following is true:
   a. While environmental common law generally protects private interests in land, statutes are designed to protect public interests.
   b. Generally, the government brings suit for violation of a statute, although citizens may sue where a citizen suit provision is included in the statue.
   c. The measure of remedies under a common law suit is private harm, while statutes usually provide for civil or administrative penalties.
   d. All of the above.

87. P brings a suit under nuisance for pollution of his land by D. in defense, D asserts that P's common law suit is foreclosed by a state statute covering the same kind of pollution. Which is the correct statement of the rule the court will apply?
   a. Statutes always prevail over the common law.
   b. Statues that occupy the same area as common law remains.
   c. Where common law and statues conflict, common law always prevails, because it is court-made law.
   d. None of the above.

88. A criminal prosecutor will pursue an environmental case when:
 a. it is certain to create political problems and upset constituents
 b. it is unlikely that the government will win
 c. the time it will take to handle the case can be justified given the violation and the government's evidence
 d. no one really knows who is responsible for the violation

89. Corporations are rarely charged with Refuse Act violations because they are difficult to prove:
 a. true
 b. false

90. In a Clean Water Act case against XYZ Ltd., an independent subsidiary of ABC Corp., the court finds that XYZ violated the Act and sets the penalty at $4,000.000. XYZ has assets totaling only $2,500,000. Which of the following is true?
 a. The government can't seek the whole penalty, because that would be inequitable to XYZ.
 b. The government is limited to the assets of the corporation; it may not seek the balance from XYZ's shareholders.
 c. The government can seek the balance of the penalty from ABC, simply by showing that ABC created XYZ five years ago.
 d. b. and c.

91. *U.S. v. Park* involved a suit against the president of a grocery store chain for violation of a federal health statute. The Supreme Court:
 a. affirmed the conviction, holding that Park should be held liable because of his authority and responsibility to correct the problem
 b. affirmed the conviction, holding that a corporate executive is liable for any statutory violation that occurs anywhere in the corporation
 c. reversed the conviction, holding that Park did everything he cold in checking with his subordinates about corrective action
 d. reversed the conviction, holding that for $50, it wasn't worth it

92. The U.S. Constitution does not include a right to a clean environment.
 a. true
 b. false

93. In *Florissant v. Park Land Company* a public interest group successfully used the public trust doctrine to prevent a development company form bulldozing unique fossil beds in Colorado. This case demonstrates that:
 a. the public trust doctrine can impose trustee obligations on private property owners as well as the government
 b. the public trust doctrine can be sued to protect values other than water right
 c. the public trust doctrine can be extended to protect treasured man-made artifacts, like paintings
 d. a. and b.

94. Land-use regulations that affect private property may by unconstitutional if they:
    a. prevent a landowner from using its land in the most economically beneficial manner
    b. prevent a public nuisance
    c. result in a decline a land value
    d. leave the property owner with no reasonable remaining use

95. The best argument for upholding regulations that restrict development of wetlands is that:
    a. wetlands need to be preserved in order to prevent harm to the public
    b. wetlands typically have lower land values so restrictions on development don't result in a significant loss in value
    c. wetlands can be easily filled and made into more productive land
    d. wetlands are difficult to value

96. When a court reviews a land-use regulation to determine if it is unconstitutional it will:
    a. not consider why the regulation was enacted
    b. only look at whether the state had the authority to regulate
    c. consider if the regulation reasonably achieves the stated purpose
    d. always overturn a regulation that burdens private property owners

97. A state law will always survive a Dormant Commerce Clause challenge provided the regulatory system it creates is facially even-handed.
    a. true
    b. false

98. Dormant Commerce Clause cases show that states may:
    a. never enact legislation that discriminates against out-of state commerce
    b. only legislate when there is a grant of authority to do so from cóngress
    c. only create laws that protect n-state interest
    d. enact legislation so long as the burden on interstate commerce does not outweigh the local benefits

99. Which of the following statements are true about administrative agencies?
    a. agency actions are not subject to judicial review, because they are part of the executive branch
    b. agencies typically act through rulemaking (issuance of general regulations) or adjudication (applying regulations to disputes)
    c. the "delegation doctrine" states that once an agency is crated, it wields wide powers unrelated to its organic act
    d. when a court reviews an agency action, it always takes over the case completely, in a trial de novo

100. In *Overton Park v. Volpe*, the environmental groups argued that the Court should apply the "substantial evidence" test or engage in de novo review of the agency's action. These arguments relate to:
    a. whether the planned highway was a good idea for Memphis
    b. whether the agency had been delegated the authority to build

highways

c. the standard of review that should be applied to the agency by the Court

d. none of the above

101. Section 102 of NEPA states that:
"... all agencies of the Federal Government shall ... nclude in every recommendation or report on proposals for legislation and other major Federal actions significantly affecting the quality of the human environment, a detailed statement ..."

Which of the following phrases from this section is most important, from the point of view of someone who wants to know if she can sue for an agency's failure to file en Environmental impact Statement (EIS)?

a. "shall"

b. "major Federal action"

c. "significantly affecting"

d. "detailed statement"

102. In 1968, the Department of the Interior began construction of an overnight lodge for visitors in Yellowstone National Park. NEPA was passed on January 1, 1970. The Department never filed an EIS. Now, in late 1970, all that is left to do is remove leftover building materials. In your citizen suit to enjoin continued work on the lodge, a court will likely:

a. issue the injunction, because construction of a lodge is clearly a "major Federal action significantly affecting the quality of the human environment"

b. deny the injunction, because citizens can't sue under NEPA

c. deny the injunction, because there is no significant work left to be done that would be affected by the EIS requirement

d. none of the above

103. The Endangered Species Act only affects species that are indigenous to the United States.

a. true

b. false

104. NEPA and the Endangered Species Act are similar in that:

a. they both were enacted during the Nixon Administration

b. they both require impact assessments

c. they both target the actions of federal agencies

d. all of the above

105. Which of the following statements are true about the management of federal lands by the bureau of Land Management (BLM)?

a. management of land is to be conducted based on "multiple use-sustained yield"

b. the "capture" of the BLM by grazing and ranching interests was a problem for much of the agency's history

c. enforcement of FLPMA is hampered by a lack of personnel and resources.
d. all of the above

106. The State of Grimes has failed to meet the Clean Air Act NAAQS for particulate emissions. If the entire state is considered a non-attainment area which of the following is true:
a. no new sources of particulates will be permissible
b. the state will be designated as ineligible to receive federal funds until it achieves compliance
c. the state must show that it will continue to make reasonable further progress towards meeting the standards
d. the state will be fined

107. One of the problems with allowing states to design pollution control strategies under the Clean Air Act is that:
a. states have too much knowledge about who the polluters are
b. states will be inclined to consider cost and technological feasibility
c. pollution knows no state boundaries
d. the federal government can do it more quickly

108. Under the Clean Water Act (CWA) effluent limitations are set based on what is technologically available , under the BAT or the BCT standard.
a. true
b. false

109. Which of the following would not need a NPDES permit under the CWA?
a. a U.S. Steel plant that discharges treated waste water in to Lade Michigan
b. a housing developer whose bulldozers deposit fertilizer–laden dirt into a small river
c. a farm which deposits agricultural runoff into the Mississippi River
d. none needs a permit

110. You are planning to start a business producing high-quality stationary from old newspapers. Unfortunately, the process involved creates waste water with high concentrations of sulfuric acid. Concerned, you consult the Regional Office of the EPA, only to find out that EPA has not issued guidelines for the newspaper recycling industry. Under the CWA, what happens next?
a. you must wait until EPA issues guidelines: then you can get a permit and start your business
b. you can get a permit, which EPA will issue based on "Best Professional Judgment" (BPJ)
c. as long as the waterbody you plan on discharging into is clean, you can go ahead without obtaining a permit
d. none of the above

111. To supplement the technology-based provisions of the CWA, the states are to designate Water Quality Standards (Was) for their waters, consisting of uses and criteria to meet those uses. This quality-based system has had little effect, because:
   a. States are free to set uses as low as they want to attract industry
   b. it's difficult and expensive to work backwards from desirable levels of water quality to limits on individual sources
   c. it's very difficult to enforce the provisions of the CWA, because violations of permits are hard to detect
   d. all of the above

112. The comprehensive Environmental Response Compensation and Liability Act (CERCLA) addresses three major problems associated with harmful releases of hazardous substances into the environment. Which one of the following is not included in CERCLA:
   a. a Superfund to finance the cleanup or contaminated sites
   b. a response system to identify cleanup alternatives and select one
   c. a manifest system to keep track of where the waste originated and came to rest
   d. a liability provision, whereby potentially responsible parties must cover the cost of cleanup and damage to the environment

113. Citizen enforcement under most federal pollution control statutes requires proof of personal harm.
   a. true
   b. false

Greentown has long been a center for the chemical industry. Over the years, most of the industrial wastes from Greentown have been deposited in the Greentown Dump. In 1954, the Dump obtained a licensee from the community to operate its facility. In 1982, pursuant to RCRA, the Greentown Dump got a permit form the federal government to operate as a hazardous waste landfill.

The Greentown Dump, despite having several permits, has been a source of complaints from its neighbors. During the 1950s and 1960s, the dump burned some of its wastes in open pits. The open fires were permitted by the local authorities, but, in response to complaints, the Dump stopped the burning of waste. In the 1970s, neighbors complained about irritating fumes, especially during the summer. This problem, again in response to community complaints, was solved. The current problem is that huge dust clouds are raised along the dirt roads in the dump by the trucks bringing in the waste. This problem has gotten worse in the past two years, as a new fleet of huge waste-hauling vehicles has started being used to bring in waste.

The trucks are not owned by the dump. The owners of the Greentown Dump say that they have discussed the problem wit the truckers and the chemical plants in the area, but that the new trucks will continue to be used. If the Greentown Dump refuses to allow the large trucks to use the dump, the waste will go to another dump and the Greentown Dump will be forced to close.

The closure of the dump will affect the community adversely. Not only will there be a loss of 120 employees at the dump, a large loss for Greentown, but the chemical plants in the area will be much less likely to invest in the modernization of current plants or the construction of new plants. Several chemical plant managers have predicted that the closure of the dump will cause 1) the loss of jobs and 2) the eventual stagnation of the economy in Greentown. The plant managers say that the chemical plants have an overriding incentive to locate close to disposal facilities (to minimize the chances of having a spill during the transportation of the waste). There is a consensus in town that the chemical industry in town, the major employer, will gradually wither away if the dump closes.

114. The Greentown Dump needs to have permits to operate. We might expect that the Dump has applied for the received permits under each of the following statutes except:
   a. the Clean Air Act (due to emissions of volatile organic substances)
   b. NEPA (because there is a major local action at the dump)
   c. the Clean Water Act (for the leachate treatment system)
   d. a local Sewer District (to link the waste water treatment system to the local sewage treatment plant)

115. There are several acres of wetlands on the dump's property. The Greentown Dump has never disturbed these wetlands and there is no indication that the wetlands have been degraded by the activities at the Dump. The state government, however, wants to pass a law that will prevent major industrial activities located within 1000 feet of wetlands form changing operations in any way that might jeopardize the wetlands. Such legislation could severely restrict or even halt operations at the Dump (which must continually change operations as portions of the landfill are filled. You are an attorney advising the state Senator proposing the legislation. You will need to consider all of the following legal theories except one in order to draft state legislation that will survive scrutiny in court. Which theory can most safely be ignored?
   a. the state has a right to pass regulation to promote the health, safety, and welfare of state and its citizens
   b. if the state forces the landfill to close, there may be no remaining economic uses for the property and a taking may have occurred
   c. the general theory of ;the common law prevents states from passing statutes that might interfere with judge made law
   d. wetlands issues may be pre-empted by federal law (the Clean Water Act)

116. Suppose that the Dump has started to leak some leachate into an underground aquifer. The EPA does not plan to add the site to the Superfund list and does not plan to close the dump, but it has ordered some remedial action to occur. Which of the following is not true?
   a. This administrative act cannot be taken without specific statutory authorization.
   b. This administrative act cannot be taken without specific authorization by the President.
   c. This administrative act cannot be taken without notice to the general public of its proposed action.
   d. This administrative act cannot be unconstitutional.

117. The following is an example of an economic externality:
   a. the right provided under CERCLA to dump hazardous substances off-site
   b. coal beds in a National Forest
   c. emitting air pollutants into the air without paying for such a right

d. emitting air pollutants into the air and paying for such a right

118. A court may issue injunctions:
   a. only in the system of the Federal Courts, since courts may not issue injunctions
   b. only after a balancing of the equities has occurred
   c. only in public trust cases
   d. only pursuant to hedonic damages

119. A class action lawsuit requires:
   a. a possible finding of joint and several liability
   b. that at least one of the causes of action be in toxic torts
   c. a "preponderance of the evidence" standard of judicial review
   d. a substantially identical legal in a number of cases.

120. All criminal provisions of environmental laws require
   a. an element of criminal intent
   b. a prior administrative proceeding
   c. that the corporation as well as the corporate official be indicated
   d. none of the above

121. A taking by the federal government
   a. cannot apply to corporations, since corporations do not have rights under the Fifth Amendment
   b. may require an application of a "diminution" test
   c. requires compensation when there is an exercise of the state police power
   d. occurs when the government raises taxes

122. The following is an example of a "small handle problem" under NEPA:
   a. issuing a permit for a small part of a large project
   b. a significant federal action which a court has hound to be not a major federal action
   c. a Congressional inquiry into a given EIS
   d. the last permit or EIS issued by the EPA

123. Placing a strict time limit on the enforcement of strict roll back provisions in the Clean Air Act will not result in:
   a. penalizing companies who are already environmentally conscious
   b. the development of catalytic converters not new types of engines
   c. a need for extensions
   d. new cleaner technology
   e. a race for laxness between states

The following fact pattern should be used to answer Questions 124-126.

For years Joe Truck Driver has been picking up barrels form GF Chemical a company he knows produces hazardous waste. The barrels say "Hazardous waste" on the side. Joe decides which landfill to take them to and places them in the fill. Susie Kick lives next door to the landfill and she gets her water form a well near the fill. Susie has become ill, apparently because of the chemicals.

124. What causes of action could she sue Joe under to receive compensation?

I. Private Nuisance
II. CERCLA
III. Trespass
IV. NEPA

a. II. only
b. IV. only
c. I. and III. only
d. none of the above
e. all of the above

125. What may be the toughest element of the cause of action to prove?
a. causation
b. intent
c. harm
d. duty to prevent the harm

126. GF Chemical might also be sued because RCRA specifically imposes
a. a manifest system for transporters
b. a cradle-to-grave liability system for hazardous waste
c. a disposal system of mandating that hazardous waste must go into a landfill
d. a disposal system prohibiting hazardous waste from going into landfills

127. You decide to sell your land. Before you do you have it surveyed. You find out that your neighbor has been dropping old batteries and oil cans onto your land. You clean up the area and decided to sue your neighbor under CERCLA. The result may be:
a. Your award goes directly into the Superfund.
b. You lose because the land cannot be a facility under the definition set forth in CERCLA.
c. You are thrown out of court because an individual doesn't have standing to sue in CERCLA.
d. You win because you are able to show that you cleaned up the area which was polluted by your neighbor.

128. The Clean Air Act can be called "harm-based" because:
a. It applies only after there has been a prima facie showing of harm.
b. The primary standards set for national ambient air quality are based on

a measure of pollution at which harm may occur to human beings.

c. There are economic incentives to harm violators.

d. Once there has been a prima facie showing of harm, technology forcing provisions come into play.

129. To promote safety, a federal statute says that at most 50 freight cars can be attached to each other at one time. To promote energy efficiency, at state statute says at least 100 freight cars must be attached at a time. This is an example of which kind of preemption?

a. implied

b. express

c. policy

d. none of the above

130. A federal statute is silent on how many freight cars can be attached to each other any one time. A state statute says 50 freight cars can be attached at a time. This is an example of which kind of preemption?

a. implied

b. express

c. policy

d. no preemption

131. "Technology forcing" refers to

a. a statutory provision that requires achievement of statute not yet technologically feasible.

b. a public trust doctrine against new technology

c. a doctrine in favor of research development in causation

d. a technological breakthrough that must occur or stiff penalties will be applied

132. A Clean Air Act "bubble" refers to

a. a trade to allow a large source to "float" just under the statutory requirements for large sources

b. a banking and offsetting system that will create new types of emissions in statutory sources

c. a theory by which multiple causes of action may apply to a particular set of facts

d. a one for one trade-off within a multi-source plant where total plant emissions remain nearly the same

133. CERCLA defenses will allow a landowner to escape liability for the improper disposal of hazardous substances only where

a. the hazardous substances were disposed of by mistake

b. the hazardous substances were carried under the property by the ground water

c. a foreign war has resulted in contamination from enemy bombs

d. where a chemical manufacturer puts in its waste disposal contract that the hazardous waste must be disposed of in a specific properly licensed and well-run landfill

134. *Boomer v. Atlantic Cement Company* present an example of the one common law tort, in which the plaintiff must prove that the defendant acted in a way that caused the plaintiff harm to his use and enjoyment of property, such that the plaintiff should receive a remedy. This is a prima facie case of

a. private nuisance
b. public nuisance
c. trespass
d. negligence

135. Peter (P0 sues Dependable Electric Co. (D) for physical harm suffered because of polluted drinking water. In his complaint, P alleges that 10 months ago there was an accident at D's power plant, which caused a two-day power outage. During that time the local water treatment plant shut down, resulting in untreated water spilling into the local reservoir. A bottling company sold bottles of contaminated water from the reservoir. As a result of drinking the water P experienced intestinal problems that have cost him $15,000 in hospital and doctor bills. The court dismisses his claim. Which is the most likely basis for the court's dismissal?

a. P failed to show cause-in-fact
b. P failed to show proximate cause
c. P failed to show sufficient harm
d. P is suing the wrong party

136. Possible defenses to a claim of negligent private nuisance may include all of the following except:

a. lack of a showing of causation
b. Plaintiff contributed to negligence
c. Defendant followed industry standard
d. Defendant did not intend to infringe on plaintiff's property rights

137. A court will most likely award punitive damages when a defendant:

a. acts intentionally
b. acts with malice
c. follows industry standards
d. acts negligently

138. Natural resource damages are difficult to assess, but may be recoverable through an award of the following except:

a. shadow pricing
b. punitive damages
c. loss of economic use
d. cost of restoration

139. You live downwind from a major industrial park and have recently suffered health problems from the air pollution. However there are five factories in the park that could be contributing to your injuries. What legal doctrine is most likely to help you overcome this problem?

a. permissive joinder of claims
b. a class action suit

c. right of contribution
d. joint and several liability

140. A foreign investor decides to buy a priceless Cezanne painting. It becomes clear to him that he can sell pieces of that painting for more than he can sell the painting as a whole. He tells you he is about to cut it up in to 20 mini-paintings. You sue for an injunction in equity arguing the public Trust Doctrine. You will most likely
a. lose because the theory of public trust doctrine arises out of law pertaining only to water right.
b. lose because he owns the painting and under the 5th amendment, there are no circumstances in which the government may infringe on his property right.
c. win because the judge feels that equity demands that the historic and artistic integrity of the painting be saved for future generations in perpetuity.
d. win because the Public Trust Doctrine is widely recognized cause of action where the government must act a §trustee over items of particular historic or environmental value.

141. The Endangered Species Act is considered a crude blunt instrument for all of the following reasons except:
a. The statute allows no balancing of equities
b. The work "shall" gives no discretion to agency administrators as to when to apply the provisions of the Act
c. Congress intended to protect all endangered animal, ugly unmediagenic ones and cute, endangered baby seals alike.
d. The statute proves a strict prohibition against the destruction of the habitat of endangered species.

142. Each of the following are generally recognized as competing interests in International Environmental Law except:
a. Environmental Protection vs. Third World Development
b. The North vs. The South
c. United Nations vs. International Treaties
d. National Sovereignty vs. The power of International Organization

143. A district court found the president of a very large grocery store chain criminally liable for a violation of a federal health statute taking place in one of the company's warehouses and fined him $50. The Supreme Court will most likely:
a. affirm the conviction, holding that the president should be held liable because of his authority and responsibility to correct the problem
b. affirm the conviction, holding that a corporate executive is liable for any statutory violation that occurs anywhere in the corporation
c. reverse the conviction, holding that the president did everything he could in checking with his subordinates about corrective action
d. reverse the conviction, holding that for $50, it wasn't worth it.

144. In prosecuting an individual for environmental harm, it is a cardinal rule that "scienter," or criminal intent, must always be shown.
a. true
b. false

1992 Rutgers University

[Final Examination, Second Half of the course]

Part I (50%, 1 hour)

Concisely explain each of the following:

1. Statutory hammer
2. Pollution Prevention Act of 1990
3. ARARS (applicable, relevant, and appropriate requirements)
4. Legal control of agricultural water runoff
5. National Contingency Plan (NCP)
6. Control of pollution from new motor vehicles
7. Antidegradation
8. Control of interstate air pollution
9. Premarket Notification (PMN)
10. *De Minimis* consent decree
11. Definition of "Solid Waste' under RCRA
12. Tradeable sulfur oxide emissions allowances
13. Section 404 of the Clean Water Act

Part II (50%, 1 hour)

Company X, located in northern New Jersey, is a large pesticide manufacturer that produces numerous pesticide products for use in the United States and abroad. In manufacturing its products, company X produces wastes that are disposed of into (1) the air, (2) a nearby river, (3) the local Publicly Owned Treatment Works, (4) a hazardous waste landfill located in a remote corner of the X plant site, and (5) by shipment for disposal at the Emelle incinerator facility in Alabama and for land disposal in the African nation of Malawi. X's onsite landfill has been in use since 1940, and there is evidence that the wastes buried there are leaching into groundwater. From time to time X has allowed other local companies to bury waste at this site on a "one-time payment" basis.

Company Y is about to merge with company X by purchasing all of X's outstanding stock. Y wants not only to continue the profitable pesticide business, but also to enter the hazardous waste disposal business (i.e. treat, store, and dispose of hazardous waste generated by other companies) by upgrading the onsite hazardous waste landfill and by building a hazardous waste incinerator. Y would then also be able to stop its waste shipments to Emelle and Malawi and dispose of this waste onsite. The proposed hazardous waste incinerator would be a source of nitrogen dioxide, a highly toxic material. Incinerator residues would be disposed of at the onsite landfill.

Company Y has hired you — knowing that you are a Cook College graduate having taken Environmental Law — to act as a liason between Y's production executives and the bank and the law firm retained by Y to carry out the merger with X. Which federal and New Jersey environmental statutes do you consider to be relevant to the merger? How would you define and outline the issues with regard to each statute? What further information would you need to assist you in your identification and discussion of these issues? Do you see any opportunities for using ADR in this situation?

[Mid-term Examination, Second-half of the course, 1992]

Part I (50%, 45 min.)

Briefly explain each of the following:

1. Paper hearing.
2. "Considerable adverse effect" on public lands by ORVs.
3. Interagency Testing Committee.
4. Exhaustion of remedies.
5. Worst Case Analysis.
6. "Taking" of an endangered species.
7. General and restricted pesticide regulation.
8. Suboptimization.
9. "Certificate of Conformity."
10. ESA consultation.
11. functional equivalence doctrine.
12. "Small handle" problem.

Part II (50%, 45 min.)

Analyze, compare, and contrast the application of benefit-cost analysis in the following federal environmental protection statute: (1) NEPA; (2) ESA; (3) FIFRA; and (4) ToSCA.

March 13, 1991
[THE EXAMS THAT FOLLOW ARE NOT KEYED TO NLS]

<u>Midterm Examination, I</u> (50%)

Explain each of the following as briefly as possible:

1. Noncompliance penalties.
2. "...to any prevailing or substantially prevailing party."
3. "...so long as there is a feasible and prudent alternative consistent with the reasonable requirements of the public health, safety and welfare."
4. Worst Case Analysis.
5. "...the fact that particular environmental interests are shared by the many rather than the few does not make them less deserving of legal protection through the judicial process."
6. "...use all practicable means, consistent with other essential considerations of national policy...."
7. Suboptimization.
8. "Secondary impacts" doctrine under NEPA.
9. Paper hearing.
10. The "clientele" of an administrative agency.
11. Tiering.
12. Counsel On Environmental Quality (CEQ).

II (50%)

The Hunting Creek incident began in 1962 and ended in 1969. Assume the accuracy of all facts presented by Sax except the ending of the case study. That is, assume that the Fish and Wildlife Service had finally refused to withdraw its "No Opposition" policy and the Corps of Engineers had granted the dredge and fill permit. Under this modified scenario, what would have been the likely result of a lawsuit brought by the project's opponents in federal court for judicial review of agency action?

In your estimation, would the Hunting Creek issue have evolved differently if the permit application had been submitted in 1972 rather than 1962? If not, why not? If so, what would the differences have been?

(90 minutes)

March 5, 1990
<u>Midterm Examination,</u> I (50%)

Explain each of the following as briefly as possible:

1. Presumption regarding meaning of enabling act
2. ". . . the fact that particular environmental interests are shared by the many rather than the few does not make them less deserving of legal protection through the judicial process."
3. ". . . use all particular means, consistent with other essential considerations of national policy,. . . "

4.5.6. Three criteria for determining whether an agency action is "arbitrary and capricious"
7. Paper hearing
8. Payment of attorney's and expert witness' fees under environmental statutes
9. Insider perspective
10. "Causation" under NEPA
11. Scoping
12. "Crystal ball" inquiry

II (50%)

The following set of facts is a combination of excerpts from the district court's and circuit court's opinions in Foundation on Economic Trends v. Heckler (1984, 198510. This case involved the National Institutes of Health (a federal agency that funds scientific research) and its requirement that all federally-funded researchers must receive NIH approval before deliberately releasing recombinant DNA material into the general environment.

After you have read this material, please answer the following question: 1) What should the plaintiff want? 2) What should be its major legal argument? 3) What should be defendant's counterarguments? 4) Who should win, and why?

December 18, 1990 FINAL EXAMINATION

I (50%)
Briefly explain or answer each of the following:

1. Tenth Amendment to the United States Constitution.
2. Broad Form Deed.
3. Occupation of the field.
4. Affirmative defense to suit under the Michigan Environmental Protection Act.
5. "Wisconsin Rule" in public trust law.
6. Negative (or Dormant) Commerce Clause.
7. Possible defendants in a suit by the beneficiary of a public trust.
8. The United States Supreme Court's view of the legality of TDRs.
9. Prior Public Use doctrine.
10. Express preemption.

II (50%)

Although it has not happened, nor is it likely to happen, assume for the purposes of this exam that the New Jersey Legislature, in Matthews v. Bay Head Improvement Association, has enacted a statute to the effect that each private owner of beach front property must create a ten-foot corridor, for public access to the beach, across her/his property form the street to the high-water mark, between her/his property lines, for public beach-related recreation.

Set out all the legal arguments that an attorney for a private beach front landowner might rely on in contesting the statute in court. How would the Deputy Attorney General, defending the action for the State, respond to these arguments? Who do you think would win, and why?

(90 minutes)

December 19, 1989 FINAL EXAMINATION

I (50%)

Explain or answer each of the following in a succinct manner:

1. Constitutional right to a healthful environment.
2. Police power.
3. "The 27 million tons of coal do not constitute a separate segment of property for takings law purposes."
4. "...no feasible and prudent alternative...."
5. The United States Supreme Court's view of the legality of TRDs.
6. Does the public trust doctrine forbid the transfer of public trust lands to private parties?
7. Average reciprocity of advantage.
8. "If, by mining anthracite coal, the owner would necessarily unloose poisonous gasses, I suppose no one would doubt the power of the state to prevent the mining, without buying his coal fields."
9. Reasonably related to an appropriate governmental purpose.
10. Commerce Clause of the United States Constitution.
11. Can New Jersey prohibit the importation of hazardous wastes originating in Pennsylvania?
12. Occupation of the field.
13. "An owner of land has no absolute and unlimited right to change the essential natural character of his land so as to use it for a purpose for which it was unsuited in its natural state and which injuries the rights of others."

II (50%)

Mr. X purchased a 30-acre piece of property (P) in 1950 for the purpose of investment. P is located within the boundaries of the 100-year flood on a major river. In 1970 the state where P is located enacted a Flood Plains Act prohibiting all new development, including residences and pipelines, within the 100-year floodlines of major rivers in the state. Company Y is a pipeline company that has been granted condemnation power by federal statute. Y has served a notice of condemnation on Mr. X for a pipeline right-of-way through P.

Mr. X wants to build townhouses on P. Naturally, he also wants to prevent the pipeline right-of-way through P. Friends Of The River (FOR), a local citizens' group, wants to prevent the construction of the pipeline and the townhouses in order to preserve P in its present state.

What would be the likely lawsuits involving P? What would be the plaintiffs' arguments in these lawsuits? What would the defenses be? How would a court go about deciding these issues? Who would win and why? Would it make any differences if the state involved here was Michigan?

If you feel that you need more information, do not ask the instructor for it. Describe what information you need and why you need it. Then may reasonable, explicit assumptions. (2 hours)

October 23, 1989 MIDTERM EXAMINATION

I (50%)

Explain each of the following briefly but accurately:

1. Three differences between law and science.
2. Grand jury indictment.
3. Fear of increased risk of cancer.
4. Remand.
5. Amicus curiae.
6. Res ipsa loquitur.
7. Removal.
8. Burden of ultimate persuasion.
9. Presumption regarding a trial court's finding of fact.
10. Summary judgment.

II (50%)

Company X is a small pharmaceutical manufacturer that produces only one drug, called "Wonderdrug", without which 10,000 people who suffer from a rare kidney disease would not survive. In the process of manufacturing Wonderdrug, X discharges mercury into the Green River. Mercury is a bioaccumulative, persistent pollutant that can be toxic to humans if ingested. Company X is discharging mercury in amounts that violate its state discharge permit, and despite repeated orders by state officials to reduce its mercury discharge to the level specified in the permit. Company X's president responds that, because of the unique process employed in producing Wonderdrug, it would cost $5 million to reduce the mercury discharge and that an expenditure of this magnitude would force Company X to close down.

Boat Rentals, Inc. (BR) owns a rowboat livery on the Green River downstream of the X plant. BR's business has declined by 90% because the state has closed the river to fishing due to mercury pollution.

Mr. and Mrs. Jones have rented one of BR's rowboats for a day of boating on the river. While standing up to take a photograph, Mr. Jones, who cannot swim, falls overboard. As he struggles to return to the boat, Mr. Jones swallows a quantity of water. A few days later he experiences blurred vision, tremors, loss of coordination, and deafness in his left ear. Mr. Jones' physician examines him, takes blood samples, and informs him that he is suffering from mercury poisoning. Moreover, his hearing can only be partially restored, and that will require three months of full-time rehabilitation.

Discuss the advantages and disadvantages to both BR and the Joneses (treat BR separately from the Joneses) of suing Company X based on 1) private nuisance, 2) trespass,

3) negligence, 4) public nuisance, and 5) abnormally dangerous activities. Next discuss the appropriateness to each lawsuit of the following remedies: 1) injunction; 2) temporary damages; 3) permanent damages; and 4) punitive damages. Are criminal sanctions a possibility in this situation?

If you feel you need more information than is provided above, do not ask the instructor for it. Instead, explain why this information is necessary and make reasonable assumptions. Be sure to clearly identify each assumption that you make.

(80 minutes)

FINAL EXAMINATION December 18, 1991

I (50%)

Briefly explain each of the following:

1. The "Massachusetts Rule" in public trust law.
2. The "Wisconsin Rule" in public trust law.
3. Prior Public Use doctrine.
4. Reasonably related to an appropriate public purpose.
5. Police power.
6. Average reciprocity of advantage.
7. Broad form deed.
8. "An owner of land has no absolute and unlimited right to change the essential natural character of his land so as to use it for a purpose for which it was unsuited in its natural state and which injures the rights of others."
9. "The 27 million tons of coal do not constitute a separate segment of property for takings law purposes."
10. Legislative history of a statute.
11. The United States Supreme Court's view of the legality of TRDs.
12. Access to dry-sand beach areas in New Jersey.

II (50%)

The X Corp, in 1979, bought a 5.000 acre parcel of bayfront property, stretching for one mile along Delaware Bay in the State of Delaware, for the purposes of building a marina and a transfer facility for loading hazardous wastes from trucks onto incinerator ships, which would incinerate the wastes at high temperatures 200 miles of f the coast. The hazardous wastes would be coming from Superfund sites located throughout the mid-Atlantic region. X Corp subdivided the original parcel into two 2,500 acre parcels and built a marina on one of the parcels while planning for the transfer facility on the other parcel.

The State of Delaware, like many coastal states, has developed a coastal planning process using federal grant money provided under the federal Coastal Zone Management Act (CZMA). The CZMA does not dictate the result of state coastal planning; it provides that a state receiving federal funds must give "full consideration to ecological, cultural, historic, and esthetic values as well as to needs for economic development."

Delaware's coastal planning process convinced the state legislature that at-sea incineration transfer facilities should be banned in the coastal zone. In 1985, just as X Corp was preparing its application for a United States Environmental Protection Agency (USEPA) permit for the transfer facility, the Delaware legislature prohibited all future transfer facilities of this kind.

What legal arguments would X Corp make in a lawsuit against the State of Delaware? What would the State's counterarguments be? Who would win, and why? Would it make any difference if this case arose in Michigan?

If you feel you need more information, do not ask the instructor for it. Describe what information you need and why you need it: then make reasonable, explicit assumptions.

(90 minutes)

MAY 9, 1988 FINAL EXAMINATION

Discuss the following federal and New Jersey statutes that attempt to protect the public from the risks associated with toxic/hazardous substances:

1. TSCA
2. SARA Title III
3. Clean Air Act
4. Clean Water Act
5. Safe Drinking Water Act
6. RCRA
7. CERCLA
8. ECRA (NJ)

Be sure to cover in your discussion: 1) how each statute regulates hazardous/toxic substances; 2) how each statute minimizes false positives or false negatives or balances these approaches; 3) how each statute is ambient quality-based or technology-based or combines these approaches: and 4) how well or poorly, in you opinion, each statute has achieved its goals.

October 24, 1990 MIDTERM EXAMINATION, 2 hours

I (50%)

Explain each of the following briefly but accurately:

1. Three differences between law and science.
2. A plea of nolo contendere.

3. Dicta.
4. Clean hands doctrine.
5. Criteria for federal court jurisdiction.
6. Preliminary injunction.
7. Post-traumatic stress disorder.
8. Presumption regarding a trial court's finding of fact.
9. Easement.
10. Remand.
11. Amicus curiae.

II (50%)

The X family lives in Sunny Acres, a residential development located in the Township of East Sludge, New Jersey. The Xs, like their neighbors, draw their household water fro ma private well. Next to Sunny Acres is a landfill owned and operated by the Grosstout Corporation, which holds a landfill permit from the New Jersey Department of Environmental Protection (NJDEP). The landfill was in operation when Sunny Acres was constructed.

The Grosstout facility is the only landfill in New Jersey that is permitted to accept hazardous materials for burial. The company was allowed to accept these materials because it had installed a plastic liner and a leak--detection system, at a cost of $5 million. When the liner was installed it was thought to be "impermeable," that is, not subject to leakage.

Last month, NJDEP ordered the Xs and their neighbors to discontinue use of their private wells because the groundwater beneath their homes was found to be contaminated by toxic chemicals, some of which are known carcinogens. NJDEP tested the groundwater because its routine annual inspection of the landfill and Grosstout's records disclosed that the landfill was leaking but that Grosstout had ignored the warnings given by its leak-detection system.

NJDEP has not closed the landfill because it is the only permitted hazardous waste landfill in the State. Furthermore, repairing the liner, pumping and treating the contaminated groundwater, and installing a leach ate collection and treatment system in case of future leaks would take one year and cost $15 million, an expenditure that Grosstout claims would force it to close down.

The East Sludge Board of Health is providing water to the residents of Sunny Acres by daily deliveries of bottled water. Ultimately, a water main will be run to Sunny Acres, with construction and hookup costs to be paid for by the NJDEP.

Discuss all causes of action potentially available to the Xs in a lawsuit against Grosstout Corp., commenting on the advantages and disadvantages of each to the lawsuit's success. Then, discuss all possible remedies that a court might grant to the Xs, and evaluate their likelihood of being awarded in this lawsuit.

Notes

Notes

Notes